# Negotiating Identity

Symbolic Interactionist Approaches
to Social Identity

## Susie Scott

polity

The right of Susie Scott to be identified as Author of this Work has been asserted in accordance with the UK Copyright, Designs and Patents Act 1988.

First published in 2015 by Polity Press

Polity Press
65 Bridge Street
Cambridge CB2 1UR, UK

Polity Press
350 Main Street
Malden, MA 02148, USA

ISBN-13: 978-0-7456-6972-4
ISBN-13: 978-0-7456-6973-1 (pb)

A catalogue record for this book is available from the British Library.

Library of Congress Cataloging-in-Publication Data

Scott, Susie, 1977–
   Negotiating identity : symbolic interactionist approaches to social identity / Susie Scott.
pages cm
   Includes bibliographical references and index.
   ISBN 978-0-7456-6972-4 (hardback) -- ISBN 978-0-7456-6973-1 (pbk.) 1. Group identity. I. Title.
   HM753.S326 2015
   305--dc23

                                                          2014048138

Typeset in 10.5/12 Plantin by
Servis Filmsetting Ltd, Stockport, Cheshire
Printed and bound in Great Britain by CPI Group (UK) Ltd, Croydon

The publisher has used its best endeavours to ensure that the URLs for external websites referred to in this book are correct and active at the time of going to press. However, the publisher has no responsibility for the websites and can make no guarantee that a site will remain live or that the content is or will remain appropriate.

Every effort has been made to trace all copyright holders, but if any have been inadvertently overlooked the publisher will be pleased to include any necessary credits in any subsequent reprint or edition.

For further information on Polity, visit our website:
politybooks.com

# Contents

# Acknowledgements

I would like to thank Jonathan Skerrett at Polity for his conscientious support for and helpful advice with this book, from proposal through to publication. I am also grateful to the three anonymous reviewers who provided extremely positive and encouraging feedback on the first draft of the manuscript.

Earlier versions of some of the writing in Chapters 7 and 8 appeared in my book *Total Institutions and Reinvented Identities* (Palgrave, 2011) and article 'Intimate deception in everyday life' (*Studies in Symbolic Interaction*, 39, 251–79), so I appreciate the publishers' permission to reproduce this material. I am also grateful to my students Sarah Hamilton and Sophie Bishop for allowing me to cite examples from their excellent research projects.

Thank you to my Sussex colleagues, family and friends who have been kind and encouraging throughout the writing process: particularly Hilde, Karin, Dagmara and Vuokko (the Nordic contingent) and James, Liz, Karl and Lucy.

# 1

# Interacting selves

*Symbolic interactionism encounters identity*

Identity is an evocative and intriguing concept, replete with paradoxes. On the one hand, it refers to something private and personal – our understanding of ourselves – yet, on the other hand, it remains intangible, elusive and resistant to definition (Strauss 1969). We may think we know who we are, but these ideas are constantly changing, shaped by our experiences, relationships and interactions: who I am now is not the same as who I was yesterday or who I will be tomorrow. We also tend to think of identity as something highly individual, which marks us out as unique – yet in forming these self-images we inevitably draw on wider cultural representations, discourses, norms and values, which we share with those who inhabit our social worlds.

Sociologists have always been interested in identity, because it resonates with many of the issues and debates that characterize our discipline. Interpretivist sociology, in particular, is concerned with the relationship between self and society (Hewitt 2007), which is mutually constitutive: the social world is created by people interacting in routinized and orderly ways, while the meanings they attach to these experiences are shaped by those very patterns, in the form of socially constructed structures, institutions and normative frameworks. Max Weber, on whose work this tradition is based, argued that sociology should involve the interpretive study of social action: the process by which individuals organize and make sense of their behaviour by taking into account other people's meanings and motivations (Weber 1904). We think, feel and behave not as isolated individuals, but as social actors with a relational consciousness. Meanwhile, sociology's aims to 'make the familiar strange' (Garfinkel 1967) and relate 'private troubles to public issues' (Mills 1959) are relevant to the study of identity as an aspect of everyday life that we often take for granted, despite its social and political dimensions. The latter have come to prominence since

the mid-twentieth century through the rise of identity politics, citizenship debates and civil rights activism, reminding us that, aside from
academic theorizing, we have a moral and ethical duty to investigate
identities (Wetherell 2009).

## What is identity?

Identity can be defined as a set of integrated ideas about the self, the
roles we play and the qualities that make us unique. Ostensibly, this
implies a relatively stable entity, which we perceive as internally consistent (Allport 1961; Gergen 1968), and use to sustain a boundary
between ourselves and others. However, this very image may just be
a construction: one that is constantly changing and whose existence is
more illusory than real. Lyman and Scott (1970) conceive identity as an
aggregate of social roles that one has played across different situations,
which together create the impression of something 'trans-situational',
or greater than the sum of its parts. Turner (1968), similarly, points
towards a succession of 'situated selves' that we inhabit as we move
between social settings, which are 'averaged out' to create an overall
sense of identity. Here we encounter what Lawler (2008) suggests is a
central paradox of identity: that it combines notions of sameness and
continuity with notions of difference and distinctiveness.

A similar duality is recognized by Williams (2000), who makes a distinction between *identity,* a sense of oneself as a coherent and stable entity,
and *identification,* a social process of categorizing ourselves as similar to
certain social groups and different from others. Social identity is therefore
relational: defined relative to other people or groups. I find out who I *am*
by knowing what I am *not*: understanding where and with whom I do (or
don't) belong. For example, the Twenty Statements Test, devised by
Iowa sociologists Kuhn and McPartland (1954), asked students to write a
list of twenty words to describe themselves. The overwhelming majority of
these referred to social categories, roles, statuses and group memberships,
such as gender, age, ethnicity, occupation and family relationships. Other
common descriptors that were found, such as ideological beliefs, interests,
ambitions and self-evaluations, can also be seen as socially shaped.

We can distinguish identity from two closely related concepts: *selfhood* and *personhood. Selfhood* is a reflexive state of consciousness about
one's internal thoughts and feelings, while *personhood* is a set of publicly presented or externally attributed characteristics that others use
to determine our status (Jenkins 2004), with moral, philosophical or
political connotations. Cohen (1994) similarly points to the primacy of
the *self,* as those aspects of experience which are private, internal and

subjective, over *personhood*, as a set of publicly externally attributed characteristics, rights or statuses. Jenkins (2004) suggests that self and personhood are interconnected dimensions of experience which are mutually constitutive. Identity is the dialectical process of their articulation, an umbrella that encompasses them both. Lindesmith et al. (1999: 218) also distinguish between the *self*, a reflexive, communicative subject who witnesses him- or herself through a succession of transitory moments of interaction, and *identity*, or the meanings individuals give to these experiences as being unified.

Jenkins (2004) suggests four features of identity: *similarity* (a sense of one's uniformity and consistency), *difference* (a sense of one's uniqueness and distinctiveness from others), *reflexivity* (the ability to think about ourselves) and *process* (agency, independence and change over time). Lindesmith et al. (1999) agree that identity is multi-layered, incorporating different types of self: the *phenomenological self* (an internal stream of consciousness about one's current situation), the *interactional self* (as presented and displayed to others), the *linguistic self* (representations of the self to oneself or others through language and biographical stories), the *material self* (the body and externally visible parts of the self, which are potentially commodifiable) and the *ideological self* (broader cultural and historical definitions of what it means to be a good citizen in a particular society).

Then, there are different types of identity, which have been theorized across the social sciences. The social philosopher Harré (1998) saw *social identity* (externally applied categorizations or attributions) as being different from *personal identity* (the belief individuals have in their own self-consistency). In social psychology, Tajfel (1982) defined *social identity* in terms of affiliations with reference groups and the processes to which this gives rise, such as social comparison, in- and out-group relations and prejudice. Meanwhile Hewitt (2007) distinguished between *personal identity* (a sense of uniqueness and difference, together with integrity and consistency), *biographical identity* (the self as recounted through narratives and stories), *social identity* (group memberships and affiliations that forge connections and shared values) and *situational identity* (produced through the presentation or 'announcement' [Stone 1962] of particular versions of the self in specific interaction settings, and the extent to which these are accepted by those we encounter therein). In sociology, Goffman (1963a) made a distinction between *personal identity* (the 'single, continuous record of facts' that documents an individual's life, for example in photographs), *social identity* (the 'complement of attributes' seen as ordinary, natural and normal for members of a recognized category) and *ego identity* (a person's subjective sense of their own character, developed over time).

This book is concerned with social identity, but even this has different theoretical interpretations. Macro-level sociologists emphasize the *collective* identities through which we understand ourselves as members of social groups, and which are mobilized in political arenas. Demographic factors like social class, family and kinship, religion, and so on, formed the focus of 'traditional' sociological studies of identity in the context of workplace relations (Goldthorpe et al. 1969; Beynon 1973), local communities (Willmott & Young 1960) and gender divisions (Walby 1997), and continue to be hotly debated today. Meanwhile, 'new', more nuanced forms of collectivity have been recognized as shaping contemporary identities, for example through subcultural affiliation (Hebdige 1979), idiocultures (Fine 1987), fan cultures (Hills 2002), neotribes (Maffesoli 1996) and contested ethnic classifications (Lentin & Titley 2011). Bourdieusian theory shifts our attention towards the social processes of distinction (Bourdieu 1979) and positioning (Lury 2011), whereby people define themselves through their *relative* social class status, in terms of tastes, possessions and lifestyle practices: identifying with one social category often goes hand-in-hand with demonstrating one's disidentification with another. Last but not least, micro-level perspectives like symbolic interactionism theorize social identity as something that is formed through face-to-face encounters in everyday life. This is the approach I will be taking throughout this book, as we explore the *negotiation* of identities through processes of social interaction.

## The social self

Symbolic interactionism is concerned with the social dimensions of the mind: imagination, motivation, perception of others, self-consciousness and emotions. Empirically, we can study the mind through its effects on behaviour, which is understood as not merely habitual or instinctive but rather 'minded, symbolic, self-reflective conduct' (Lindesmith et al. 1999: 21) – in other words, Weberian social action. This can be contrasted to psychological approaches, which include the 'theory of minds' (the cognitive and developmental processes through which we can imagine the world from someone else's perspective), and philosophical approaches that focus on metaphysical questions of ontology and consciousness. Rationalists, such as Descartes, emphasized the introspective primacy of the thinking subject, located in the ideal rather than the material realm, while empiricists claimed that only knowledge acquired through the senses could be verified as true (Williams 2000). The empiricist Hume (1739) questioned the notion of an underlying self, the transcendental subject, who interprets these experiences. Ryle (1949) similarly disputed the rationalist 'ghost in the machine' as a 'category mistake' of Cartesian dualism, arguing for the interconnectedness of mind and body. Locke (1689) conceded that we may have a *sense* of our own sameness and continuity from recurrent empirical experiences, but that this was just an illusion. Harré (1998) made the similar point that our sense of self may just be based upon linguistic conventions, such as the use of the pronoun 'I', which locates the speaker/thinker in relation to others. However, this is an elusive and slippery agent. If we can only reflect on our conduct retrospectively, we can never witness our own subjectivity acting in the present moment: as Mead (1934: 174) put it, 'I cannot turn around fast enough to catch myself.'

The symbolic interactionist concept of the 'social self' centres on the idea that selfhood is relational, arising through social interaction at the micro level. This is a symbolic and communicative process by which actors understand themselves through their relations with others. It involves reflection and perspective-taking, definitions and judgements; the self is an active agent, capable of manipulating objects in the social world. Hewitt (2007) adds that the social self is processual: it is not a fixed object or entity but, rather, fluid, emergent and mutable. Selfhood is never finished but in a constant state of becoming. Identity, similarly, is 'never gained nor maintained once and for all . . . it is constantly lost and regained' (Erikson 1959: 118) through social negotiation.

These theories stem from the philosophical tradition of pragmatism: the study of human praxis, or meaningful activity. Ontologically, pragmatism teaches that social reality is constructed through human action: we define the social world and the objects within it in terms of their use for us, or practical effects upon situations (Dewey 1922). The term 'object' here incorporates people, and, most crucially, one's own self: we can reflect upon ourselves as social objects in other people's worlds, and imagine their perceptions and judgements of us. James (1890: 295) argued that this is a key means of understanding ourselves, which also suggests multiplicity: an actor has 'as many social selves as there are distinct groups of persons about whose opinions he [*sic*] cares'.

Pragmatism suggests that the self has two sides: it is both subject and object simultaneously. The mind has a reflective capacity: we think, feel and act, but also reflect upon the social consequences of this, and modify our self-image accordingly. Cooley's (1902) concept of the Looking Glass Self had three elements: imagining how we appear to others, imagining how they might judge us, and the resultant self-feelings, such as pride or shame. This in turn shows that the self is a dynamic *process*, which is never complete: we do not simply 'have' selves but rather 'do' or 'make' (and re-make) them, through constant reflection.

Animation and personification help us to imagine this process more clearly. James (1890) made a distinction between two phases of the self: the 'I', the agent of thought and action, and the 'Me', the version(s) of oneself that were presented to others. Mead (1934) developed this idea further, arguing that the self unfolded through an inner conversation between 'I' and 'Me', as alternating phases of the self. He defined these as subject and object, respectively. The 'I' is the creative, impulsive agent of social action, while the 'Me' is an image (or collection of images) of oneself, viewed from the perspective of others. This is internalized into the self-concept as the 'organized set of attitudes of others which one himself [sic] assumes' (Mead 1934: 175). For Mead, mind, self and society were all intertwined parts of the same process: we import 'society' into the mind through an internalized set of attitudes and responses from others, which we then use to guide our conduct. The self, then, centres on the ability to take oneself as an object of reflective thought, to be both subject and object simultaneously. We cannot experience the self directly, but only through the imagined responses of others.

This reflective intelligence is used as people imagine and mentally rehearse possible courses of action and anticipate likely responses. This involves the manipulation of symbolic social objects (Blumer 1969) in the mind, which are translated into communicative gestures. Mead (1934) suggested that humans have a unique capacity to use 'significant symbols' (such as language), which convey a shared meaning to those in our immediate milieu: actors can be said to be making a communicative gesture when they understand the meaning it will have for the other and can anticipate the response it will 'call out' in them. Mead proposed the analytic concept of the 'act' (and, more specifically, the social act) as the most elementary unit of conduct: the smallest meaningful unit we can extract from the ongoing stream of human behaviour (Hewitt 2007). The act is a discrete unit with a beginning and an end, which begins when a previous act ends or is interrupted; it is also functional, purposive and goal-directed in helping the actor to express or realize an intention. The act has four stages – perception, impulse, manipulation and consummation – whereby we identify symbolic objects, indicate these to ourselves, design intentions and carry them out.

Mead (1934) proposed that the self developed through a sequence of stages in childhood socialization. The first stage is *play*, when the child begins to 'take the view of the other', imagining situations from another person's perspective. This enables them to engage in fantasy and role-play, orienting their conduct towards what they think the other person perceives (this echoes the 'theory of minds' in psychology). However, this perspective-taking is limited to discrete, specific other individuals whom the child has directly encountered, such as parents or friends. The second stage, called the *game*, occurs when the child is able to take the view of a whole group or a collective perspective. Mead used the term '*generalized other*' to describe this symbolic object, which we use as adults to organize our conduct: we have a tendency to orient ourselves towards what we think 'people in general' will think, say or do.

The social self can be broken down further into several components (Hewitt 2007). Each of these is imaginative, relational and emergent, as we consider alternative ways of knowing or viewing ourselves through the eyes of others. Charon (2007) distinguishes between the *self-concept* (an image of oneself), *self-esteem* (feelings about one's status or worth) and *self-judgements* (the processes by which we arrive at these things). Rosenberg (1979) similarly suggests that the *self-concept* refers to the totality of thoughts and feelings about the self as a stable object. This is reflected in both personal dispositions (characteristics one sees oneself as possessing) and social identities (groups and categories to which one imagines oneself to belong), and the relationship between these two comprises the basic structure of the self. Meanwhile, *self-image* involves cognitive schemas, such as the templates of 'possible selves' (Markus & Nurius 1986) that are available for us to choose between within our cultural repertoire (Gubrium & Holstein 2001). Finally, *self-esteem* refers more to the emotional aspects of identity, such as feeling accepted and valued (Gecas & Schwalbe 1983) as we evaluate how successful or 'efficacious' a course of action has been in communicating an impression of self to others (James 1890).

Of particular significance here are the self-conscious emotions (Tangney & Fisher 1995) – shame, pride, guilt and embarrassment (and, I would add, shyness [Scott 2007a]) – which arise when we evaluate our own conduct through the eyes of significant others, and consider its implications for our social and moral status. Scheff and Retzinger (1991) argue that shame signifies a perceived threat to the social bond (that which exists between the individual and their reference group), while I define shyness as a perception of oneself as being relatively incompetent at managing social interaction, with the anticipation of negative judgement by others (Scott 2007a).

What happens when the social self enters into interaction? The phenomenologist Schütz (1972) pointed out that we need to align our 'streams of consciousness' so that we can co-ordinate our behaviour in situations. This in turn contributes to social order, by allowing the social world to flow smoothly, in an orderly and predictable fashion. Schütz argued that while individuals inhabit their own subjective reality, this is an imported microcosm of the wider social world. The 'lifeworld' is a sphere of mundane, everyday practices and common-sense knowledge, on which we rely to make our lives as orderly and predictable as possible. We do not consciously reflect on the contents of the lifeworld but, rather, take them for granted: it constitutes a 'paramount reality' in which we believe unless convinced otherwise by disruptive and unexpected events. The actor translates this stock of background knowledge into action by adopting the 'natural attitude': as we cannot consciously attend to every possible interpretation of events, we assume that the most likely and common meaning is true, and bracket out our awareness of all alternatives. This means that we encounter the social world as if it were real, external and objectively verifiable, beyond our control. In their theory of the social construction of reality, Berger and Luckmann (1966: 89) called this process 'reification': '. . . the apprehension of human phenomena as if they were things'. An important component of this capacity is the stock of generalized schemas or representations about what might be meant in familiar kinds of situations: these include *typifications* about the types of people (or roles) that we expect to find in certain contexts, and *recipe knowledge* about the chain of interaction that is likely to unfold (Schütz 1972).

## Multi-dimensional subjects: fixity or fragmentation?

An important debate concerns the question of whether or not there is a core, essential, 'true' self, which is fixed and stable, below the levels of discourse, performance and interaction. Social constructionist theories pose a challenge to the essentialist assumptions underlying more traditional theories, which are seen as having been produced from a position of white, male, heterosexual privilege. Hall (1996) argues that identity can no longer be taken for granted as something fixed, stable and internally coherent, for it is now subject to fragmentation, uncertainty and doubt. Calhoun (1994: 13) contests the notion that individuals can have 'singular, integral, altogether harmonious and unproblematic identities', while others have challenged representations of social groups as having a collective identity based on a set of core or essential features, such as gender (Connell & Pearse 2015), sexuality (Weeks 2003) or ethnicity (Gilroy 2000). These theorists point instead to the instability of the self as something that is fragile, fragmented and dispersed rather than integrated, as well as fluid, mutable and resistant to definition. Meanwhile, postcolonial writing on race, ethnicity and citizenship has pointed to the way in which nationalist and racist discourses constructed notions of the 'other' as a threatening outsider (Said 1978; Hall 1996). Challenging and rethinking these culturally inscribed boundaries, and in some cases reclaiming stigmatized identities, has been central to the rise of civil rights activism and identity politics since the late twentieth century (Plummer 2003; Lentin & Titley 2011).

The anti-essentialist ontologies of these theories challenge not only the idea of unity, totality and sameness, but also the agency of the human subject (Williams 2000). Identity can be viewed not as something that we have, but as something that we do, or that is made and bestowed upon us. There may be no underlying referent or subject, but merely surface-level representations, descriptions and images of groups of people. This poststructuralist view is epitomized by the work of Foucault (1971), who, drawing on Nietzsche's nihilistic pronouncement of the 'death of the subject', argued that identities – or the idea of them – were discursively produced. Identities come into being through cultural and linguistic conventions, which in turn are a reflection of dominant systems of knowledge and power. That is, discourses (ways of seeing, thinking and writing about a cultural object [Hall 1996]), which are created within cultural and historical contexts, come to define certain ways of being. Foucault (1961, 1976) referred to 'subjectivities' or 'subject positions' rather than 'identities', and argued that a succession of these emerged in different historical eras: for example, the hysterical woman, who was a discursive product of nineteenth-century psychoanalytic theory. Moreover, these 'discoveries' reflected not absolute truths, or the triumphant march of progress in scientific knowledge, but rather the interests of the powerful in each era. They indicated who held the power to define what was normal, natural and inevitable, and, conversely, what was abnormal or deviant. The post-Enlightenment birth of the human sciences (clinical medicine, psychiatry, criminology, economics and demographics), with their emphasis on reason and rationality and systematic logic, led to attempts to map out the terrain of social characteristics through systems of classification and categorization (Foucault 1963). This reflected a desire to know about, gaze at, penetrate into, understand, monitor and regulate the behaviour of populations (Foucault 1975).

This is a rather nihilistic view in suggesting that there can be identity without agency (Williams 2000), but some more contemporary poststructuralist theorists have attempted to bring the autonomous subject back into the debate. Hacking (1999), for example, argued that discursive texts and practices create identity categories by defining the conditions of personhood, or ways of being a certain social type. Individuals may then fit themselves into these categories and find meaning in them as identity monikers.

Another example of this is Judith Butler's (1990, 1993) model of gender identities. For Butler, there is no pre-discursive subject, or core essential self, lying beneath the level of surface appearances. The self has no fixity, stability or substance; it consists merely of a series of stylized, repetitive performances that create the illusion of this: appearance precedes essence. Butler claimed that masculinity and femininity were not essential ways of being that were expressed through appearance and behaviour, but just performative effects, or ways of 'doing gender' (West & Zimmerman 1987). As Butler (1990: 25) famously argued: '. . . there is no gender identity behind the expressions of gender; that identity is performatively constituted by the very "expressions" that are said to be its results.' Butler disputed hegemonic constructions, such as the gender binary (the assumption that there are only two categories of gender, male and female), cis-gender (the state of congruence between one's biologically attributed sex and subjectively felt gender identity), the gender order (Connell & Pearse 2015) or the sex/gender system (Rubin 1975; the hierarchy of culturally preferred gender identities, with male heterosexuality at the top), and heteronormativity (the assumption that heterosexuality is the default 'normal' state of being). She advocated the subversion of these through disruptive and dismantling acts of resistance, such as transvestism and drag, as well as the recognition of identities that lie outside the 'heterosexual matrix' (Butler 1990), such as transgender, gender-queer, non-cis-identified and pansexual.

However, these apparent signs of agency may just reflect the insidiousness and pervasiveness of social control. Rose (1989, 1990) argued that the Foucauldian disciplinary gaze was not only internalized by subjects, but also regarded by them as positively helpful as a means of regulating their own behaviour. Through 'governmentality', individuals willingly turn the gaze upon themselves by becoming self-surveillant, while at the same time offering themselves up to knowledgeable experts, such as social workers, life coaches, solicitors and counsellors. Rose (1989) points to the curious paradox of social control and regulation being delivered through discourses of liberation, freedom and citizenship: we are obliged to be free. Disciplinary power infiltrates both subjectivity and intersubjectivity: the desire to gain knowledge of oneself, other people and the spaces in between. One of the most prominent media he identifies is the expertise vested in the 'psy' industries, with their twin weapons: the 'therapeutic culture of the self' (Rose 1989: xii) and the construction of 'neurochemical selves'. Although Rose suggests that we learn to 'assemble' ourselves and to cite motives of self-fulfilment, self-actualization and self-improvement, he attributes these motives to the 'colonization of the lifeworld' (Habermas 1981), whereby the channels of communication between genuinely free citizens have been blocked by ideology: our thoughts are not our own, and our perception of our own (and others') competence is limited.

The symbolic interactionist position in this debate is something of a compromise between the extremes of fixity and fragmentation. Symbolic interactionist scholars do refer to such notions as self and identity, which may be experienced by individuals as relatively consistent, but do not claim that this constitutes a 'pure' essential core, immune to external social influences. Instead, we refer to social actors, who are defined in processual terms, by their actions and capacities (for agency, perspective-taking, role-play, conformity and resistance). Moreover, the self is subject to ongoing challenge, definition and modification by significant others in the course of interaction, and so it is fluid and mutable, constantly evolving. Actors may even construct an assemblage of multiple selves as they move between different situations and interact with different audiences. Nevertheless, this still logically presupposes that there is some kind of agent: the actor behind the performances, or the author of the selves. This agent 'does' or creates (performs, authors, narrates, represents and reflects upon) his or her own social identities, but always through negotiation with others.

## Symbolic interactionism

Let us now take a closer look at symbolic interactionism (SI), the theoretical approach I will be taking in this book. SI is a micro-sociological perspective that focuses on small-scale, often face-to-face, encounters between social actors, and the meanings they attach to their behaviour. SI regards identity, like society more widely, as a process of negotiation: it is relational, communicative, and symbolically meaningful. Becker (1963) wrote of people not *being* but rather *becoming* social types, as their identities emerge from ongoing patterns of interaction and are never completely finished. Within this perspective, I include Goffman's dramaturgical theory (discussed more below), which focuses on how social actors present, perform and strategically manage different versions of themselves in different situations; the cumulative effect of this creates the precarious structure of the 'interaction order'. Identities are contextual, the details of their expressions varying between settings and situations, as well as dynamic, mutable and contingent. Their meanings are forever shifting in line with situational demands, group values and normative expectations. In summary, I suggest that SI describes and analyses the social processes of interaction through which identities can be *created, shaped, maintained, communicated, presented, negotiated, challenged, reproduced, reinvented and narrated.*

## Historical origins, branches and schools

SI is a broad tradition encompassing many strands. Even its most devoted advocates have pointed to its 'messy' intellectual development (Fisher & Strauss 1978), varied historiography and disputed terrain (Atkinson & Housley 2003). Nevertheless, we can trace the historical origins of SI through a number of commentaries (Meltzer et al. 1975; Rock 1979; Fine 1995; Charon 2007) that emphasize its unique, distinctive position.

SI grew out of North American sociology in the twentieth century, and so is a relatively modern perspective. In the inter-war years of 1920–40, the University of Chicago was home to some highly influential figures in the world's first sociology department (William Thomas, Robert Park, Ernest Burgess, Louis Wirth, Albion Small), as well as its new flagship publication, the *American Journal of Sociology*. The city of Chicago at this time was undergoing a period of rapid social transformation, following the Great Fire of 1871, and so constituted the perfect 'natural laboratory' in which to observe how social processes of urbanization, migration, crime and poverty were affecting the everyday lives of ordinary people. This new interest in 'urban ecology' lent itself to empirical field studies of 'social problems' and their effects upon the experiences of those on the margins of society, such as Polish immigrants (Thomas & Znaniecki 1918), homeless people (Anderson 1923), criminal gangs (Thrasher 1927) and juvenile delinquents (Shaw 1934). The emphasis on empirical field research was something novel and unique to this group, who would conduct ethnographies in particular local settings, based on interviews and participant observation (Bulmer 1984).

Initially, there was a bifurcation between this Chicago School, with its emphasis on interpretivist theorizing, humanist ontology and pragmatist epistemology, and the lesser-known Iowa School, whose approach was more positivistic and quantitative (Meltzer et al. 1975). However, the latter did not survive beyond one generation as it was absorbed into other disciplines like social psychology. By contrast, the Chicago School continued to thrive. After the initial flurry of activity, the first generation of scholars were replaced by a more geographically dispersed 'second Chicago School' (Fine 1995). This consisted of iconic figureheads like Everett Hughes, Howard Becker, Anselm Strauss and Erving Goffman, who set up new SI-inspired departments around the USA.

Another distinction can be made between two branches of SI that focus on either the regular, patterned and normative aspect of interaction or its fluid, processual, contingent character (Hausmann et al. 2011). The former is represented by structural symbolic interactionism (Stryker 1980), which focused on how the structure of society – albeit one envisaged at the micro level as merely 'the pattern of regularities that characterize most human interaction' (Stryker 1980: 65) – shapes the self. For example, through normative routines and practices of socialization, we learn culturally shared rules of behaviour or roles that we are expected to play. The latter branch is represented by interaction ritual theory (Collins 2005), an approach inspired by Durkheim's (1912) functionalist theory of religion. Durkheim argued that collective worship took a ritualized form that symbolized and reinforced its followers' adherence to shared *social* values, thus strengthening their cohesiveness and solidarity. Collins developed this by suggesting that the same processes occur in mundane everyday situations insofar as these involve ritualized forms of interaction (e.g. greetings and farewells, or apologies). Interaction rituals involve similar states of mutual awareness and a shared focus of attention; they can also generate a collective mood of 'emotional energy', which is dynamic in instigating further action. As we shall see in Chapters 2 and 4, Goffman (1959, 1967) showed how interaction rituals like displays of civility, politeness and decorum reveal actors' common commitment to upholding the interaction order.

## Key concerns

Epistemologically, symbolic interactionism is concerned not with making objectivist claims about what is 'out there' in the 'real' world, but rather with grasping participants' subjective experiences of their own situations. This illustrates Weber's (1904) notion of *verstehen*, or the interpretive understanding of social action. In terms of its substantive subject matter, Atkinson and Housley (2003) suggest that SI studies the interdependency of *social action, social order and social identities*. This in turn lends itself to two domains of empirical study: the *production and distribution of social identities* through micro-social processes, such as the creation and use of moral types, labels and social categories, and the *relationship between social actors and social organizations*, for example when members of an institution become socialized into role-identities that are defined by that structure. We shall consider these, but also other, aspects of identity in the chapters of this book.

## Blumer's symbolic interactionism

The term 'symbolic interactionism' to denote a distinct theoretical perspective was introduced in a classic text by Herbert Blumer (1969). Atkinson and Housley (2003) suggest that Blumer inherited the dual traditions of Chicago thought – Mead–Cooley pragmatism and Park–Burgess empiricism – and blended them into an original approach.

Blumer took Mead's rather abstract notion of the social self and showed how this was grounded in the practical, everyday world of social interaction (Manis & Meltzer 1978). While Mead had emphasized the human capacity for reflexive thought, Blumer argued that this was not merely introspective but, rather, shaped by and emergent from the social process (Rock 1979). For example, the 'social objects' that comprise our everyday world, including representations of self and others, were constructed, defined and modified by processes of communicative interaction.

Blumer (1969) identified three key principles of symbolic interactionism: firstly, humans act towards social objects on the basis of the *meanings* that these things have for them; secondly, these meanings arise out of social *interaction*; and, thirdly, meanings can be modified by *interpretation*, or the *interpretive process*. In this way, he said, humans create the worlds of experience in which they live: a constructivist ontology of social reality.

Blumer introduced the concept of the communicative *gesture*, making a distinction between gestures that are *non-symbolic* (instinctive and unreflexive) and those that are *symbolic* (having a meaning that is reflexively understood and shared between participants). For example, compare a blink and a wink. The social world is mainly symbolic rather than non-symbolic: we respond not merely to conditioned stimuli but to actively constructed meanings (Charon 2007), which are subjectively perceived, negotiable, mutable and open to constant redefinition. Hewitt (2007) refers to symbols as being 'conventional' in that they are socially constructed, shared, mutually known about and therefore normative; they are learned through socialization, and designed for a communicative purpose. The most obvious example of symbolic gestures is the use of language.

Blumer extended Mead's original notion of the act: a four-phase process of perception, impulse, manipulation and consummation, by which individuals exercised their will in relation to objects. Blumer argued that acts were not simply individual but often co-operative: what he called *joint acts* involved people using symbolic gestures and drawing on shared meanings to co-ordinate these. Joint action is a collaborative venture of making sense of situations together, constructing order out of perceptual chaos. This involves considering the action from all sides and seeking to find common ground between different perspectives. Thus the internal dialogue that Mead posited between the 'I' and 'Me' of the self was re-imagined by Blumer as a 'conversation of gestures' between different selves. Actors make constant indications to themselves and others about how their symbolic gestures should be interpreted, whilst simultaneously reading meanings from the gestures that these others give. SI theorists agree that through this interactive process of mutual perspective-taking, meaning-making and communication, social situations emerge: 'We modify our lines of action on the basis of what we perceive alter's implications to be with respect to our manifest and latent plans of action' (McCall & Simmons 1966: 136); 'Interaction means actors taking each other into account, communicating to and interpreting each other as they go along' (Charon 2007: 140). This in turn allows SI to theorize micro-level structures and social order. 'Society' is not an objective, external structure, but rather just a subjectively perceived semblance of such. This is based upon regular patterns of interaction: routinized, habitual ways of doing things that come to be regarded as normal, natural and inevitable. The phenomenologists Berger and Luckmann (1966) called this 'the social construction of reality', which involved both *reification* – the apprehension of constructed objects as if they were external – and the *negotiation process* – an ongoing cycle of definition, redefinition and mutual adjustment.

## Goffman's dramaturgy

Dramaturgy can be understood as a theoretical perspective in its own right, but I find it helpful to think of it as a variant of symbolic interactionism, with which it shares some key concerns: the micro-sociological study of face-to-face interactions; actors' collaborative work in creating definitions of reality; and the idea that social identities can be produced, negotiated and performed through these situated encounters. We shall examine Goffman's theory in more detail throughout the book, particularly in Chapters 4 and 5, but an overview of the approach may be helpful at this stage.

Erving Goffman (1922–82) was a graduate student of sociology at the University of Chicago in the late 1940s, in the aftermath of the Chicago School's heyday, and was taught by some of its key figures, most notably Everett Hughes. The fieldwork Goffman carried out in the Shetland Isles on 'the social structure of an island community' would later form the basis of his most famous book, *The Presentation of Self in Everyday Life* (1959). In attempting to catalogue and analyse the minutiae of human behaviour, using typologies, taxonomies and classification systems (Løfland 1980), Goffman was heavily influenced by anthropology, ethology and game theory (Smith 2006). Although he went on to teach in the sociology departments of Berkeley and Pennsylvania, he remained reluctant to describe himself as a sociologist, much less as a symbolic interactionist. However, this may have been less a question of fervent occupational identity than one of mere disengagement and disinterest: Ditton (1980) suggests that Goffman was largely indifferent to disciplinary boundaries, and kept himself away from the 'turf wars' of academic identity politics.

Goffman's perspective of dramaturgy was inspired by Kenneth Burke's (1945) dramatism, as outlined in his book *A Grammar of Motives*. Burke argued that everyday interaction consisted of actors trying to interpret and align their different motivations, work out frames of meaning and establish modes of co-operative action; all of this was unpredictable and dynamic. Apart from studying the narrative design and format of situations, Burke said that we should examine people's motives. Mirroring the key questions of 'who, what, where, when and how' that characterize mystery detective stories, he proposed an analytical 'pentad' of five elements that could be found in ordinary social situations. These were: the act (what happened), scene (where this took place), agent (who was involved), agency (how the action was accomplished) and purpose (why the actors were motivated).

Goffman's writing style was also imitative of Burke's 'perspective by incongruity', in that he sought to highlight the dramatic elements of social interaction by drawing analogies to mundane phenomena with which readers would be familiar from their everyday lives. Seeing the juxtaposition of the routine and the remarkable forced readers to make associations and draw parallels between the two, jolting them into a new state of awareness and generating fresh insights into social reality, by 'making the familiar strange' (cf. Garfinkel 1967). To this end, Goffman employed various metaphors, such as the con game, the service industry, ritual worship and animal behaviour (Lofland 1980). Most famous, however, was his theatrical metaphor.

Dramaturgy is based upon the idea that social life is like a theatre, with many comparable features. Goffman (1959) described social actors as being like actors on the stage, who are constantly performing: playing their part, or role, in the drama of each situation, and presenting various different characters to the audiences they encounter therein. This tendency is called *self-presentation*. We try to control the images of ourselves that we convey, using the skill of *impression management*: we devise moves, lines, gestures and tactical displays of information. One of the greatest contributions of Goffman's work was his systematic and exhaustive cataloguing of these myriad tactics and strategies. He showed how actors manipulate social objects, settings and definitions of reality as instruments of communication (Perinbanayagam 1985). Identities, in this model, are situated and performative: it is difficult to ever know the 'true' self, or the person behind the mask, the actor behind the characters they play, because in every social situation we encounter we will be performing one persona or another.

Performances can also be collaborative: actors work together like members of a theatrical cast to uphold a collective group impression or definition of the situation. Goffman (1959: 85) defined the 'performance team' as 'any set of individuals who co-operate in staging a single routine'. The reference here to 'a single routine' reminds us that these formations are contextual: fellow actors may be supportive team-mates in one situation but strangers or even adversaries in another. Team-mates are those on whom we rely to help us out of embarrassment, tactfully save our face and get encounters back on track. They repair the damage caused by disturbed expectations, for whatever happens, 'the show must go on'. In Chapter 5, we explore the intricacies of this 'dramaturgical loyalty' (Goffman 1959), to see how team-mates manage matters of casting, recruitment and boundary monitoring.

Audiences have an important role to play in accepting or rejecting these performances. While actors make identity claims, or 'announcements', audiences interpret these with 'placements', which may or may not be 'coincidental' or congruous (Stone 1962). They may decide an identity performance is not convincing and be suspicious that an actor is not who they appear to be. This may mean that audience members refuse to co-operate in supporting it through their own lines of action: remember that they are simultaneously actors, and the protagonists in their own dramas. Audiences are always scrutinizing the performances they see, trying to interpret their significance and read characters' identities correctly. Goffman therefore thought it was important to study not only the impressions people 'give' deliberately but also those they 'give off' unintentionally. For example, in a job interview, we may attempt to create an image of competent professionalism, but feel betrayed by nervousness and self-doubt leaking out.

The physical context in which individual and team performances are given is very important. Goffman (1959) suggested that the self is divided into two main parts, or regions, which correspond to areas of a theatre. The *frontstage* region is where public performances are given, and where we enact carefully scripted role-identities. The 'front' of a performance consists of its *setting* (location, scenery and décor), which is fixed in one place, and the *personal front* that actors bring to the situation (items of identity equipment, such as clothes, material objects as props, and facial expressions). Meanwhile, the *backstage* region is where actors relax out of character, and may contradict their public identities: this is a private space to rehearse, dissect and reflect upon one's role performance and recharge one's batteries before going back on stage. When alone in these backstage regions, actors might become aware of their 'true', private self-identities, but this is a rare and privileged insight.

## Criticism and defence

Of course, symbolic interactionism is not without its limitations, which have been identified both within and outside of the perspective (Meltzer et al. 1975). One of the most obvious and major criticisms is that SI, in its focus on the micro-sociological level of analysis, neglects to examine wider or deeper macro-level structures. This is important because it implies a lack of recognition of social inequality, power and conflict (Gouldner 1973). However, this may be an over-simplistic (mis)interpretation of the perspective that misses the subtler ways in which SI and dramaturgy do theorize these concepts. Indeed, Jenkins (2008) describes Goffman as a major theorist of power. Goffman's work is replete with commentaries on unequal power relations in different interaction contexts, such as the 'institutional arrangements' of the psychiatric hospital (Goffman 1961a; see Chapter 7 below) and the attribution of stigma (Goffman 1963a; see Chapter 6 below). Neither does SI make the rose-coloured claim that social actors are free to interpret their roles and perform their identities in whichever way they choose: power relations and social divisions can be found at the micro level, through patterns of interaction, normative conventions and dominant, agreed-upon definitions of reality. These impose constraints upon individual agency and limit the repertoires of action that are open to social actors: for example, when a person's role within an occupational setting is prescribed by formal regulations (Hewitt 2007).

A related criticism is that SI is fixating on the trivial. The analysis of micro-level encounters, interaction dynamics and the minutiae of social life can appear superficial to some, who argue that SI 'fetishizes' everyday life (Brittan 1973) or celebrates image, style and performance at the expense of substance (Gouldner 1973). At the same time, the perspective has been described as 'quaint' and out-dated for its emphasis on face-to-face, localized encounters, which seem less relevant in a contemporary, media-saturated, globalized and virtual world (Gergen 1991). Whether or not these criticisms are valid is debatable – as noted above, such dismissive readings of SI neglect to appreciate how the perspective does theorize deeper issues and social problems, albeit more subtly – but even if so, we might counter, does this matter? There is no obligation for social theory to be politically effective or morally worthy, and some social phenomena are simply interesting to study.

Taking this further, Denzin (1969) defends SI against its criticisms. He argues that the perspective has been accused of not doing what it had never intended to do anyway, such as examining macro-level structures or offering political analyses of inequality. As outlined earlier in this chapter, SI has never claimed to be concerned with the 'why' of social action or to have a radical, transformative political agenda; its focus is on the 'how' of social order: how the semblance of structure is created and maintained, and how this is experienced by people. Methodologically, its focus is on observing rather than explaining, from a neutral or detached position, the mechanics and dynamics of social interaction.

Other criticisms that have been levelled at SI include that the perspective is overly rational, even cognitive, in its analysis of how people logically appraise social situations and decide upon courses of action. This implies a neglect of the emotions (Lupton 1998), unconscious motivations (Craib 1998) and embodiment (Williams & Bendelow 1998), suggesting a rather complacent model of the self as one-dimensional and unproblematic. Related to this is a charge of ethnocentrism: SI's 'Americana bias' (Shaskolsky 1970) was evident in the way that its empirical studies have tended to focus on contemporary Western societies and liberal democracies, where actors can take for granted their rights to full citizenship. The early theorists enjoyed a privileged position as white, middle-class, able-bodied heterosexual males, whose universalistic claims belied a Western, ethnocentric bias (Brissett & Edgley 2005). The rational, pragmatic, self-contained, instrumental model of the self that they presented may not fit with the subjective experiences of those who occupy less privileged positions of marginalized or excluded 'otherness' (Hall 1996).

Goffman's dramaturgical perspective has encountered some more specific criticisms, as well as those above levelled at SI more widely. Some argue that the theatrical analogy is overstated: not everything in social life is so rationally calculable and strategically controllable, and often human experience feels quite the opposite: messy, chaotic and spontaneous (Dodd & Raffel 2013). That said, Goffman himself recognized the limitations of dramaturgy and was careful 'not to make light of its obvious inadequacies. The stage presents things that are make-believe' (Goffman 1959: 9), whereas social life confronts us all directly, and we experience it as real.

Goffman's methodology was also a little 'unpolished', to say the least. Although it is a delight to stumble across the little gems in his magpie collection of illustrative examples (Scott 2007c), Goffman did not explain his sampling strategy and methods of data collection in the rigorous manner that would be expected of social scientists today (Smith 2006). However, Zerubavel (2007) disputes this, arguing that reading across the various examples reveals common features and general patterns of interaction that are trans-contextual. Nevertheless, there is an absence of a singular, distinctive methodological approach in Goffman's work (Manning 1992), and no systematic scientific way of verifying his theory (Psathas 1996). As Smith (2006: 110) puts it, Goffman may be too empirical to be considered a 'pure' theorist, yet too theoretical to be 'just' an ethnographic researcher. Lofland (1980) adds that Goffman's writing can be difficult to follow: as a body of work, it lacks internal consistency as he moved about between concepts and analogies in different books without cross-referencing his ideas, and so the reader must do the interpretive work of putting this all together into a coherent overall theory.

Despite these qualifications, many would agree that dramaturgy is incredibly powerful and evocative. As Burns (1992) explains, Goffman's approach is enormously valuable in highlighting those aspects of everyday life that were previously considered unremarkable. By showing that these 'micro' matters were essential to the maintenance of the social interaction order, Goffman made the familiar world refreshingly new (Manning 1992).

## Symbolic interactionism and identity

To summarize, there are three main features of the symbolic interactionist and dramaturgical approaches to identity. Firstly, identity is a *process*. It is not something that people have, or are ascribed to, or that stays the same throughout their lives, but rather something that continuously unfolds and evolves. This process is mediated by social interaction, as actors perceive and respond to the symbolic meaning of each other's actions, and so identity is negotiated through interaction. Maines (2001: 242) defines identities as the 'social categories through which people may be located and given meaning' in a situational context.

Secondly, identity is *performative*. We have seen from Goffman's dramaturgy how SI envisages social actors working together and alone to display versions of themselves, and using a myriad of strategies to this end: impression management, information control, facework gestures, and so on. Identity is therefore something that is actively accomplished, worked at and 'done' by individuals in the course of interaction, and this is a self-conscious, reflexive process. The SI meaning of 'performance' is different from the word 'performative', used in poststructuralism (e.g. Butler's gender theory), where there is a deconstructionist, anti-essentialist ontology of selfhood. SI puts a more pragmatic emphasis on what actors do and what is shown (the performance that can be observed) rather than the abstract capacities or potentials of subjectivity. This retains the idea of a core self as the agent authoring these choices: there has to be an actor behind the character.

Thirdly, identity is *pragmatic*: something that does not just exist at the abstract level of image and perception, but rather is tangibly expressed through concrete lines of action, which can be observed and analysed. SI research involves empirical studies that illustrate how identities are negotiated, performed and managed in specific interaction contexts, and uses these data as evidence to support or challenge theoretical ideas. Lofland (1970) identifies this as a key strength of the approach, immunizing it against accusations of abstract armchair theorizing. Such empirical studies are exactly the kind of material on which I shall be drawing throughout the book, to bring the theoretical concepts to life and ground them in relatable examples.

These three qualities of process, performance and pragmatism lie at the heart of the SI approach to identity and characterize the shape of its research.

## Outline of the book

Taking a symbolic interactionist perspective, this book is concerned with an overall theme, as noted above: the social processes of interaction through which identities are *created, shaped, maintained, communicated, presented, negotiated, challenged, reproduced, reinvented and narrated.* Each of the chapters that follow focuses on one such process or dimension of interaction to elucidate different aspects of social identity.

Chapter 2 considers how social interaction is organized in public places and settings, using Goffman's concept of the 'interaction order'. We shall see how actors co-operate to stage versions of reality, or 'definitions of the situation', to which they tacitly agree to adhere. However, these may only be 'polite fictions' that are belied by what everyone knows is really the case. We shall explore how these collaborative performances are staged through the interaction rituals that characterize what Goffman called 'focused' and 'unfocused' social encounters. This will be illustrated by studies of the management of public nudity, in swimming pools, naturist camps and gynaecological examinations. Finally, we will consider attributions of rudeness to behaviour that breaks these rules of everyday civility.

Chapter 3 looks at the role of language, especially talk-in-interaction, as a tool of identity performance. Using theoretical ideas from ethnomethodology and three methodological techniques (conversation analysis, discourse analysis and frame analysis), I examine how social actors carefully design what they say and how they say it to convey symbolic meanings. This can be studied in relation to roles and institutional settings, such as broadcast journalism and academic science. In more mundane, everyday contexts, we can observe the techniques of 'aligning actions' by which actors demonstrate conformity to social norms and values. These include motive talk, accounting procedures (excuses and justifications), reparative actions (apologies, requests and identity repair work), and disclaimers.

Chapters 4 and 5 explore Goffman's dramaturgy in relation to individual and group identity performances, respectively. After revisiting the dramaturgical concepts of self-presentation and impression management, Chapter 4 examines how this relates to the performance of social roles. The SI notion of role-making suggests that actors interpret, construct and perform social roles according to situational motives and concerns. This may involve dramaturgical techniques of idealization, mystification, misrepresentation and defensive facework, as we shall see in a study of students' self-presentation upon receiving exam results. We shall also consider the extent to which actors themselves believe in the parts they are playing, using Goffman's distinction between cynical and sincere performances and Hochschild's surface and deep acting; this is illustrated by Van Maanen's insightful study of Disneyland.

Chapter 5 examines Goffman's notion of teamwork: that actors work co-operatively like members of a theatrical cast, to support each other's performances and create collective group impressions. We look at the rituals, gestures and material props used to accomplish this, drawing on studies of musical bands and sports clubs. Revisiting Goffman's concept of facework, we consider the protective and collective variants of this, whereby team-mates tactfully save each other from embarrassment or avoid unwanted attributions. This is illustrated by a study of how colleagues participating in a workplace-based exercise group dealt with role conflict by defining themselves as 'familiar strangers'. We also consider how team-mates manipulate each other into giving supportive gestures, through the taxonomy of 'response cries'. Finally, we look at Goffman's concept of 'communication out of character', whereby team-mates can present two lines of action simultaneously, their tacitly understood subtext undermining the version of reality presented to the audience. Techniques of team collusion are found in studies of the retail and service industries, along with staging talk, coded cues and realigning actions.

In Chapter 6, we look at how identities change over the life course, this process being mediated by experiences of social interaction. Identity can be imagined as a 'career' or 'trajectory' that is constantly unfolding and never finished. Individually, we engage in self-reflexive biographical work, seeking to impose order and meaning on our lives. Critical moments, epiphanies and turning points can be identified and narratively reconstructed, along with the ritual processes of status passage that mark transitions from one social identity to another. Then we consider Goffman's notion of the moral career, whereby value-laden social reactions to a person's conduct shape the way their identities are regarded. Hardie-Bick's ethnography of skydiving illustrates how participants carefully negotiated attributions of risk-taking by learning to perform seriousness. This leads on to a discussion of Goffman's stigma, a discrepancy between the 'virtual' identity the actor seeks to project and the 'actual' identity they think they have backstage. Stigmatizing attributes can be visibly discrediting, potentially discreditable or vicariously felt as courtesy stigmas, each affecting interaction differently. Through studies of disability and sexuality, we see how actors devise techniques for managing these encounters, such as information control and passing. The concept of the deviant career, meanwhile, was popularized in the 1960s by labelling theory. Aside from criminal activity, I argue, deviant careers affect other, more routine experiences of feeling different, as illustrated through my study of shyness. Finally we consider whether and how it is possible to halt the progress of a career and step off the trajectory; the process of role exit is also mediated by significant others in interaction.

Chapter 7 examines how identities change through the experience of being in an institution or organization. I focus particularly on Goffman's concept of the total institution (TI) – places to which people are confined around the clock, and subjected to coercive resocialization. Through studies of psychiatric hospitals, we see how inmates undergo a symbolic 'mortification' of their previous identity before a new one is imposed upon them, but also how they may resist this to retain a sense of authentic selfhood. Updating this concept somewhat, I propose an alternative model of the reinventive institution (RI), whereby inmates voluntarily commit themselves and fervently adhere to the resocialization process. Positive meanings of self-improvement, enhancement and transformation are associated with this as an ostensibly benign process, although we can also detect the influence of a more subtle and pervasive form of social control. Power operates in the RI through peer surveillance, discipline and monitoring, as we see in studies of the interaction dynamics between members of therapeutic communities, religious cults and military-style training camps.

The final chapter of the book concerns identity deception, questioning whether, how and why we might present fake versions of ourselves to others. This involves the study of lying, secrecy, tactful or benign fabrications and betrayal. A central debate is whether such deception can be functional for social interaction, regardless of its moral right or wrongness, insofar as it makes situations flow more smoothly. Drawing on Simmel's fascination–fear dialectic, I argue that this depends on the depth of connection that exists between actors. This is illustrated by an examination of how deceptive interaction can unfold at five different levels of relationship intimacy: polite relations between strangers; collusion between rival teams; competitive game-play between members of the same team; betrayal by an intimate accomplice; and the ultimate possibility of self-deception.

In all of these discussions, we see how social identity is not a simple 'thing' that people 'have', but, rather, a complex process, which is constructed throughout social life in relation to others. Furthermore, it is precariously contingent on these connections and bonds for its survival. Versions of ourselves can be claimed, displayed and performed, but they must also be accepted and supported by others; thus identity is *negotiated* at the micro level of everyday life. Through our rituals, routines, interactions and encounters, we navigate paths around possible selves and different identities, managing social reactions alongside private reflections. Symbolic interactionism and dramaturgical theory help to make sense of this dangerous and delicate feat, elucidating the mutual dependency between social identities and the interaction order.

# 2

# Relating in public
## Rudeness, civility and polite fictions

This chapter explores how social identities are performed and managed through interaction in public places, where participants encounter each other as strangers yet still significant objects, to whom their conduct must be oriented. Public places include the street, waiting areas, public transport and recreational facilities, where the rules are ambiguous and have to be negotiated *in situ*. Without the supportive frameworks of trust, familiarity, intimacy and routine, actors are rendered vulnerable to their identity claims being challenged or misread, to making unintended blunders and creating unwanted impressions. Yet often we find that audiences are supportive and accommodating, sharing a common motivation to uphold the immediate 'definition of the situation' and the wider semblance of the 'interaction order'. We shall examine the mechanisms behind this, such as displays of tact, civility and ritualized observance of social norms, which show how even apparently 'unfocused' interaction (Goffman 1967) is actually governed by routine, predictability and rule-following behaviour.

## The interaction order

The title of this chapter refers to one of Goffman's books on the micro-processes of interaction, *Relations in Public* (1971). This, along with other titles such as *Encounters* (1961b), *Behavior in Public Places* (1963b) and *Interaction Ritual* (1967), serves as a catalogue of the forms of expressive behaviour – verbal speech, facial expressions, bodily gestures and demeanour – that can be observed in any situation, as an index of the underlying social structure. Goffman emphasized the patterning of rules, norms and values across situations that govern orderly conduct; these are ceremoniously observed and followed as pragmatic guiding principles for action.

The term 'interaction order' was coined by Goffman in his 1982 presidential address to the American Sociological Association, which was published as a journal article after his death (Goffman 1983a). Here, he argues that the interaction order constitutes a distinct domain of social life that can be studied in its own right, as a structure of moral and institutional order (Heritage & Clayman 2010: 8). While comprising a plethora of discrete, localized social settings, each of which unfolds as a self-contained drama, when put together, these constitute a broader, deeper pattern of social organization.

This realm encompasses a wide range of social interaction, from the 'merely situated', where events unfold that are incidental to the co-presence of the particular actors and could conceivably take place without them, to the 'situated', where actors come together to pursue a common purpose. Elsewhere, Goffman (1967) referred to these as 'unfocused' and 'focused' encounters, respectively. He also distinguished between levels of interaction, according to the situation's format, collective organization and distribution of roles. At the first level, embodied individuals are merely 'vehicular elements' or 'ambulatory units', moving around social space and navigating a path around others (Goffman 1971). They follow a set of tacitly understood 'traffic rules' to protect their personal territories and avoid encroaching into others' spaces. The second level involves 'contact' between interactants, such as the physical touching of bodies or eye contact and glancing. At the third level, there are conversational 'encounters' marked by ritual exchanges, where people come together 'as ratified participants in a consciously shared, clearly interdependent undertaking' (Goffman 1983a: 9). Fourthly, the 'platform' entails a scene staged before an audience, such as a meeting, a formal address or service transactions in occupational settings. Finally, the 'celebrative social occasion' demands that actors display deference towards some 'jointly appreciated circumstances' (Goffman 1983a: 11); these are highly ritualized and generate a collective mood of excitement.

Behaviour in public places can be located within the first, second and third of these levels. Goffman (1963b) suggests that conduct in such encounters, whether they be focused or unfocused, is nevertheless orderly as it is governed by 'situational proprieties': the rules, norms and expectations of how one ought to behave in order to demonstrate respect and courtesy to others. These 'enabling conventions' establish a backdrop of shared understandings and normative expectations, which serve as a pragmatic resource for action and which all participants can draw upon. Thus 'orderly interaction [emerges as] . . . a process of normative consensus' (Goffman 1983a: 7). Although these interaction arrangements are designed to withstand occasional violation, overall there is a collaborative effort to maintain the micro-structure's stability.

## Politeness and civility

Central to the maintenance of this tacit moral code is the notion of *civility*. This refers to the motivation behind rule-governed conduct, namely a respect for the principle of orderliness and a commitment to upholding that appearance. Civility entails an attitude of politeness: not merely as a superficial adherence to conventional etiquette, but as a display of shared morality, demonstrating one's reliability and trustworthiness as a member of the group. Behaviourally, civility includes the practices of manners, observing situational proprieties and following appropriate decorum, all of which, Burns (1992) suggests, points to a concern with behaving predictably and co-operatively and avoiding embarrassment. Apart from keeping face ourselves, we try not to undermine others' self-presentational claims or interfere with their lines of action.

Politeness is an art form: a set of skills that people learn to defend themselves against embarrassment, compromised dignity or interactional strain. Goffman (1967: 47–96) referred to the dramaturgical techniques of deference and demeanour. Deference is an attitude of respect towards those in higher-status positions; it is how we convey appreciation of the other or the 'sacredness' of their face. This might involve rituals of avoidance (such as servants avoiding eye contact with their employers) and rituals of presentation (compliments, invitations and minor services). Demeanour describes the means through which deference is communicated, such as facial expression, courteous language and appropriate dress. The appearance of a civilized order spreads a veneer of pleasantness over potentially frosty encounters, disguising any underlying tension. Spiers (1998: 32) suggests that politeness provides 'the means for performing face-threatening acts whilst still maintaining each other's face'.

## Definition of the situation

The performance of civility in interaction is an example of an important concept in symbolic interactionism, the 'definition of the situation' (Thomas & Thomas 1928). This describes a stage of examination and deliberation that occurs between actors in a social situation as they strive to achieve a working consensus of what is going on. It results in a subjectively perceived reality, regardless of what may objectively be the case, which is meaningful to and has pragmatic consequences for those involved. Thomas and Thomas (1928: 575) famously said: 'If men [sic] define situations as real, they are real in their consequences.' Beyond the immediate setting, this has wider implications for the interaction order. Thomas (1923) suggested that social morality is not a matter of universal truth but rather one of social convention, specific to a local group or culture: an emergent set of rules or normative codes of conduct that is built up over time by a group's successively agreed definitions of situations.

As a process of negotiation, the definition of the situation involves actors orienting themselves towards their common goals, the symbolic objects around them, the roles they should be playing, and the actions that accompany these. Hewitt (2007: 61) summarizes the concept as an 'organization of perception in which people assemble objects, meanings, and others, and act toward them in a coherent, organized way', while Ball (1972: 63) points to 'the sum total of all recognized information, from the point-of-view of the actor, which is relevant to his locating himself [sic] and others, so that he can engage in self-determined lines of action and interaction'.

The function of this within the situation is to make it comprehensible, predictable and easy to participate in. Recalling Schütz's (1972) phenomenology (see Chapter 1), actors draw upon shared stocks of background knowledge to interpret and make sense of situations together. This consists of normative assumptions and expectations based on previous occasions, such as role 'typifications' and 'recipes' of scripted action (Schütz 1972). Following these rules allows actors to assume the 'natural attitude' (Schütz 1972) of habit and routineness, proceeding with the situation as unremarkable 'business as usual'. Ontologically, this state of unreflexive consciousness enables actors to 'carry on being' (Giddens 1984), bracketing out their awareness of the arbitrariness of their agreed-upon reality.

Not surprisingly, actors share a common motivation to uphold this version of events and protect it against threat or challenge. They selectively perceive aspects of the setting to confirm their definition, and tactfully ignore information that refutes it. Goffman (1969) wrote of the importance of preserving 'normal appearances' and staging 'normalcy shows': depictions of whatever was happening as if it were completely unremarkable, even if the opposite were true. Paradoxically, actors may present an air of casual nonchalance ('acting natural' and 'at home' in a scenario) whilst self-consciously monitoring their conduct and managing the show as a contrived performance. Burns (1992: 98) suggests that this is 'a virtually universal social skill which we put to frequent, and legitimate, use'.

## Ritualized observance

Socially constructed realities are precarious accomplishments that have to be repeatedly re-enacted to survive. This is achieved through *interaction rituals*: regular, stylized and conventional ways of acting towards one another in situated settings, drawing upon normative codes of conduct. As we saw in Chapter 1, Collins' (2005) interaction ritual theory suggests that this ritualized observance of the interaction order is crucial to its maintenance, through the celebration of common values that strengthens social solidarity within a group or culture.

This was illustrated in an ethnographic study I conducted of a public swimming pool in the UK (Scott 2009a). Here I argued that the pool constituted a local social world, with its own distinct culture: a set of complementary roles (swimmers, lifeguards, supervisors, managers, receptionists, and so on), values (the pursuit of fitness, leisure and recreation) and code of conduct (how staff and customers were expected to behave towards each other). I argued that this structure was maintained from within, by the members of the setting, through a process of negotiated order (Strauss 1978; see also Chapter 7 below). Swimmers in particular are a self-governing performance team (Goffman 1959), who monitor, regulate and sanction each other's behaviour in the pool.

Behavioural etiquette in the pool centres on three social norms, to which swimmers pay ritualized observance. These are: respect for personal space; respect for disciplinary regimes; and the desexualization of encounters. Firstly, individual lane swimmers respect each other's 'territories of the self' (Goffman 1971: 51): the body itself; the area surrounding it; and the possessions people use to mark this, such as goggles, floats and bottled water. Swimmers show respect for this rule by keeping as much distance as possible, avoiding bodily contact (or apologizing if this accidentally occurs) and queuing up to swim lengths.

Secondly, there is a tacit understanding that those 'serious' swimmers occupying the three lanes will have their own exercise agenda, such as a certain quota of laps to complete. It is expected that swimmers will choose a lane appropriate to their ability and speed (fast, medium or slow) and not inconvenience others by getting in their way. For example, when confronted by a swimmer faster than oneself, it is considered polite to give way and allow that person to overtake, while rude to stay defiantly in front, slowing them down. Sociability is restricted to the open area, and it is inappropriate to strike up conversations in the lanes:

> Bit of a moral dilemma today – arrived late so was keen to get my lengths in before the whistle, but then Laura (friend) arrived and wanted to chat.

I wanted to listen and see how she was, but time was ticking on. When she said, 'Anyway, how are you?' I took my cue and said, 'Actually, do you mind if we talk later, in the showers? Sorry, I'm running a bit late today!' Blushed and cringed like mad, but luckily, as a seasoned regular, she immediately 'got it' and said, 'Oh yes, of course,' put on her goggles and sped off. (Field notes, September 7, 2008) (Scott 2009a: 133)

The third rule frames the setting with a 'civilized' definition of the situation: the desexualization of encounters between swimmers. This 'elephant in the room' is a strange paradox of the pool: everyone is nearly naked, yet nobody refers to the fact, because its implications would be too embarrassing to address explicitly. Nudity is disattended to, and actors bracket out their awareness of each other as embodied, sexual beings (though see the discussion later in this chapter). Bathing costumes provide a tokenistic nod to modesty but leave little to the imagination. Those who swim with their heads above water avoid eye contact with each other, and present blank, emotionless faces, giving the impression of being 'away' in a reverie (Goffman 1963b: 69). Connected to this is a taboo on physical contact between bodies: any accidental brushes of the skin evoke embarrassment and mutual apologies to restore the definition of the situation:

I was turning in the shallow end and accidentally kicked a woman in the leg. It wasn't my fault – she wasn't looking where she was going and stepped backwards – but I instinctively apologized, because that's what you do. Reminded me of another time when a man did the same to me but looked really embarrassed and apologized profusely, as if I might think he was trying to touch me. (Field notes, July 3, 2008) (Scott 2009a: 134)

## Unfocused encounters: regulating involvement

The swimming pool example is illustrative of how actors uphold the interaction order in *focused* gatherings: settings that bring people together to co-operate towards a common goal with a shared focus of attention (Goffman 1967). Many situations in the realm of public places, however, fit more neatly into Goffman's category of *unfocused* interaction: where actors happen incidentally to be co-present but are pursuing independent lines of activity. Even if these lines are actually identical (e.g. waiting for a service), people seek to engage in them alone rather than co-operate in joint activity. Waiting rooms, bus stops, parks, streets and public transport are all examples of this kind of setting. Morrill and Snow (2005) point to the myriad ways in which people seek to be 'together alone' – or perhaps we might say 'alone together'. This typically means bracketing out their awareness of each other's presence and ignoring the social aspects of the scene, such as bodily proximity and visibility within the sweep of a gaze. In unfocused situations, then, actors seek to continue pursuing separate lines of action and avoid the deeper obligations of a focused encounter.

## The stranger

Unfocused interaction implicates a certain kind of social actor, or at least a role or attitude that actors can assume. Schütz (1964) analysed interaction in terms of the degree of mutual knowledge actors hold about each other's role-identities and likely courses of action. He identified certain subject positions defined by actors' levels of familiarity with the setting and the types of knowledge they could take for granted. These included the 'expert', the 'well-informed citizen' and the 'man on the street'.

Occasionally, however, individuals find themselves in the position of the 'stranger' (Schütz 1971). This is someone who feels excluded from the common stocks of background knowledge that those around them appear to take for granted. This has pragmatic implications in making it difficult for the individual to partake in joint action (Blumer 1969): they might not know which role to play, the normative code of conduct or the recipe knowledge needed to help the situation flow smoothly. Simmel (1908a), too, wrote about the stranger as a social archetype, characterized by its marginal position. Encountering a ready-formed group from the outside, the stranger represents two of Simmel's interactional 'forms' simultaneously: proximity and distance. This experience is central to the feeling of shyness (Scott 2007a). As one of my participants, Urchin, reported, it is common to find oneself 'hovering on the fringes, attracting suspicious looks' (Scott 2007a: 71).

However, Simmel also suggested that there were advantages to this position, in that one might be regarded by group members as a confidant(e): someone so remote as to be harmless, who could therefore be trusted with their team secrets (Goffman 1959). In fact, Simmel argued, on the contrary: the stranger who was indulged thus was actually in a powerful position as they could potentially betray these confidences to another party. We revisit these ideas in Chapter 4 in the discussion of Goffman's 'non-person' role, and in Chapter 8's discussion of deception.

## Civil inattention

A common technique used in unfocused encounters is civil inattention (Goffman 1963b). This pattern of behaviour occurs amongst strangers who enter into one another's space through chance meetings, such as passing on the street. Like other techniques in this dramaturgical subset, its purpose is to regulate the level of engagement and mutual involvement between interactants, and avoid unfocused encounters turning into focused ones. Civil inattention is a ritual dance of non-verbal symbolic gestures, particularly the careful use of eye contact. It is a display of non-involvement in other people's business and absorption in one's own affairs. Thus two strangers will glance briefly at each other and then look away, as if to signal that they acknowledge the other's presence and right to be there, but pose no threat to them. Goffman (1963b) suggested that whether it was possible to use civil inattention was partly dependent on the density of a situation's population. He identified a critical threshold of 150 people, called the 'nod line', below which actors felt obliged to acknowledge each other with eye contact and personal greetings, but over which they could get away with feigned ignorance of each other's presence.

Civil inattention is a trademark gesture of urban life, whose busy public places frequently bring strangers into situations of unwanted proximity. Simmel (1902–3) wrote a famous essay on the 'metropolis', or modern city, and its effects on those who live there. He argued that the fast-paced, hectic, media-saturated nature of the urban street created a sensory overload that was difficult to endure, especially when combined with the superficiality of human contact fostered by a series of anonymous, fleeting encounters. City dwellers responded to this by affecting a blasé demeanour: an expressionless face, the avoidance of eye contact and a brisk walking pace, as if to communicate that they were too busy to stop and get involved in any deeper form of interaction. Wirth (1938) made similar remarks about the anonymous and superficial nature of encounters between strangers, and the isolated experience of urbanism as a way of life.

Writing some decades later, Lofland (1973) argued that we were now living in a 'world of strangers': as cities had expanded, the metropolitan mentality had become the normal mode of interaction throughout society. There had been a shift from occasional dealings with the infrequent stranger to routinized encounters with the 'constant stranger'. More optimistically than Simmel, she suggested that this might come as a relief to some, as unfocused interaction was less dramaturgically demanding to perform: it allowed 'co-presence without co-mingling, awareness without engrossment, courtesy without conversation' (1973:

462). Lofland argued that skilled urbanites had developed a range of tactics and strategies for managing this change, beyond mere civil inattention, which centred on creating private spaces for themselves within public scenes or settings. These included 'locational transformations', which changed the actual physical place or the objects within it, for example when we bring personal items from home to decorate our desks at work and carve out a little individual territory. 'Symbolic transformations' meant adapting one's attitude to the landscape to alter its meaning and make it easier to navigate; civil inattention is an example of this.

## Territory, accessibility and space

As unfocused encounters tend to involve relatively little speech, much of the work that people put into regulating the distance between themselves is performed through the body. Sometimes this means moving the whole body around social space – Goffman (1971) imagined embodied selves to be 'vehicular units', navigating their way through the 'traffic' of crowded scenes – but often it is managed through subtler gestures of eye contact, facial expressions, positioning and angling the body, and using material objects as props. This back channel of communication is always being used but varies in its salience. Goffman (1963b) said that when talk is used in interaction, it becomes the main focus of attention, but without it, non-verbal gestures rise to prominence. Whichever is the case, whenever we are in another's presence we cannot stop communicating; we can say the right thing or the wrong thing but we must say something. Unfocused encounters rely on participants' shared understanding of the 'body idiom' (Goffman 1971), a common repertoire of symbolic gestures that actors display and audiences interpret.

Actors show their 'accessibility', or willingness to be drawn into interaction, in various ways. Looking up and around at others, making eye contact and smiling, all demonstrate to onlookers that an individual has time to spare for superfluous engagements. Conversely, actors may endeavour to dissuade others from encroaching on their attention by ostentatiously busying themselves with other activities. 'Auto-involvements', especially, are those focused on one's own self or body, such as playing with hair, examining fingernails and picking imaginary fluff off clothes. In my research on shyness, one participant, Georgia, told me that she would avert her eyes from anyone who seemed to be heading in her direction and exert a studied gaze elsewhere: 'It's almost like we [shy people] have a "Please don't approach me!" look' (Scott 2007a: 58).

Material props can also be used to communicate the same gestures of (in)accessibility. Goffman (1963b) referred to 'involvement shields' that actors place in front of themselves as barriers between their own and others' bodies. Reading a newspaper while sitting on a park bench, or fiddling with a mobile phone whilst waiting for a train, are ways in which actors convey the message that however bored and at a loose end they are, they would still rather be left alone than be drawn into a social encounter. The irony is, of course, that secretly the actor may not be immersed in these activities at all but surreptitiously monitoring the social scene, exercising dramaturgical discipline (Goffman 1959) as they remain vigilant and poised for action.

Props can also be used as boundary markers, delineating areas of personal space around the body. Goffman (1971) described the 'territories of the self' that we build like fortresses to guard our privacy when out in public places, and which we fiercely defend against invasion. This is an attempt to create a minimal, sometimes token or symbolic, enclave of privacy away from the social gaze. It is a strategy often used when practicality necessitates a move from comfortable backstage regions to crowded frontstage ones, which we would prefer not to have to share. On the beach, Goffman observed, people will set out their belongings, such as rug, picnic food and sunbathing equipment, as if to delineate a patch that is entirely theirs, ostensibly ignoring (but actually carefully regulating) the proximity of others doing exactly the same. On buses and trains, we seek to find a 'double seat' to avoid having to sit next to someone (the comedian Ben Elton wrote a great sketch about this), and put our bags on the seat next to us to discourage anyone from sitting there. Students have confessed to me that they sometimes pretend to be asleep, in the hope that passers-by will not want to disturb them.

Sometimes a person's level of accessibility is determined by factors outside of their control. Actors may find themselves circumstantially located in *open positions* where they are helplessly exposed to public scrutiny, for example when waiting for a friend on the street without any distracting props to hand. Goffman (1963b) also pointed to *open regions*, or places in which it is difficult to exercise civil inattention, because etiquette demands that those present be 'on show': for example at parties, where one is supposed to 'mingle' with strangers. Then there are *open roles*, such as reception desk staff, shop assistants or police officers, whose occupants are obliged to make themselves accessible to approach by anyone, regardless of their private attitudes. As soon as the performance is over and they come out of role, however, these obligations stop, and the actor can revert to being socially removed if they so wish. A swimming pool lifeguard once explained to me what a relief it was to reach the end of his shift and drop his 'public face', with the responsibility that this entailed. Five minutes earlier he had been busy teaching swimming lessons, herding children into the showers, talking to inquisitive parents and rearranging lane ropes, but as soon as the whistle blew marking the end of the session, he was able to walk away, leaving his colleagues to tidy up the scene. He could later be found in a quiet corner of the foyer, curled up on a sofa reading a book and evidently 'off duty'.

These ideas are illustrated by a wonderful ethnographic study by Kim (2012) of social interaction on Greyhound buses, a mode of public transport that people use to travel long distances between cities in the USA. These vehicles bring together a collection of strangers from diverse social backgrounds into a situation of co-presence for an extended period of time. This evokes many of the aforementioned features of unfocused interaction in public places – civil inattention, strangerliness, in/accessibility and territory management – but as Kim suggests, these are performed in a distinct way because of the unique circumstances of the setting. What she calls 'nonsocial transient spaces' are those in which strangers are forced into each other's intimate co-presence for a temporary spell, yet still seek to avoid engaging in focused encounters. Paradoxically, however, this in itself is a performance demanding carefully studied interaction rituals.

Sharing a long-distance bus journey creates a blurring of the boundaries between Goffman's front- and backstage regions, as passengers are forced to carry out normally private activities (eating, sleeping, going to the bathroom) in public, and it becomes harder to sustain a glossy front of civility. Over time, tiredness and frustration supersede the urge towards politeness that would normally restrain actors' behaviour: the mask slips and they neglect to conceal private aspects of their selves, such as emotional expressions and bodily 'creature releases' (Goffman 1959) like yawning, scratching and breaking wind. Acts whose privacy would normally have been fiercely protected are regarded with an attitude of wearily resigned acceptance, so passengers make no attempt to hide washing their hair in the sink of a bus station washroom, or wiping sweaty armpits with a dampened paper towel (Kim 2012: 273).

Greyhound passengers actively perform disengagement, avoiding both acknowledging the presence of others and being acknowledged by them. For example, Kim noticed a deviation from the normal rule of 'restrained helpfulness' (Morrill & Snow 2005: 11) in public places. While waiting in the bus terminal, passengers would decline to ask others to 'watch their stuff' while they went to the bathroom, and would sit on the floor rather than ask someone to move their belongings from a seat. This was because making such polite requests would force them to acknowledge each other's presence, which they had hitherto ignored:

as they would then be spending the next few hours in a confined space together, this would cause embarrassing ambiguity about whether or not to continue acknowledging each other. However, there may be exceptions to this. Raudenbush (2012) found that black minority groups living in poor, urban areas of Chicago were more likely to breach civil inattention on public transport by talking to each other, in a symbolic display of social cohesion.

When choosing a seat on the bus, Kim reports that passengers would endeavour to sit alone, extending the territories of the self to demarcate a protected area of private space. Those first onboard would take a double seat, placing their belongings next to them as an involvement shield (Goffman 1963b). The unlucky ones who boarded the bus later, when it was nearly full, would have to negotiate the delicate balance of finding someone to sit next to without appearing intrusive, whilst protecting their own position from expectations of involvement. They would carefully select a person to sit next to according to their presumed level of 'normalness'. Experienced riders knew how to spot the risk factors of an undesirable seat partner: those who broke the rules by taking up too much space, either physically, with their bodies, or socially, with their demands for involving conversation. As one respondent, Ty, explained, 'Yea, there are some crazies. You don't wanna sit next to a crazy person, a fatty, a chitchatter, and especially not a smelly one' (Kim 2012: 274). Another jaded regular, Loretta, was able to recount the list of tacitly understood rules for managing accessibility and using the body as a shield of privacy (cf. Lofland 1973: 140):

> Avoid eye contact with people getting on the bus; lean against the window and stretch out your legs on the other seat; place a large bag or sleeping bag on the empty seat; sit on the aisle seat and blast your iPod, and if someone asks for the window seat, pretend you don't hear them; place several small items on the empty seat so that it's clearly difficult and not worth their time to wait for you to clear the seat; pretend to sleep; sit on the aisle seat and look out the window with a 'blank stare' (makes you look crazy); put your coat there and make it look like the seat's already taken. . . . If all else fails, you can lie and say that you are saving the seat for someone. (Kim 2012: 274–5)

Occasionally, these rules would be broken by somebody who had not grasped them: like Schütz's and Simmel's archetypal stranger, they did not have access to the common stocks of background knowledge that others took for granted. Someone who sat down next to another passenger when there were other empty seats would be regarded with wide-eyed disbelief and branded a 'weirdo' (Kim 2012: 275), while hostile glares would be directed at those who disturbed the peace with loud mobile phone conversations. Occasionally there would be a direct confrontation, but immediately afterwards the situation would revert to normal appearances: '. . . someone may even overtly complain, "Hey, keep it down!" or try to silence the speaker with a "Shh!" These cues serve as a reminder to violators to uphold the rules' (Kim 2012: 279).

## Queuing and waiting

Queuing, or waiting in line, is another fascinating piece of social theatre to observe. Strangers are once again forced into uneasy co-presence, as everyone is pursuing the same line of action but seeks to bracket out their awareness of others. They perform the paradoxical strategy of 'studied non-observance' (Goffman 1963b): making a show of not looking and appearing immersed in their own private affairs, whilst surreptitiously keeping an eye on the scene. In elevators, for example, passengers pretend to ignore each other, standing in silence and facing the doors at the front. Felipe and Sommer (1966) call this 'diversionary action', as actors seek to convey the impression that their attention has been momentarily distracted elsewhere, and hence that they are neither culpable of looking nor available to be looked at.

Schwartz (1975) argues that queuing represents inequalities in the social distribution of time: making somebody wait for the service you will provide is an act of power, conveying the implication that your time is more important than theirs. Conversely, being kept waiting is boring and frustrating, as it reminds us of our relative powerlessness. Nevertheless, queuing is accepted as what we have to do in the situation; not just pragmatically but morally, it is the *right* thing to do. This is because it represents what Fox (2004) called the fairness principle, or 'first come, first served'. Schwartz agrees that we rarely object to the principle of queuing, because we can see that everybody is being treated fairly, with the exception of those in an urgent predicament: there is an unspoken rule of priority allocation.

From an organizational perspective, various tricks and strategies can be used by service personnel to regulate their customers' waiting behaviour. Many of these are aimed at managing either expectations or perceptions of the service delivery, thus preventing customer dissatisfaction. This reduces the risk of challenges, complaints and disruptive behaviour, which would threaten the interaction order of the situation. This is an example of what Goffman (1952) called 'cooling the mark out': helping people adjust to a loss of status or rejected identity claim, and to resultant feelings of degradation, disempowerment or disappointment (see Chapter 8 below).

Maister (1985) catalogues some of these strategies and identifies the principles on which they are based. Firstly, there is the idea that occupied waiting time feels shorter: if we are kept busy with a task whilst standing in a queue, we will be distracted from the frustration and indignity of waiting. Often these time-wasting 'filler' tasks will be cleverly disguised to appear as if they are contributing to the final outcome, as if the process of the service has begun. Hence restaurants hand out menus to customers who are queuing to be seated, while call centres make use of numbered dialling systems: by choosing the required option each time, pressing buttons and stating personal details, the customer feels as if they are actively doing something to participate in the process and to make it more efficient.

Secondly, explanations, apologies and politeness appease frustration. In Goffman's (1967: 47–96) terms, these platitudes serve as gestures of deference, albeit merely feigned, to the supposed dignity of the customer. Hence railway stations pipe out announcements over the loudspeaker to explain *why* a train is late (a broken-down train further ahead, a missing driver, the wrong kind of leaves on the line). Recorded messages on telephone helplines reassure the customer that they 'thank you for your patience' and that 'your call is important to us'. The fact that these are clearly just 'McDonaldized' (Ritzer 2004) uniform sound-bites pumped out in a standardized, impersonal manner is an irony rarely lost on those forced to listen to them.

Thirdly, Maister suggests that uncertainty and anxiety make waits seem longer: it is stressful not to know how long we will have to wait, whether we have joined the fastest queue or whether we will even be served at all. This is why the supermarket queue next to us appears to move faster than the one we have joined, or why people waiting in an airport departure gate nervously huddle near the door, even though they have allocated seats – just in case they cannot get on the plane.

Finally, there is the principle that tolerance depends on the perceived value and quality of the service: people are more willing to wait for things that they really want or that they believe to be good value. This is why patients are prepared to wait months for medical treatment, and those who long to be parents persevere with navigating the cost and bureaucracy of fertility clinics or adoption agencies. Conversely, those waiting in line at the Pound Store will have much shorter attention spans and thresholds of tolerance; their impatient foot-tapping and sighing begin after a matter of minutes.

## Polite fictions and presented realities

So far we have seen a myriad of ways in which we co-operate to uphold the interaction order. But what if we are not convinced? Are we naïve in assuming, simply because actors appear, behaviourally, to uphold a definition of the situation, that they actually believe in it? In some interaction contexts, it seems that actors may juggle two social realities simultaneously: ostensibly adhering to one version of events whilst privately believing in another state of affairs, which they know to be 'really' true. Burns (1992) refers to the 'polite fictions' on which we rely to keep social scenes flowing smoothly, and which actors tacitly agree to uphold, but which 'everyone knows' are not really the case.

### Disattending to nudity

By way of illustration, we can consider a type of situation in which this duplicitous awareness of incongruent realities often takes place: scenes involving nudity or nakedness. Sometimes it is appropriate for, and normatively sanctioned by, the circumstances of a situation that one or more actors present should be unclothed, and yet this reality is still not explicitly acknowledged.

This is usually because of embarrassment. Actors may feel self-conscious through *conspicuousness* (if they are the only person naked amongst a group of clothed people), *unfamiliarity* with the setting and its local norms (when a new member enters a sauna or open-plan locker room), or anxiety about the *alternative meanings* that onlookers might read into the event (especially that the naked body could have sexual connotations).

To manage this embarrassment, people either disattend to the state of nudity completely, acting as if they were fully clothed or otherwise oblivious, or choose to acknowledge their condition but redefine its meaning as non-threatening. In both cases, actors are colluding to create and uphold an official definition of the situation that is objectively false but – insofar as it is upheld through their ritualized observance – becomes subjectively 'real in its consequences' (Thomas & Thomas 1928: 575) for the interaction order.

#### Conspicuousness and power: gynaecological examinations

Three empirical studies serve to illustrate these three sources of embarrassment and its collective management through interaction rituals. Firstly, with regard to self-consciousness through conspicuousness, Emerson (1970a) observed how (male) doctors and (female) patients

behaved in gynaecological examinations. Here, the 'real' state of affairs
was that the patient was unclothed and exposing her body to a stranger, in
a very unnatural and invasive situation that was potentially humiliating.
This was anticipated and managed at an institutional level by routinized
clinical practices that served to convey an alternative, face-saving definition of the situation. Emerson (1970b) calls this the 'nothing unusual is
happening stance', and shows how it was maintained through interaction rituals. For example, the medical staff's manner communicated
to patients an air of reassuring professionalism and neutral disinterest;
this was just a routinized, everyday clinical procedure, and the patient
was in safe hands. The doctor avoided talking to the patient beyond a
brief greeting and explanation of the procedure, and used costume and
props, such as the white coat and surgical instruments, to create social
distance and emphasize his strictly professional role.

However, the patient was not powerless in this encounter, for she
could challenge the presented version of events. Occasionally, a woman
would be so overcome with pain, anxiety or emotional discomfort that
she would 'break frame' and interject an incongruous line into the
script, countering the 'nothing unusual' stance and disrupting the show.
For example, in the extract below, a patient has just asked a worried
question about the technical procedure, which implicitly challenges
the doctor's claim to competence and trustworthiness, before adding
bluntly, 'I hate this.' In asserting that, in fact, something unusual *is*
going on, the patient threatens to disturb the polite fiction, and breach
the interaction order. The doctor's response is interesting here, as he
ignores the interjection, replies with another technical explanation and
continues with the examination. In refusing to engage with the patient's
attempt at reframing the situation, he retains control of it: a symbolic
exercise of medical power:

> *Doctor*: You have some pain already, huh?
> *Patient*: It's just that I hate this.
> *Doctor*: Okay, try to spread your legs apart. Okay, I'm going to try to touch
> this and see where it is.
>
> (Emerson 1970b: 215)

## Unfamiliarity with local norms: the nudist camp

Secondly, we can consider actors' unfamiliarity with a setting and its
local norms through studies of naturist or nudist camps. Weinberg
(1965) suggested that the ideology of nudism subverted a widely
accepted normative institution of sexual *modesty* (that in everyday life,
a naked body has sexual connotations, and so should be treated with

restraint and reserve), making adherents vulnerable to accusations of immodesty. To avoid this, naturists sought to redefine their own situation as modest, or, as he put it, 'decent', according to four principles: that nudism and sexuality were unrelated, that there was nothing shameful about exposing the human body, that the abandonment of clothes could create feelings of freedom and natural pleasure, and that nude activities could enhance physical, mental and spiritual wellbeing (Weinberg 1965: 314).

This was upheld through the ritualized observance of a code of rules, involving normative proscriptions and prescriptions for social conduct. Firstly, organizational precautions served to filter out new members with questionable motives: for example, some camps did not allow single men to join, or required letters of recommendation. Secondly, there were norms regarding interpersonal behaviour, such as 'no staring', 'no sex talk', 'no alcohol' and 'no photography'. Thirdly, any attempts to cover up the body were regarded as unnecessarily prudish and subjected to ridicule, such as teasing new members who kept their clothes on.

In their ethnographic study of Eden Beach in California, Douglas et al. (1977) investigated some of the ways in which patrons translated these kinds of rules into action, to avoid shame and embarrassment. When accounting for their lifestyle in the abstract, they were able to cite an 'ethos of naturalism', citing values of honesty, sincerity and righteousness, which presented a 'counter-moral front' in refuting and foreclosing any more dubious interpretations of their motives (Douglas et al. 1977: 85). However, there remained great potential for misperception when the bathers were confronted 'in the flesh', as it were, by outsiders, who could be variously categorized as unsuspecting tourists, moral outragees and smirking voyeurs (1977: 71). Many such sceptics held preconceptions that the nude beach was merely a pretext for a 'wild sex orgy', but were surprised to find it a 'perfectly ordinary beach scene' that was 'depressingly normal' (1977: 93).

The campers were at pains to normalize their behaviour to these audiences with a front of breezy nonchalance, to redefine the situation as decent. 'The nude beach is a *scene of suspicion* and of continual misinterpretation' (1977: 99, emphasis in original). However, this appearance was only a polite fiction, concealing an underlying awareness of their deviance. There was a contradiction between 'two polarized public views' of what was going on, which could be defined as either an 'orgy scene or a family social' (1977: 96). The nudists were 'especially anxious to look like they are doing respectable or normal things' (1977: 94), while being aware that they were really not, and so tacitly agreed to present a 'normalcy show' to onlookers. Moreover, as a consciously contrived performance, this involved exaggerated gestures (strolling around in full view of passers-by, stretching out with a loud yawn) that, to the researchers, seemed overplayed and unconvincing. Even the audience were implicated in staging this normalcy show, as observers sought to distance themselves from the shameful attribution of the 'peeping tom voyeur' and present themselves as 'straight' onlookers (e.g. staring out to sea with binoculars in the name of 'bird-watching' [1977: 114]).

## Ambiguous motives: the swimming pool

Thirdly, with regard to rule ambiguity and the risk of misinterpreted meanings, let us return to my own ethnographic study of the swimming pool (Scott 2009a). Earlier, we saw how the interaction order was maintained by three norms, the last of which was the desexualization of encounters. Swimmers performed ritualized observance of this by wearing bathing costumes, using civil inattention and avoiding eye contact, but occasionally this definition of the situation was challenged by behaviour that acknowledged the near-naked state of swimmers' bodies. It was as if, like the young boy in Hans Christian Andersen's (1837) fairy tale, they were pointing to the obvious 'elephant in the room' and shouting 'But the emperor has no clothes!'

Such breaches of etiquette may have occurred because of the ambiguity of the setting and its rules. Certain areas were 'liminal zones' (Turner 1967), positioned between other, clearly delineated regions, where conduct norms were open to interpretation. When leaving the pool and entering the changing rooms, swimmers were ambiguously placed between the naked and the clothed, the shameful and the civilized. There were some awkward moments when people were walking to their lockers, from the lockers to the showers, back to the lockers to collect their clothes, and on to the changing cubicles. Actors making any of these trips looked distinctly uncomfortable and tended to scurry rather than walk slowly, from embarrassment as much as coldness (Scott 2009a: 135).

In the pool, meanwhile, the nudity taboo was broken by flirtation between swimmers, who did not always welcome the attention. Crossley (2006a) similarly found evidence of 'ogling' at the gym and identified it as an implicit motive for attending. I observed that flirting often occurred in the late-evening Adults-Only session at the pool (known sardonically by regulars as 'pick-up time'), and was a largely heterosexual dynamic of men gazing at women: '*Home safely. Pervert Parade tonight – they all crawled out of the woodwork! That "reclining" one only swam 3 lengths. I counted.* (Text message to female friend after 'Adults Only', November 21, 2007)' (Scott 2009a: 19). Flirting redefined the situation as a sexualized encounter and brought the erstwhile absent body of the swimmer into full view. It also drew attention to the body of the flirter, however, and rendered him or her as vulnerable to losing face as the flirtee. Consequently, the ritual dance was carefully managed by both parties through a conversation of symbolic gestures (Blumer 1969) and tentative interpretations. The flirter gave off subtle signals by swimming only a minimal number of lengths, pausing for long periods and eyeing up their prey. If the gaze was returned and conversation ensued, then all was well, but if the objectified swimmer was not interested (or oblivious), the flirter could realign themselves with the official definition of the situation by pretending that they were just pausing for a rest, adjusting goggles or doing something else innocuous.

## Awareness contexts

The discrepancy between manifest and latent definitions of reality can be used to create analytical taxonomies of situations according to the orientations actors have towards them. Scheff (1968) made a distinction between 'believed realities', wherein we convince even ourselves that the ostensible scene is true, and 'presented realities', which are acted out with an air of sceptical detachment. For example, in Weinberg's (1965) and Douglas et al.'s (1977) studies of nudist groups (see above), we saw how members cited earnest beliefs in the situation's moral decency, but were at pains to convey this meaning through contrived displays of nonchalance. We revisit this in Chapter 4 with Goffman's (1959) distinction between 'sincere' and 'cynical' role performances.

Schütz (1964) argued that when negotiating definitions of inter-subjective reality, actors have different levels of insight into the tacit knowledge embedded in a scene and their respective role-identities within it. Sometimes this knowledge distribution is unequal, as one party knows more about the other and/or the situation than that other knows about them. This idea was developed by Glaser and Strauss's discussion of awareness contexts: 'the total combination of what each interactant in a situation knows about the identity of the other and his own identity in the eyes of the other' (1964: 670).

In their study of encounters between terminally ill patients and medical staff in a hospital, Glaser and Strauss (1964) identified four possible scenarios. Firstly, an *open* awareness context occurs when both parties are fully aware of each other's identities and/or the real meaning of the situation. In this case, both the patient and the staff knew that the former was terminally ill and could talk openly about the prospect of death, for example by discussing palliative care. Here there is no discrepancy between the official version of reality to which all actors are orienting themselves and the true state of affairs in which they privately believe. By contrast, *closed* awareness contexts occur when one interactant does not know the other's true identity or their own identity in the eyes of the other: in this case, the patient did not know that they were dying but the doctors and nurses did, and so there was an inequality in their access to relevant knowledge. This meant that the question of the patient's dying could not be talked about, and the medical staff had to work hard at concealing this information from them. Thirdly, a *suspicion* awareness context arises when one interactant suspects that things are not as they seem – either the other is misrepresenting their identity, or they are being duped as to the real meaning of the situation – but these concerns are not expressed, and so both remain focused on the manifest definition of the situation. The patient realized they were being lied to by staff but felt scared to confront them, so played along with what they were told. Finally, a *pretence* awareness context occurs when all actors are fully aware of the true state of affairs and/or their true identities, but tacitly agree not to mention this, instead co-operating in upholding the official definition of the situation. This might happen if a patient had been told that they were dying but felt too frightened to talk about it; the staff would tactfully collude with their denial by keeping the conversation on other topics.

## Familiar strangers

One interesting example of a pretence awareness context is the relationship known as familiar strangers (Milgram 1977). This refers to a group of people who regularly encounter one another but do not interact; it often occurs in public places where people cross paths in the course of their daily lives, each pursuing individual lines of action. A common example is commuters who catch the same train every day and so recognize each other on the station platform. Familiar strangers may take comfort from seeing the same faces and scenes every day, yet know nothing about each other's 'real' selves. It can be tempting to imagine fantasy characters and backstories for them, because this incongruence feels so curious. The film *Eternal Sunshine of the Spotless Mind* exploits this romantic potential by exploring what would happen if two regular train passengers were to finally strike up a conversation.

Familiar strangers comprise a pretence awareness context because although they recognize each other, they pretend not to. They make a show of civil inattention, acting as if they were 'pure' strangers meeting for the first time: glancing briefly at each other and then away, before busying themselves with auto-involvements such as sorting through their bags or checking their mobile phones (Paulos & Goodman 2002).

But why do people go to so much trouble in these situations: why not simply greet each other and initiate a civil relationship? Perhaps this is due to embarrassment and the potential for interactional strain: if they were to acknowledge each other once, they would have to continue doing so every time they met, and this could become awkward because (so they imagine) they probably have nothing else in common and would have little to talk about (Fox 2004). It is easier to behave as if they are absolute strangers with no mutual obligations to support each other's role performances, nor shared responsibility for making the situation flow smoothly. In Chapter 5, we revisit this idea through Rossing and Scott's (2014) study of a workplace-based exercise class.

An interesting exception to this ritual occurs when familiar strangers meet in *another* social context, outside of their usual setting. This can be momentarily confusing, as the actors know that they recognize each other, but because of their superficial relationship, cannot think how. I have occasionally met fellow regulars from the swimming pool in a different place, on the street or in the supermarket. There is a short pause as we look at each other, realize who the other is and then – curiously – exchange shy smiles and say hello. It is almost as if by being removed from their familiar environment and encountering each other out of context, the two actors share a common state of disorientation, which actually brings them a little closer together.

## Rudeness and incivility

Sometimes the veneer of politeness can be scratched away, revealing the ruthless of individualism beneath. Rudeness is something that we often assume to be a quality that certain people possess: there are rude people, and then there are the rest of us who are polite and civilized. From a symbolic interactionist perspective, however, we can re-imagine rudeness as something that emerges out of social relations and situational encounters: it is a perception of others' behaviour, a definition of the situation that is negotiated between actors. This relates to the labelling theory of deviance (Kitsuse 1962; Becker 1963; Lemert 1967; Schur 1971; see also Chapter 6 below), which moves away from assumptions about there being inherently deviant people or acts, and looks instead to the process through which social attributions of deviance are created and applied (Becker 1963).

This model of rudeness as a situationally defined attribution is explored by Smith et al. (2010) in their study of incivility in everyday life. Their 'routine activity theory' of rudeness describes it as an opportunistic, situation-specific form of conduct that is defined by its audiences: those who are offended by what they perceive as rude behaviour. Furthermore, in suggesting that rudeness is an emergent property of situations rather than individuals, Smith et al. echo Matza's (1964) point that everyone has the potential to drift in and out of deviant behaviour: there are no inherently 'rude people'. Smith et al. suggest that rudeness is something universally acted out as well as experienced, and it is a relatively ordinary and commonplace occurrence. Rude offenders and their victims are in fact all the same group of people (Smith et al. 2010). Nobody likes to think of themselves as a rude person, however, and it is much easier to regard ourselves as upholders of social morality, whilst being quick to indignantly ascribe rudeness to others.

Smith et al. (2010) conducted a secondary analysis of data from Everyday Life Incivility in Australia Survey (ELIAS) in 2005, which had asked people to recall recent episodes in which they felt they had experienced rude behaviour. The first thing the researchers noted was that, indeed, rudeness seemed to be universal: there was not a distinct group of people who were most likely to have behaved rudely (e.g. stereotypically we might expect those accused to be young people), but rather the characteristic was attributed across the whole demographic spectrum. Thus Smith et al. suggest that rude offenders and victims are socially similar. Secondly, they refer to the time/space patterning of rude incidents: most happened not in particular places or scheduled events, but at the moments in between, when people were moving between one activity and another, often in a hurry, and in spaces of high population density – for example public transport. Related to this, rude incidents were found to occur most often when people were in transit between places; they were associated with movement rather than destinations. Smith et al. suggest this is because such liminal zones (Turner 1967) or non-places (Augé 1992) between other scenes have ambiguous rules, which are open to misinterpretation.

Smith et al. analysed these data to identify four main categories of rude events, as perceived by their 'victims', or audiences. Firstly, there was blocked motion, or invaded space. This often happened on public transport when a person was seen to be standing in the way, with a presumed obliviousness to others' interests. They might also have jumped a queue, evoking moral indignation at an abuse of the fairness principle (Fox 2004), or invaded the intimate zones of another's personal space (Hall 1959). Secondly, people reported inappropriate non-verbal actions, which offended their ideas about modesty, self-containment and civilized behaviour (Elias 1939). As such, these often involved a perceived undignified lack of control over the body and its aforementioned 'creature releases' (Goffman 1959), such as belching or breaking wind, chewing gum noisily, spitting and poor personal hygiene. Thirdly, there were intrusive sounds, such as people holding loud conversations on mobile phones, or playing music that was audible beyond their headphones. Finally, there was unwanted verbal communication, such as swearing, abusive language, inappropriate (e.g. sexual) talk for the situation, and sometimes there was an objection to any talking at all.

A widely publicized example of rudeness occurred in Britain in July 2013 when a Sainsbury's supermarket cashier made the headlines for refusing to serve a customer because she was talking on her mobile phone (*Guardian* 2013). The cashier interpreted this behaviour as rude because she perceived herself and the customer to be engaged in a focused encounter (Goffman 1967), with all the moral implications of politeness, civility and mutual regard that this implies, and yet the customer was conducting an exchange with someone else. By neglecting to greet and interact with the cashier and instead simply expecting her to silently and dutifully scan the shopping, the customer was failing to acknowledge the cashier's presence and worth as a fellow actor. Service personnel and indeed servants are often rendered this lower-status position, which Goffman (1959) called the 'non-person' (see Chapter 4 below).

What is equally interesting is the way in which both people in this situation viewed themselves defensively and sought to justify their behaviour: in line with Smith et al.'s theory, each thought that they were in the right, that the other party was rude, and so they both claimed the moral high ground. Comedian and columnist David Mitchell (2013) reported the alleged dialogue between them and argued that both parties could be interpreted as equally polite – or, indeed, equally rude:

> It's a curious exchange . . . between two people who place a high value on politeness . . . . [The cashier] obviously felt it was rude of [the customer] to talk on the phone when she should have been interacting with people who were physically present. But . . . it was also rude to passively-aggressively freeze until [the customer] put the phone down. I wonder if, on sober reflection, she thinks the phrase 'I will not check your shopping out until you get off your mobile phone' is exactly charm school material either. Clearly she was indulging in retaliatory rudeness. Which is just as rude as the rudeness she was retaliating about.

Rudeness serves as an exceptional case that 'proves the rule' of the normal, everyday interaction order. Most people, most of the time, try to observe and uphold the normative conventions of social behaviour. It is only on the rare occasions when these norms get broken that we realize what they are, or even that they exist at all. As Garfinkel (1967) argued, rules only become visible 'in the breach', and most of the time they remain 'seen but unnoticed'. Social reactions to rudeness, as with any form of norm-breaking behaviour, reveal much more about the values and morality of a social group, the norms of a local culture. In this case, indignant reactions to 'rude' behaviour underline how much we rely upon the assumption that everyone will follow the unspoken rules of conduct. This principle – and its ritualized observance through symbolic gestures of politeness and civility – is what creates orderliness in public places, contributing to the social structure of the interaction order.

## Conclusion

This chapter has explored the myriad ways in which social actors co-operate to uphold the interaction order in public places, and their motives for doing so. Civility is an important definition of the situation that helps to facilitate the smooth flow of social encounters, making them orderly, predictable and apparently natural. Actors tacitly agree to play along with this official version of events, even when it is merely a 'polite fiction', belied by private sentiments about what they know is really going on. We have examined some of the strategies people use to maintain this show of the interaction order in focused and unfocused encounters, such as civil inattention, territorial accessibility and interaction rituals, and seen from empirical studies of nudity, waiting areas and public transport how these reinforce the local norms of each interaction context. Finally, we have considered what happens when an actor breaches these assumptions and acts in a way that others perceive to be rude: the reactions they evoke are even more revealing of the reverence with which we hold micro-social order and how we will leap to its defence. In the next chapter, we focus on the role of language and discourse in creating these interpretive frames around situations, and consider how enacting this helps individual actors to deliver their identity performances.

# 3

# Framing pictures

*Definitions, accounts and motive talk*

In this chapter, we turn to the role of language in constructing social realities and making identity claims. These processes unfold through the verbal expressions and (para)linguistic devices that can be found in spoken or written texts. Conversation analysts argue that the social business of interaction gets done through the media of talk and text (Sacks 1992), as people employ all kinds of tacitly understood rules, techniques and strategies to accomplish their aims. Language is therefore a tool of social action, which has consequences for identities, situations and institutional arrangements. 'Talk-in-interaction' constructs versions of reality that are preferred, dominant or normatively conventional, although it can sometimes be used to challenge these; like all definitions of the situation (Thomas & Thomas 1928; see Chapter 2 above), these are precarious constructions that have to be constantly recreated and reaffirmed to survive. We shall also examine the ways in which language can be used to perform different identities, according to the setting, the audience and the actor's situational motives, beliefs and assumptions. Methodologically, we will consider three analytical approaches, of discourse analysis (DA), conversation analysis (CA) and frame analysis (FA), with illustrative examples of each.

## Language and the social construction of reality

The approaches outlined here share a social constructivist ontology. This means a view of social reality as multiple, fluid and contingent upon human activity: reality is whatever people believe it to be and represent it to themselves as being. This echoes the principles of phenomenology (see Chapter 1 above), but also applies to a range of disciplines in the social sciences, such as discursive psychology, poststructuralism, semiology, linguistic philosophy, ethnomethodology and frame analysis. Constructivist approaches regard mental processes not as essential, innate capacities but rather as shaped by a person's social experiences. Attitudes, beliefs, motives, perceptions and emotions are 'constructed by people conceptually, in language, in the course of their performance of practical tasks' (Edwards 2005: 258). Moreover, these social representations (Moscovici 1984) of symbolic objects in the world around us are shaped by cultural ideas and discourses (Billig 1996). They are 'manifestations of discourses, outcrops of representations of events upon the terrain of social life. They have their origin not in the person's private experience, but in the discursive culture that those people inhabit' (Burr 2003: 66).

## Semiotics

The branch of linguistic constructivism known as semiotics is defined as the 'science of signs' – or the semantic relations between concepts. This approach suggests that there is a structural relationship between culture and language, whose meanings are contextually dependent, and an underlying system of rules, which are stable and constant, of which the former are surface-level expressions. Saussure (1916) argued that each culture had its own set of beliefs about the ways in which cultural phenomena (such as food or music) could be combined or sequentially ordered. These were 'syntagmatic' rules, which set the conditions for meaning, while 'paradigmatic' rules were like templates, allowing people to generate further examples of the phenomenon once it had been defined (Potter & Wetherell 1987: 24). So although there were culturally universal principles governing the way people thought about materials in their culture, these phenomena only acquired meaning from their place within a wider system or sequence of related things. Saussure talked about the 'arbitrariness of the sign': there was no essential relationship between *signifiers* – linguistic expressions, such as speech sounds or written words – and *signified* concepts – their underlying referents.

Barthes (1957) suggested there could be further levels of signification beyond this, whereby the signified concept became the signifier of another signified, which was often abstract or symbolic (e.g. clear skin signifying 'beauty', or expensive jewellery signifying 'luxury'). Barthes called these 'connotative' meanings, as distinct from the first-level 'denotative' meanings, but the model also resonates with the symbolic interactionist idea of symbolic meaning being attached to social objects. For Barthes, these second- and further-order levels of signification (which he called 'myths') could go on indefinitely, in an iterative sequence, so that what was observable in the expressions of a culture or language was far removed from the original meanings. This is what created such diverse variation between cultures' beliefs, values and practices, and gave the appearance of incommensurability.

## Performative speech

Meanwhile, at the micro level, linguistic psychology and philosophy consider how the specifics of language use (the words chosen, the order in which they are put together and the way they are vocalized) can create different versions of reality in the minds of those who articulate or hear it. Chomsky (1965) argued that the mind contained a cognitive structure that provided a set of rules for generating grammatical sentences. This Language Acquisition Device (LAD) was genetically inherited and culturally universal, so that everyone had the capacity to learn one language – their first, native tongue – intuitively, with an innate tacit knowledge of its correct grammar and syntax. Importantly, though, Chomsky made a distinction between linguistic competence (the abstract, idealized potential) and linguistic performance (the actual expressions of language that people make, which can be prone to error, memory lapses and irrelevant tangential details). Speakers have creativity in their linguistic performances, as the number and variety of possible combinations of words are endless.

Words are not only performative but also powerful. Language is partly a tool we use to 'get things done' in social life (Potter & Wetherell 1987: 18), but it is also constitutive, and potentially transformative, of social reality. Austin (1962) disputed the presumption that language was merely a tool of verification, describing states of affairs that could be proven true or false. His view was that language was productive or constructive, rather than merely reflective, of social reality. Austin revealed the power of words to 'do things', or perform social actions such as orders, challenges, changes of status, requests and apologies. He made a distinction between two types of linguistic statement, or utterance: the *constative* (describing or asserting something that could be verified) and the *performative* (having practical consequences or creating a new state of affairs). Constative and performative utterances are analytically but not empirically distinct, however, for speech can both describe and do things, simultaneously. The line in a marriage ceremony 'I now pronounce you husband and wife,' the court jury's judgment 'We find the defendant guilty,' or the wager 'I bet you £100' all bring about a change in the participants' definition of the situation and understanding of their roles therein, whilst simultaneously describing the new state of affairs.

Speech acts can of course fail, insofar as they depend on not only the speaker's intentions, but also the listener's interpretation and compliance. Austin (1962) used the term 'felicity conditions' to describe the social ingredients that must be combined for performative language to accomplish its goals. For example, there may be a conventionalized procedure (such as a ritual exchange) for sequences of utterances, and the persons involved must be playing legitimate roles. We study this below in the discussion of apologies and other 'aligning actions'.

This reminds us of the symbolic interactionist concept of negotiating meaning, as a collective endeavour. Speech acts, like any form of social action, are joint (Blumer 1969), negotiated (Strauss 1978) and contingent upon audience interpretations (Goffman 1959). Thus Potter and Wetherell (1987) point to the contingency and variability of surface-level expressions, arguing that the rules of language are not a universal grammar but rather defined locally by actors in situated interaction contexts. The 'natural' language we observe in everyday life is used pragmatically, according to actors' motives and interests. Its form is messy, imperfectly composed and complicated by tangential details, which add contextual meaning but carry the risk of misunderstanding. As Potter and Wetherell (1987: 152) argue: '. . . rules [are] a flexible strategic resource, open to many interpretations.'

## Interpretive repertoires

Potter and Wetherell (1987: 138) present an alternative concept of the 'interpretive repertoire', which they define as 'a lexicon or register of terms and metaphors drawn upon to characterize and evaluate actions and events'. The concept stems from the work of Gilbert and Mulkay (1984), who studied the ways in which biochemical scientists used different discourses (word choices, styles of expression and underlying meanings) to describe their research, depending on the context and medium through which they were performing or rehearsing these accounts. Gilbert and Mulkay identified two contrasting discursive styles, or interpretive repertoires, on which the scientists drew to describe their work. These reflected self-presentational concerns with their own professional accountability and the reputation of 'science' as an institution. The *empirical repertoire* was used in academic journals, presentations and other 'official' settings, while the *contingent* repertoire was used in more informal discussions amongst themselves, and in the research interviews.

These repertoires could be used to describe the same events or activities but in different ways, according to the actors' concerns. For example, the empirical repertoire represented the scientific process as data-driven, based on the discovery of objective facts about the 'real', external, physical world, and thus independent of human (mis)interpretation. Scientists used a linguistic device called 'the truth will out' or 'that's how it is' (Potter & Wetherell 1987: 152–3), in suggesting that science unfolds logically and consistently, according to disciplinary conventions and unaffected by researcher bias. There was an implicit claim to neutrality, trustworthiness, credibility and authority on the part of both individual scientists and the scientific establishment.

Meanwhile, the contingent repertoire revealed the human and social aspects of how science got 'done' in the everyday practices of laboratory work. Acknowledging the messy unpredictability of human action, it showed how apparently objective scientific knowledge was socially produced through interaction and identity work. Such accounts made reference to charismatic personalities, scientists' beliefs, emotions, theoretical values and biases, prejudices, group loyalties, rivalries or funders' interests, which shaped how research was designed, data were gathered and results were analysed. The contingent repertoire was used more often to account for errors or discrepancies in scientific research – which would be attributed to the individual characters of the scientists who had conducted the research, their faults, mistakes or failings – while the empiricist repertoire was used to explain research findings that confirmed the dominant paradigm (cf. Kuhn 1962).

The contrast between these two interpretive repertoires resonates with Goffman's (1959) dramaturgical theory, as there was a clear difference between the former, 'frontstage' depiction of what science 'should' be about, its official face and the values and principles on which it is based, and the latter, 'backstage' confessional account of how science really happened, through social processes of interaction.

## Ethnomethodology: talk-in-interaction

When examining the role of language in conversation, analysts draw on the perspective of ethnomethodology. This is a theoretical tradition that emphasizes social actors' (or 'members'') capacity for shared understandings and tacit knowledge, which they use to skilfully accomplish the interaction order. Literally, the name refers to the study (ology) of the 'methods used by people' (ethno-methods) to produce and make sense of everyday social life (Potter & Wetherell 1987: 18). Pragmatically, it studies how these capacities are reflected in everyday use: the ways in which members see, describe and explain their local worlds (Zimmerman & Wieder 1970) and the practical methods they use to accomplish micro-social order and build constructed worlds (Garfinkel 1967). Empirically, meawhile, ethnomethodologists study the role of 'talk-in-interaction' (Psathas 1995), or what conversation 'does' for situations.

This involves a reconsideration of what previous researchers had considered a 'resource' for researchers (participants' lay explanations and accounts as data tools, or as media through which to access the underlying realities they described) as instead being a 'topic' in its own right (the features of talk can be analysed as an object of study). Simultaneously, however, language is re-imagined as a resource used by lay members: a practical tool or shorthand code on which they draw to direct each other's attention to the relevant meanings in a situation (Potter 1996). A social constructivist ontology is employed to disregard the idea of an essential, true, underlying social reality, focusing instead on how participants construct their particular versions of the world. Talk is seen as actively produced, with certain motives or interests, as well as with practical consequences for identities and interaction. Speakers use rhetorical devices and linguistic formulations to comment on the conversational event itself as having a particular meaning or significance (Heritage & Watson 1979), to render their motives accountable, or to otherwise demonstrate the 'reasonableness' of their intentions (Potter 1996).

Ethnomethodology regards everyday interaction as *work* – an active process of sense-making, which uses tacit methods of practical reasoning, stocks of background knowledge and taken-for-granted assumptions (Garfinkel 1967). The aim is to make visible these processes of interactional work – showing how realities get constructed through joint social action – and identify the organizing principles that underlie them. These implicit rules are shared between members, holding the same meaning and being potentially accessible to everyone; they function as a practical repertoire, like Mills' (1940) vocabulary of motives (see below). Members have the capacity to reflect upon and account for their conduct in these terms, although most of the time they are not required to. This is because there is an implicit social and moral obligation that everyone will adhere to the rules and behave 'normally' – in line with social expectations about what is 'reasonable' or 'common sense'. Knowing that others will be interpreting their actions in these terms, actors seek to produce actions that will be accountable (recognizable, sensible and describable) in the present interaction context (Heritage & Clayman 2010).

Thus the *rules* governing social conduct in any interaction context (what is considered comprehensible, meaningful, accountable and normative) are simultaneously shared *resources*, to which all participants have access and on which they can all draw, both to make sense of each other's actions and to present themselves in ways that will make sense to these others. As Heritage and Clayman (2010: 10) put it: '. . . the

same methods organize both action and the understanding of action.'
Rules of talk are templates or social guidelines for typified actions,
and are simultaneously *descriptive* and reflective of existing, familiar or
conventional social reality, and *constitutive* or productive of the situated,
emergent, new one.

We can identify three key principles of ethnomethodology. Firstly,
*indexicality* (Garfinkel 1967) is the idea that the actual utterances
observable in speech are surface-level expressions of a deeper, underlying set of meanings, rules and taken-for-granted assumptions. The
former are an 'index' of the latter, in that we can study the manifest
content of conversational exchanges (the words chosen, the syntax of
their composition, the proximity of different utterances, and non-verbal
gestures such as pauses, sighs and overlaps) as a means of accessing the
underlying rules and resources of which they are expressions.

Secondly, the *et cetera clause* (Garfinkel 1967) built into talk means
that beyond everything said there is a wealth of information that is left
unsaid but presumed to be understood by all. Conversation partners are
able to fill in the gaps between utterances by drawing on their common
stocks of background knowledge (Schütz 1972). Members follow tacit
understandings and normative expectations without conscious reflection; the rules they observe are 'seen but unnoticed' (Garfinkel 1967).
Although the specific instances of talk will vary in their content, the
general organizing principles on which they are based are universal, and
can be studied across different examples. These rules provide general
guides for talk-in-interaction, incorporating an infinite range of potential modes of expression and actors' motives.

Thirdly, the principle of *reflexivity* (Garfinkel 1967) refers to the
quality that language has of not merely describing the world but also
producing it: insofar as talk performs social actions, it constitutes the
reality to which it refers. For example, some linguistic formulations
allow speakers to comment on the conversational event itself, in order
to do something with it (Heritage & Watson 1979). As we shall see, this
might be to reorient participants to the focus of a discussion that has
wandered off track, to render accountable the motives or intentions they
have just indicated or to demonstrate their own normality and rationality (Potter 1996). Language and discourse feed back into the very same
structures of society that have helped to produce them. Giddens (1984)
called this the 'hermeneutic circle', and argued that it showed the
mutually constitutive relationship and effects of (social) structure and
(individual) agency. Actors are skilled and knowledgeable because they
have a reflexive capacity to use language in creative and novel ways, but
this capacity is constrained by normative structures, such as traditions,
institutions and social conventions. As Potter and Wetherell (1987:

21–2) put it: '. . . talk is not merely about actions, events and situations, it is also a potent and constitutive part of those actions, events and situations . . . [It] *formulates* the nature of the action and the situation and has a number of practical consequences' (emphasis in original).

## Conversation analysis

The method of conversation analysis (CA) was developed in the late 1960s through the work of Harvey Sacks, Emanuel Schegloff and Gail Jefferson (e.g. Sacks et al. 1974; Sacks 1992; Schegloff 2007), who were students and followers of Goffman and Garfinkel. Their aim was to empirically document the procedural rules underpinning ordinary talk in everyday situations, and through this to identify the patterns and principles organizing interactive talk more generally. The whole system of conversational talk is highly organized by these implicit rule structures, while the properties of this system are embedded in observable sequences of talk (Potter & Wetherell 1987: 81). The same social mechanisms can be observed in all forms of talk, from the informal, spontaneous exchanges of everyday conversation to the more formal or ritualized, scripted exchanges in institutional settings (Heritage & Clayman 2010).

Methodologically, CA scrutinizes verbatim transcriptions of 'naturally occurring' data (i.e. actual, recorded conversations), which are presumed to have more ecological validity than the hypothetical models presented by linguistic philosophers. The aim is to discover 'what is going on' beneath the surface-level utterances: What social actions are performed, and whose identity performances are accomplished? What work does the talk do for the speaker, the listener, the audience and the situation? Conversation analysts look at each utterance and its position relative to those preceding and succeeding it in the sequence of talk, and ask themselves, 'Why that, now?' (Heritage & Clayman 2010: 14).

One of the most important features of talk that CA examines is turn-taking (Sacks 1992) and turn allocation (Sacks et al. 1974). Through the positioning and sequencing of utterances, speakers demonstrate a tacit awareness of each other's situational roles, institutional statuses, relative positions and rights to speak. Each turn in a sequence 'projects' the next and generates further speech options, according to mutually understood rules (Schegloff 2007): for example, a question sets up the expectation that it will be met with an answer.

Changeovers between speakers (Sacks et al. 1974) are also rule-governed and orderly. There is often a brief pause, providing a temporal space for participants to shift positions, although when they know each other well, there may be an overlap between the end of one person's line and the start of the next person's. Speakers embed subtle verbal or non-verbal cues into the delivery of their speech to signal when this time is approaching, for example by lowering their pitch at the end of a sentence, or resuming eye contact with the listener, which cues them to take the floor. This rule can also be observed in the breach, as speakers who do not want to give up the floor give cues that discourage others from trying to break in, such as raising their voice or its pitch, and avoiding eye contact. When people start speaking at the same time, they quickly realize and halt, before negotiating turn allocation and sequencing ('Sorry, you go first').

Within the overall system of turn allocation, there are some more specific turn-taking practices (Heritage & Clayman 2010), each of which reflects its own underlying rules, assumptions, meanings and values. For example, *turn-initial address* terms (Lerner 1995) are those that invite a particular person to speak next, such as 'What do you think, Alice?' *Oh-prefacing responses* are those that imply the preceding question was inappropriate or irrelevant (e.g. 'Oh, I couldn't comment on that . . .'), which in turn serves as a register of the participants' relative claims to knowledge and rights to speak (Heritage & Raymond 2005). *Polarity items* are words such as 'many', 'some' and 'any', which qualify statements about quantity, extent or extremity (Heritage & Clayman 2010).

*Adjacency pairings* (Sacks et al. 1974) are two turns of utterances that appear together, consecutively. These include questions and answers; requests and permission-grantings; greetings and return greetings; and apologies or offers and acceptances. The delivery of the first half of the pair carries with it the expectation that the second half will be given in response, and the latter comes from a restricted range of acceptable options from a shared stock of tacit knowledge. By recognizing and interpreting this cue, the listener is prompted or primed to give such an answer: for example, 'How are you?' invokes an almost automatic response of 'Fine, thank you', and 'Sorry' is usually accepted with a 'That's okay', regardless of how the second speaker actually feels. The second part of an adjacency pair may not follow immediately, but rather is set up as a likely and anticipated response by the normative expectations embedded in the first part (Heritage 1984). It has 'conditional relevance' (Schegloff 1968) in that it is expected, socially conventional and relevant as a conclusion to the exchange.

This allows for other complicating matters to be dealt with or subsidiary social actions completed alongside the main business of interaction. Sometimes there will be an intervening 'insertion sequence' (Potter & Wetherell 1987), for example when the second speaker checks a detail from the meaning of the first person's question before answering, which can be thought of as an action-within-an-action, bracketed off within the main purpose of the exchange. When dealing with these insertion sequences, speakers demonstrate an ongoing awareness of and deference to the moral obligation of the primary adjacency pair: they deal with the query and close the figurative bracket before returning to complete the original task of the initiating utterance.

Another feature of talk is *preference structures* (Schegloff 2007). This is the idea that in the second part of an adjacency pair, there are *preferred* responses, which are normal and expected, and *dispreferred* responses, which are unexpected and unusual. For example, the preferred response to a request for information is to provide that information, while a dispreferred response would be to refuse, or to evade the question.

The use of preference structures performs important work for individual speakers in relation to their identity claims and self-presentation. Preferred responses allow the speaker to show co-operativeness, reliability and conformity to social norms, whereas dispreferred responses can indicate a disregard for these conventions, or acknowledgement and regret that one is deviating from them. These meanings are built into the delivery as paralinguistic cues, signalling to the first speaker how they should interpret the response (Potter & Wetherell 1987). Preferred responses are brief, produced with minimal delay and straightforward, with one clear-cut meaning that is usually positive. Dispreferred responses are often hesitant, lengthier and complicated by filler words ('um', 'er'), hedging ('though on the other hand . . .') and qualifications ('perhaps', 'maybe', 'at least I think so'), which soften the blow of a more negative sentiment.

The collaborative management of preference-structured pairings also performs work for the situation, and for the interaction order more widely. The ritualized performance of agreement, in particular, not only reinforces the immediate definition of the situation, but also strengthens social bonds between the speakers. For example, in Sweden there is a strong moral principle of democratic agreement that shapes interaction. People are concerned to ensure that decisions are made through genuine consensus and that everyone is happy with the outcome (Daun 1989; Booth 2014). This coincides with a motivation to keep others in face (Goffman 1967: 5–46) and avoid confrontation, challenge and embarrassment (Daun 1989). Consequently, a common word in the Swedish language is 'Precis!', meaning 'precisely', which is uttered with great frequency and excitement in everyday conversation, along with similar words like 'Absolut!' ('absolutely') and 'Exakt!' ('exactly'), in response to sentiments expressed by a principal speaker. These preferred responses are both normative and socially facilitative as they allow listeners seek to show agreement, understanding and validation of each other's thoughts and feelings.

Alongside these norms, we can consider some deviant cases, as exceptions that prove the rule. CA studies of emergency calls show these to be a distinct genre of talk that involves a curious blend of institutional rules and conversational dialogue (Whalen & Zimmerman 1987; Zimmerman 1992). Heritage and Clayman (2010) explain that emergency calls differ from ordinary telephone calls in everyday life because of two main factors: the specific, instrumental focus of the talk (there is a particular task to be accomplished in summoning help) and the urgency with which this is treated (the help needs to arrive as quickly as possible).

The result is a unique form of talk, embodying some of the features of everyday conversation but in a brief and truncated form. Zimmerman (1992) identified five phases in the sequence of an emergency call: opening, request, interrogative series (questions aimed at gathering information), response (a reassurance that help is being dispatched) and closing. Although the interrogative series in the middle is ostensibly an insertion sequence, the callers understand that it is not superfluous or diversionary: the information-gathering process is aimed at the overall purpose of dispatching assistance, and will help to do so more efficiently. There may also be 'pivotal turns' that mark the boundaries between these phases, such as 'Thank you', as speakers let each other know that a subsidiary action within the task has been completed and they can move on to the next. Rather than a politeness gesture, this is an efficiency signal that allows the action to proceed swiftly.

Emergency calls contain none of the superfluous embellishments we would find in an ordinary telephone call, such as personal identifications and recognitions, greetings and inquiries into each other's welfare (Schegloff 1968), nor any opportunities for unplanned, purely sociable talk or pleasantries (Heritage & Clayman 2010). The central adjacency pair – a request for help and the granting of this – stands alone, stark and unadorned:

[Midcity 21: Midnight-1.00am: 5a]
1   ((ring))
2   *911*: Midcity emergency?
3   *Clr*: Yes uh: := I need a paramedic please.
4   *911*: Where to.

(Heritage & Clayman 2010: 62)

Even when there are exceptions to this pattern, for example when callers are so distressed that they cannot follow the line of questioning, or when calls are put through that are hoaxes, the immediate response of the call-taker is to assume that the caller has a 'normal' set of intentions and try to make sense of what they say in terms of the expected script (Heritage & Clayman 2010: 62). This reminds us of the way that participants in talk share a tacit comprehension of the indexical meaning behind surface utterances, and use this to negotiate a skilful joint performance of the dialogue.

## Discourse analysis

Discourse analysis considers how written or spoken texts are shaped by wider structures, such as cultural values and institutional contexts, and the discourses that circulate within them. Discourses are culturally and historically specific ways of thinking, talking and writing about social phenomena, which shape people's understandings of what these things are. Foucault (1971) emphasized the power of language to produce, or constitute, the very things it describes, for example social groups like 'homosexuals' or concepts like 'madness'. Language can be used not only for the purposes of individual self-presentation, but also to serve institutional functions, such as presenting the public face of an organization, or defining the epistemological territory of an academic discipline. Potter suggests that discourses are resources on which actors draw to 'constitute events, settings and identities [and] build plausible descriptions' of these things. The aim of DA is to 'make visible the ways in which discourse is central to action' as a constitutive tool of social order (Potter 2004: 609).

The sub-branch of critical discourse analysis (CDA) studies the role of discourse as an instrument of social power. CDA theorists consider how relations of dominance are expressed, reproduced, but sometimes also challenged, through the use of language (Van Dijk 1993). This approach developed out of the Frankfurt School of critical theorists such as Adorno, Marcuse and Horkheimer, who focused on the role of popular culture as a vehicle of ideology. Gramsci's (1935) notion of hegemony is also employed to explain how dominant interests and values are presented as if they are neutral and objective, and thus legitimated. For example, CDA studies of the mass media consider such questions as who controls the agenda of television, radio and print journalism, whose voices get heard in political discussions, and who has 'discourse rights' to direct public debates (Van Dijk 1993).

In his book *Representing Reality*, Potter (1996) unpacks this process, using DA to explore how alternative accounts of social reality are produced by different actors, groups and institutions through their linguistic practices. He considers how claims to knowledge are composed through talk and text, and made to appear as if they are solid, neutral and independent of the speaker. Potter makes a distinction between *facts*, as signified referents such as people, objects or events, which are indicated by language as being real or true, and *descriptions*, as actions that construct and define facts as such. DA is concerned with the latter, asking such questions as: How are descriptions produced so that they will be treated as factual? Which versions of reality come to be accepted as true? Who has the power to make their reports 'count' and influence other people? What procedures do audiences use to interpret these accounts and establish their veracity? DA is concerned with the social, interactive process of *fact construction* (Potter 1996) and its role in the wider social construction of reality (cf. Berger & Luckmann 1966).

In giving such accounts, speakers not only present an institutional reality but also perform their own identities as witnesses to it. They seek to be trusted as sources of knowledge: to be regarded as *credible* in the way they describe an event, process or person. The apparently factual basis of the knowledge they impart is closely bound to their neutrality as a conduit, and their right to be believed. The 'work' that descriptive language does involves making claims not only about an external reality, but also about the speaker's position or perspective, and their relation to the audience. This process is called 'working up' identities: presenting a version of the self by emphasizing some qualities, abilities, knowledge or interests, and downplaying others. These accounts are occasioned (Schegloff 2007), or produced in situated contexts of interaction.

## Membership categorization, interests and stake claims

One important way in which this identity work is accomplished is the use of what Sacks (1992) calls membership categorization devices. These are linguistic strategies people use to identify themselves or someone else as a member of a social group. Zimmerman (1998) suggests that people assume *discourse identities* as they engage in discussions. These may be situation-specific *conversational* roles, such as the current speaker, listener, storyteller, audience member, questioner, answerer or repairer, or wider *institutional* roles, as we saw in the case of emergency call centres.

Antaki and Widdicombe (1998) suggest there are five principles of membership categorization. Firstly, categories have associated *characteristics*: this helps actors to organize their perceptions by 'placing' each other (Stone 1962) within distinct groups. Secondly, this casting is indexical in an *occasioned* way: its meaning emerges from that specific situation and the views those participants hold. Thirdly, the identities invoked are made relevant to the interactional business going on in the scene: their meanings are *operative* (practically used) to meet these goals. Schegloff (1992) argued that we should examine members' own categories – those that actors orient themselves to or see as relevant to their identities – rather than those we think are interesting from the outside. Fourthly, the principle of *procedural consequentiality* (Schegloff 1992) means that we should also study those categories of meaning that have some practical effect on the unfolding social interaction and/or participants' identities. Finally, members tend to adhere to sociolinguistic rules and *conventions* when displaying a categorical identity, which are easily recognized by the audience, and so prime them to endorse the claim.

One of the ways in which membership categorization devices can be used in pursuit of identity work is in relation to a person's claimed interests or stakes in the subject matter they are discussing. Potter (1996) describes a number of techniques that can be employed to this end. Firstly, *stake inoculation* is used when a speaker recognizes that what they are about to say might lead those listening to place them in an undesirable category, through attributions of value and bias. This is especially important for those whose institutional positions mean that it is important for them to be seen as fair and neutral. Actors using this technique pre-empt but then deflect accusations of bias, by first acknowledging its ostensible appearance but then demonstrating how they are not in fact in this position. This often involves stating a counter-interest or an alternative, biased view and showing that one has considered it, before dropping it in favour of one's current view. The contrast of the two positions, and the implied irrationality of the first, cleverly makes the second seem more rationally considered and likely to be true. For example, Potter (1996: 126) gives the example of a report in the *Guardian* newspaper about a scientist who 'was initially sceptical, but having looked at [the evidence]' became convinced by a theory.

A second technique is *stake confession*. This is when a person expresses a view that appears to contradict what their official line should be, given their occupational role or institutional membership. However, this is very tactical. In presenting an unexpected, 'off the record' view, the speaker attempts to convince the listener that they are being honest and authentic: not merely reciting a rehearsed standardized spiel but rather confiding their personal views. This in turn makes them seem more credible, and invites the listener to trust them. It is a classic sales technique, used to establish the semblance of a personal relationship, so that the customer feels obliged to buy something ('I tell you what, I'm not supposed to do this, but I can let you have it for a discount').

We find this technique used in advertising, when reverse psychology is used to make the producers of an item appear to be on the consumer's side, against the rest of 'them' in the industry. For example, in 1996, Unilever, the manufacturers of Marmite, a strongly flavoured yeast extract spread, began an advertising campaign that invited consumers to either 'love it or hate it'. The television commercials played humorously on the idea that many people found the taste revolting, but turned this to their advantage by using the fascination of disgust as something that would tempt viewers to try it. By 2007, the BBC reported that sales of Marmite had tripled over the intervening years, and attributed this to the success of the adverts: 'It takes a highly confident brand to acknowledge that some people don't like it, but it gives Marmite what Unilever calls "mass affinity". Even those that don't like the taste feel included and will talk about the advert and, by extension, the brand' (BBC News 2007).

A third technique is *interest invocation*. This is when values or interests (as opposed to neutrality) are explicitly acknowledged as an indicator of credibility, in that having access to insider, specialist knowledge gives someone the right to speak. In academic writing, we find the technique used as a means of establishing a researcher's personal commitment to the subject matter, and, by implication, their authenticity and reliability as a source of knowledge about it. In the late 1960s and 1970s, debates about value freedom and objectivity in the social sciences led some qualitative researchers to advocate 'taking sides' and explicitly acknowledging one's values and biases (Becker 1967) as an epistemological advantage.

The fourth technique borrows from Sacks' (1992) concept of *category entitlement*. People seek to demonstrate that they are members of a certain social group in order to lay claim to its knowledge or experiences, and thus the right to talk about this. Category entitlement occurs in the discourses of and about professional occupations, for example when medical 'experts' are designated as such by virtue of their specialist knowledge and years of education or training (Potter 1996). Journalists often refer to medics by their titles or credentials ('Doctor X', 'Professor Y'), while groups are referred to with mysteriously vague terms like 'scientists'.

This device can also occur with respect to dramatic events that a person has witnessed or been involved in. These might be traumatic experiences, such as terrorist attacks or natural disasters, or those that are simply bizarre and seem incredible. Potter (1996) discusses the recounting of urban myths about strange or unexpected experiences, arguing that these stories tend to follow a standardized narrative structure. A common element in this structure is the preface that the event happened to 'a friend of a friend'. Potter unpacks the wording of this clause, which on the surface seems unnecessarily clumsy. The allusion to the first 'friend' makes sense, as it implies a trustworthy and credible source of information, but why, Potter asks, is there the need for the second friend? Why not just say, 'a friend told me'? He suggests that locating the strange experience in this other, unknown person functions to distance the speaker from the original source of the story, and thus absolves them of responsibility for verifying it. The speaker cannot be expected to know the details of the story, and so is not at risk of being quizzed about any errors or inconsistencies in it. Potter argues that this rhetorical strategy strikes a balance between factuality and deniability: the narrator benefits from the first 'friend' connection while protecting themselves via the mediation of the second.

Wooffitt (1992) similarly analyses accounts of paranormal experiences, such as alien abductions, meeting angels or seeing ghosts. Anticipating that they will be doubted, storytellers emphasize their credibility and trustworthiness as witnesses to the unlikely event. They seek to be recognized as members of the same group as the listener – the category of normal, rational people – and to distance themselves from less desirable categories, such as 'mad', 'crank', 'weirdo' or 'New Age hippie' (Wooffitt 1992). This is achieved through the careful composition of the narrative structure to include, again, a strategic preface, which juxtaposes the ordinary with the extraordinary. The storyteller often introduces the account with 'I was just doing [something mundane and innocuous, such as "washing the dishes"] when [the unexpected event] happened.' The first part of the sentence sets up a scene that depicts the principal actor as an ordinary, normal person, doing everyday things that the listener can relate to; it emphasizes their similarity and invites understanding. When this is followed by the unbelievable consequential event, the latter becomes hard to dispute, for the reliability of the witness has been established.

## Gendered talk

DA provides valuable insights into the gendering of talk-in-interaction. Tannen (1993) critically revisits a common view that men tend to dominate in conversation: that language is a patriarchal tool of oppression, used to silence women and reinforce traditional gender divisions. This has been supported by studies showing how men speak more than women, speak louder (Spender 1980), interrupt (West & Zimmerman 1983), raise more topics (Shuy 1982) and are more adversarial, commanding and competitive (Maltz & Borker 1982). Conversely, women have been shown to be more hesitant, indirect, quiet and reticent

(Spender 1980), use their talk to pursue co-operation, negotiation and consensus-building, and give suggestions rather than commands (Maltz & Borker 1982).

However, Tannen adopts a relativist position, arguing that such linguistic strategies are not inherently associated with either power or submissiveness, but rather can be used by either gender and to different ends. Men can use silence rather than volubility to exercise power: she gives examples of men refusing to answer their 'nagging' wives. Similarly, indirectness need not signify a reluctance to assert oneself: expressing one's demands more subtly may ensure that they get met. Interruption does indicate assertiveness and even dominance in conversation, but is not solely the domain of men. Women-only friendship groups often display high levels of interruption, but they perceive it as 'overlap', which has more positive connotations of agreement and support: talking excitedly *alongside* rather than *over* somebody.

## Making the news

News journalism has a distinct style of discourse, in particular television interviews and panel discussions featuring politicians, such as the BBC programmes *Question Time* and *Newsnight*. Broadcast media make institutional claims to neutrality, which are reflected or 'indexed' by the actions of their members. According to Heritage and Clayman (2010), news interviews follow a standardized format, with tacitly understood rules of conduct. The question–answer adjacency pairing is used in a repeated turn-taking sequence, in a game-like pursuit of attack and defence. There is usually an interviewer (IR) or host, who asks the guest interviewees (IE) a series of probing questions, as if they are on the side of the audience and gathering 'facts' for them. This is an act of stake inoculation, according to Potter's (1996) schema, acknowledging potential accusations of bias and employing gestures to convey the opposite impression of neutrality. Although political journalists are actually highly knowledgeable about their subject matter, they present themselves as merely seeking information in an unbiased way. The IR takes up a relatively small proportion of the time and space allocation by keeping their utterances to a minimum, avoids making assertions or offering their own opinions, and sticks to questions that invite the IE to take the floor while they just listen.

Interestingly, IRs breach some normative rules of everyday conversation, as they do not offer the usual 'receipt tokens', such as 'yes', 'mmm', 'ok' and 'uh-huh', that listeners normally provide to reassure the speaker that they are being heard and give them permission to continue. This is a strategic action to avoid positioning themselves as the recipient of the talk, or presenting the scene as if it were a private conversation. Instead, the talk is staged as if it were for the benefit of the television audience, as a 'ratified but unaddressed audience of overhearers' (Heritage & Clayman 2010: 225).

Heritage and Clayman also consider the ways in which IEs try to answer – or evade – the IR's questions, using either overt or covert strategies of resistance. Overt strategies offer the advantage of making the IE appear honest and reasonable, willing to listen to their critics, but their success depends on the answers being accepted by the audience as credible. Covert strategies circumvent this risk by allowing the IE to evade the question, but do not allow them to explicitly defend themselves.

Overt tactics involve showing deference to the IR, for example by prefacing the answer with a request for permission to take the floor, which cleverly signposts the idea that the IE is conscientiously addressing their duties ('Can I just answer that question?', 'If I can just take that last point . . .'). The tokenistic aspect of these prefaces is indicated by the way that IEs do not actually wait for permission to be granted before ploughing on with their answer, which may be quite irrelevant. Other overt tactics include minimizing the divergence from the formal agenda or turn-taking sequence, for example when an IE interrupts out of turn with 'Can I just make one very quick comment . . .?' IEs may also seek to justify their resistance to answering a question with reference to moral principles of fairness ('I'm not prepared to answer questions about my personal life') or embargos on what they are permitted by their agents to say, which would be difficult to dispute.

Covert tactics, meanwhile, include 'furnishing the veneer' of an answer to disguise an evasion as an engagement with the question, for example by repeating the first few words of the question to make it sound as if one were answering it. Another tactic is 'operating on the question' to turn it into something else: a difficult question can be reformulated as an easier or even advantageous one that the IE does want to answer and that might enhance their public image. Heritage and Clayman give the example of US Vice President Dan Quayle evading a series of challenging questions about his willingness to step up to the presidency if George Bush, Sr were unable to continue. Quayle kept twisting the questions into enquiries about his own qualifications for leadership, rather than giving a direct answer. Such sequences of 'resistance and pursuit' (Heritage and Clayman 2010: 258) reveal the game-like nature of verbal exchanges, something we revisit in Chapter 4's discussion of Goffman's (1969) strategic interaction.

## Aligning actions

Next, we examine the role of language in providing reasons and explanations for action, either prospectively or retrospectively, in line with the norms and values of the audience. These are called 'aligning actions' (Stokes & Hewitt 1976) and can be divided into four types: motive talk, accounting procedures (excuses and justifications), reparative actions (apologies, requests and other forms of identity repair work) and disclaimers.

### Motive talk

The first set of techniques is what Mills (1940) called 'motive talk'. This involves the actor drawing on their knowledge of a shared, tacitly understood set of acceptable reasons for behaviour, called the 'vocabulary of motives'. Mills suggests that this cultural interpretive repertoire (Potter & Wetherell 1987) serves as a normative guide for action, in both its design and its *post hoc* rationalization: motives are 'accepted justifications for present, future or past programs or acts' (Mills 1940: 907). Actors appeal to their audiences for the validation of their actions as being acceptable within this normative framework; they help the actor to perform a defensible line of action (cf. Goffman 1967). As Hewitt (2007) argues, we are constantly observing and interpreting each other's behaviour, which involves imputing motives to others and avowing our own motives, but it is only when an action appears to be norm-breaking that we seek an explanation. Questionable conduct leads to requested and offered explanations for action.

The idea that motives can be constructed *after* an action in order to justify it subverts common-sense understandings of human behaviour. Mills was challenging the dominant wisdom from essentialist psychology that language is merely expressive of the underlying individual will: that thoughts, emotions and motivations drove behaviour. Instead, he argued that we act first and account for it later, if and when required to do so. Pragmatism is evident in his claim that motives are 'social instruments', designed to serve a purpose in situated interaction contexts. Epistemologically, this means that we can never know an actor's original, underlying motivations, but only the ones that are publicly manifest in their accounts: 'All we can infer and empirically check is another verbalization of the agent's which we believe was orienting and controlling behaviour at the time the act was performed. . . . There is no way to plumb behind verbalization into an individual and directly check our motive-mongering' (Mills 1940: 909–10).

McKinlay and Dunnett (1998) report on interviews with gun

collectors in the USA, who knew that the issue of gun ownership was politically controversial and socially divisive. They sought to distance themselves from stereotypical media representations of gun owners as violent, criminal and insane, seeking instead to be regarded as normal, rational, sane and reasonable. They performed verbal identity work in pursuit of 'accomplishing normality', by *working down* one (deviant, anticipated) social identity and *working up* another (socially approved and normative) one. This involved, respectively, the techniques of *identity disavowal* and *recasting*.

In the first case, the gun owners tactically acknowledged the existence of a small number of extremists who did fit the stereotype, but argued that these were exceptional and atypical cases. This performed the action of *disavowing* an undesirable motive (wildness, madness or immorality) that might otherwise have been attributed to them, and distancing themselves from the category of people with whom it would be associated: '. . . the idea of the militias and whatnot, they're the fringe, they're the minority. You're gonna have wild folks in any group that you put together and we don't condone or agree with what they believe in' (McKinlay & Dunnett 1998: 41). By distinguishing themselves from this minority of 'wild folks', the interviewees simultaneously aligned themselves with the residual category of 'normal' people: the interviewer and the imagined audience of critics. Thus in the second aspect of the identity work, the gun owners used the technique of *recasting* to alter the audience's perceptions of them and lay claim to a different, socially acceptable identity. They achieved this by contextualizing their practices within a wider discourse of moral and legal principles – a vocabulary of motives – which they believed was shared by the culture at large. Thus they referred to the American Constitution as a code of universal morality and an indisputable authority to which everyone was presumed to adhere: '[The National Rifle Association] try to protect the rights that are guaranteed under the Constitution of the United States for the average citizen to be able to carry a handgun or a rifle' (McKinlay & Dunnett 1998: 38). The use of the phrase 'average citizen' is also important here in performing an aligning action. By couching their personal choices within a broader set of shared values, and citing their allegiance to these, they deflected any potential dismissive judgement of themselves as individual 'cranks'.

Similarly, Anderson and Taylor (2010) analysed skydivers' accounts of their participation in this activity, as something that was outside the cultural mainstream and often (as they saw it) misconceived as dangerous. This evoked an ambivalent dual strategy of identity work, aimed at the two motives of 'standing out whilst fitting in'. On the one hand, the skydivers wanted to stand out positively, as different, unique and interesting, but, on the other hand, they did not want to stand out negatively, by being marginalized as deviant, strange or frightening. Consequently, their accounts worked up two sets of meanings, emphasizing originality and ambition, but also moral and social conformity. In doing so, they performatively indicated their alignment with shared values in the cultural vocabulary of motives.

For example, male skydivers hinted at the sport's association with stereotypically masculine values of power, coolness under pressure, hedonism and (hyper-)heterosexuality (Anderson and Taylor 2010: 41). They would brag about the danger of serious injury and death resulting from the activity, implying their bravery as risk-takers. However, they were careful in their presentation of this image, not wanting to be misconstrued as irresponsible. They worked up an image of responsibility by mentioning their qualifications and training, as well as their personal qualities as 'healthy' and 'family men'. One father of three was keen to impress that, 'I'm not really that much of a risk taker. I don't smoke or ride motorcycles and I'm always safety-conscious when I'm skydiving' (Anderson & Taylor 2010: 48). We revisit this idea in Chapter 6 with Hardie-Bick's (2005) ethnographic study of skydiving, which showed how members worked down the attribution of a risk-taking identity in the negotiation of their moral career.

## Accounting procedures: excuses and justifications

The second set of aligning actions, produced retrospectively, are accounting procedures. These are verbal statements people make to explain actions that are regarded as deviant (Scott & Lyman 1968), or that have caused a breakdown of normal conduct (Austin 1957). Austin (1957) suggested that studying people's accounts was important in revealing the wider mechanisms of the interaction order: fractures and failures, and social reactions to them, elucidate what the normative expectations would be. Additional insights came from studying how people make sense of the choices they have made by citing external constraints on their freedom (Potter & Wetherell 1987: 75).

There are two main kinds of accounting procedure, based on Austin's ideas but developed by Scott and Lyman (1968). *Excuses* are explanations that acknowledge an act was deviant, but deny personal responsibility for it. *Justifications* are the opposite: these accept responsibility for the act but seek to convince the listener that there was a good reason for it. Scott and Lyman argued that both excuses and justifications are 'conventional' utterances, taking a standardized form and drawing upon the vocabulary of motives as a shared cultural resource (Potter & Wetherell 1987). They often include statements of *denial* (of

various unwanted connotations) and *appeals* (to moral values, other
people and 'common-sense' reasoning).

Semin and Mansted (1983) present an exhaustive typology of both
kinds of accounts that consistently show these features. Excuses, in
their model, include *denial of intent* (claiming 'I didn't mean to' with
reference to accidents, ignorance or mistaken identity), *denial of volition*
(claiming reluctance or lack of choice in performing the act, such as 'I
was so tired that I didn't know what I was doing', or 'I was drunk'),
*denial of agency* ('It wasn't me', 'We did it together', or 'She made me
do it') and *appeal to mitigating circumstances* (referring to situational
constraints: 'I was under pressure').

Meanwhile, justifications in Semin and Mansted's typology include
a *claim that the effect has been misrepresented* (denial or minimization of
the harm done), *appeal to the principle of retribution* (claiming that the
victim deserved their injury because of something they had done or
were), *social comparison* (claiming that others did the same thing but
escaped blame), *appeal to a higher authority* (claiming that the act had
been directed by a superior person or institutional rules: 'I was only following orders'), *self-fulfilment* (suggesting that the act was an important
symbolic gesture of assertiveness, integrity or conscience), *appeal to the
principle of utilitarianism* (pointing out that the actual consequences of
the act were more beneficial than harmful), *appeal to values* (political,
moral or religious ideas, such as freedom, justice or loyalty) and *appeal
to the need for facework* (alluding to Goffman's concept of saving, keeping
or repairing social face [see Chapter 4], for example with reference to
professional reputation or credibility amongst peers).

Some of these types of excuses and justifications were observed by
Sykes and Matza (1957), who examined the ways in which juvenile
delinquents accounted for their criminal activities. The excuse techniques they used included *denial of responsibility* (similar to Semin and
Mansted's categories of denial of agency and appeal to mitigating
circumstances, such as 'The gang made me do it'), while their justifications included *denial of injury* (minimizing harm done: 'He wasn't badly
hurt'), *denial of the victim* (appealing to the principle of retribution:
'They'd threatened us before'), *condemnation of the condemners* (evoking
the appeal to social comparison: the delinquents would claim that those
blaming them were no better than themselves) and *appeal to higher
loyalties* (akin to Semin and Mansted's appeals to values, self-fulfilment
or need for facework). This study can be contextualized within the symbolic interactionist labelling theory of deviance (see Chapter 6 below),
which points to the interactional processes through which deviance is
attributed to people who may not self-define this way. Matza (1964)
argued that so-called 'deviants' and 'law-abiding' citizens were actually

similar in values and outlook: instead of there being a subcultural group of 'deviants', there was a 'subculture of delinquency' into which anyone might drift. Juvenile delinquents viewed their own deviant behaviour as relatively infrequent, occasioned by situational pressures or circumstances, and sought to align themselves with the dominant norms and values of society to which their critics adhered. The same idea is applied in Smith et al.'s (2010) theory of rudeness, discussed in Chapter 2.

## Reparative talk

The third type of aligning action aims to repair any perceived (real or anticipated) damage to the interaction order caused by a personal faux pas. This 'corrective process' forms one half of Goffman's (1967: 5–46) concept of facework, which we examine in Chapter 4, the other half being the 'avoidance process'. Facework means the techniques through which actors seek to maintain an acceptable social 'face' (public image) and prevent this from being lost, spoiled or discredited. The corrective process is what actors do to save their faces, appease those affronted, smooth over cracks in the veneer of the scene and restore it to normal appearances (see Chapter 2).

Often this takes a ritualized form, as there are certain moves that the two parties (offender and offended) are expected to make; these are co-operatively managed as 'remedial interchanges', performed in a stylized, standardized manner. Goffman describes such rituals as moral devices for transforming the meaning of a 'virtual offence': one that might potentially be committed if the pacifying addition were not given.

The most common technique in the corrective process is the apology, which Goffman (1971) says has four stages: challenge, offering, acceptance and thanks. Strictly speaking, the apology represents only the 'offering' stage, and is a gesture made by one actor to another (or others), but it must be received to be effective. This is a performative speech act in that it 'does' something, by making a statement about the deviant action and the actor's attitude towards it, which in turn performs reparative action on a fractured situation. Hewitt (2007) suggests that the apology works by making a distinction between the action and the actor, emphasizing the distance between them. As Goffman (1971: 113) says, '[There is] a splitting of the self into a blameworthy part and a part that stands back and sympathizes with the blame-giving, and, by implication, is worthy of being brought back into the fold.' An apology acknowledges that a transgression has occurred (Potter & Wetherell 1987), and accepts responsibility for it, but implies that this was out of character: the act should not be seen as indicative of the actor's general intentions and attitude towards the other, and there is an implicit promise that it will not reoccur. Apologetic actors show a willingness to recognize, even participate in, their own castigation, to emphasize their alignment with the other's moral values.

Another form of reparative talk occurs in the therapeutic discourse of media talk shows. This began with Goffman's *Forms of Talk*, which examined the 'embedding capacity' of language in allowing speakers to reflect and comment on their own conduct and thus present moral selves to their audiences. One of this collection of essays, 'Radio talk' (Goffman 1981: 197–330), showed how this process of self-presentation occurred through the way that radio announcers made and then corrected errors of speech, or 'fautables'. For example, a common strategy used to repair the mistake is humour: announcers would lapse into laughter, often together with their co-presenters. In another essay, 'Felicity's condition' (1983b), Goffman makes a play on words with Austin's concept of felicity conditions (which render everyday talk understandable) by emphasizing how actors seek not only to make the content of their speech rationally comprehensible, but also to present themselves as sane and normal: to present a competent social identity. Audiences listen for these cues in speech in order to attribute and categorize the speaker as such; felicity conditions are '[a]ny arrangement which leads us to judge an individual's verbal acts to be not a manifestation of strangeness' (Goffman 1983b: 27).

In a more contemporary study, Ferris (2004) analyses the discourse used in a US radio call-in show, *Loveline*. This was a part comic, part quasi-therapeutic programme in which listeners phoned in with problems and dilemmas about relationships, sex and other intimate matters, on which the DJ and resident 'expert' therapist, Dr Drew, gave advice. In doing so, they cited and reinforced a moral discourse about ideal selfhood: what it means to be a good person, to be happy and healthy, and to know right from wrong. This public processing of private troubles can be contextualized within a wider cultural trend in the mass media towards confession, soul-baring, conversion and recovery. Talk shows in particular work to symbolically transform guests' identities through spectacular displays and 'morality plays' with a clear moral discourse about self-improvement (Gubrium & Holstein 2001; Scott 2011).

Ferris argues that in the ritualized exchange of these conversations, there are three distinct interactional phases through which the callers and hosts negotiate a symbolic transformation of the 'troubled selves' that are presented. The first stage involves what Ferris calls 'humour and humiliation': the DJ turns the caller's problem into a joke and teases or embarrasses them, using sexual innuendo. Ferris likens this to Garfinkel's (1956) concept of the degradation ceremony (see Chapter 7 below), whereby an individual's identity is symbolically stripped down before an audience.

The second stage is 'therapeutic direction': the hosts step in and assume a directive role, providing sensible advice and asking questions to seek information from the caller. Ferris describes a young woman complaining that her boyfriend 'takes her for granted', which, after the initial joking, is taken seriously as she breaks down in tears. Advice is offered within the aforementioned moral discourse, citing broader principles such as self-worth, honesty and integrity. The doctor says, 'I'm sorry but this guy is not worthy of a relationship with you right now. . . . You should just find somebody who does care about you in the same way you care about him' (Ferris 2004: 258).

The final stage, 'symbolic transformation', represents the critical denouement of the process. Another caller, Stephanie, phones in complaining about an unco-operative boyfriend. She shows initial resistance but eventually capitulates to the hosts' advice that she should break up with him. Their response is to affirm her decision, reassuring her that it is the right thing to do as an important step in her self-development. They do this by invoking imagery from *The Wizard of Oz*, in which the Wizard gives character-building gifts (brains, heart, courage) to the Scarecrow, Tin Man and Cowardly Lion. The hosts even claim explicitly that they are 'bestowing knowledge' on the caller, indexically referencing their own ritualistic action and drawing attention to its reparative qualities. The caller humbly acknowledges this and considers herself healed:

CLR: But see, I'm, I, I'm so naïve, I'm feeling –
DR: Yes.
DJ: Alright, but now you're not naïve anymore. We're bestowing knowledge on you. Like the Tin Man. Was it the Tin Man? Or did he want a heart? No, the Lion wanted a heart.
DR: The Scarecrow.
DJ: The Scarecrow, you're now the Scarecrow, Stephanie.
DR: He got a 'Th.D.,' a Doctor of Thinkology.
DJ: Never mind the man – 'Pay no attention to the man behind the curtain!' You now have guts, and nuts, and go out on your own, and find yourself a guy who's going to treat you right. All right?
CLR: OK.

(Ferris 2004: 261–2)

Crucially, Ferris argues that what creates the transformation is not Stephanie's decision but rather the retrospective interpretation and representation of this through the hosts' speech acts. Their talk is performative: in the process of describing an apparent transformation of a troubled self, the words themselves actually accomplish the action of transformation: 'We're bestowing knowledge on you. . . . You now have guts, and nuts, and go out on your own.' By describing the caller as someone who is brave, wise and has self-belief, they are not referring to an existing identity but rather creating a new one and making it socially real.

## Disclaimers

The final kind of aligning action used in verbal identity work is the disclaimer. This is a statement used to preface another statement that the speaker anticipates may cause offence. They may be about to speak disparagingly about a social group, or reveal some disturbing information, and realize that this could reflect badly on them. Hewitt and Stokes (1975) argued that disclaimers are a technique of prospective repair work, used when an actor anticipates that their situated identity claim will be discredited by the content of their words or actions. In Goffman's (1959) terms, they want to 'give' a good impression, but worry that they will 'give off' a bad one. This involves a process of '(re)typification', whereby the actor seeks to avoid being cast or typified by the listener as a particular category of person and to redefine themselves as another, more socially desirable type.

The first type of disclaimer is *hedging*. This is the prefacing of a statement of fact, opinion or position in a debate by a comment that shows minimal commitment, in case it is judged to be wrong (factually or morally) by the audience. For example, we might say, 'Of course, I'm not an expert but I think . . .'. Hedging is often used when the speaker feels uncertain about what they are about to say, and worries that it will invite a social reaction of disapproval. This technique helps the actor to save face by setting up an escape route: if it turns out they have misjudged their comment, they can always backtrack to this prior position of ambivalence and claim that they had never really believed in the viewpoint anyway. We revisit this idea in Chapter 5 with Goffman's (1959) 'realigning actions', as a form of 'communication out of character'.

*Credentializing* is used when the speaker knows that what they are about to say is controversial, but they are nonetheless committed to expressing the viewpoint. They try to establish their credentials that give them the right to speak from this position or cite this view. Sometimes this is used when criticizing an individual: if the speaker worries that this will make them seem petty or unreasonable, they start by asserting that the view is 'nothing personal' but based on a greater moral principle, like honesty or justice: 'Don't get me wrong, he's a nice guy, it's just that . . . '. Thus the credentials invoked are not so much official qualifications, but, rather, symbolic claims to personal or social characteristics that grant the speaker membership of a certain group (such as 'nice people'). In a particularly tactical variant of this, the group invoked is the very one who stands to be offended by the dubious statement: the classic 'I'm not a racist, but . . .', or 'I'm not homophobic – some of my best friends are gay!'

The third type of disclaimer is the *sin licence*. Here the speaker stipulates in advance an acknowledgement that what they are about to say constitutes a rule violation, but points to justificatory reasons or mitigating circumstances that they hope will excuse them from blame. Sometimes this is achieved by claiming that the rule itself is too stringent or bureaucratic, and that it is only reasonable to take it with a pinch of salt. We find this in the patter of the salesperson who indulges their customers with the flattering preface, 'I'm not really supposed to do this, but I can offer you a discount.'

Fourthly, the *cognitive disclaimer* is used when the speaker believes that they are right in what they are about to say, but realizes that their actions may be misconstrued as strange, mistaken or disproportionate. They preface the statement with an acknowledgement of the apparent nonsensicality of the act but make a request for the audience to withhold their scepticism and give them the benefit of the doubt. For example, the witness to an unusual event might say, 'I know this sounds crazy, but I'm sure I just saw . . .'. We saw this in Woofitt's (1992) study of accounts of paranormal experiences (see above), where it functioned as a membership categorization device, establishing the speaker as a normal, rational, sane person.

Closely related to this is the *appeal for the suspension of judgement*. This is when an actor is aware that what they are about to say or do might be construed as offensive or cause temporary discomfort, but also knows that they can give a subsequent justification for it that will exonerate them from blame. As with the cognitive disclaimer, the speaker is asking the listener to suspend their initial reaction and wait for an explanation or demonstration of the action's 'real' meaning: 'Hear me out.' However, instead of this this being couched in terms of the actor's claim to be a rational, reasonable person, or the action's logical or practical sensibility, it is based on value-driven, moral or affective criteria, such as being a 'decent' or 'fair' person.

## Frame analysis

Frame analysis (FA) is an approach developed by Goffman (1974) when he critically revisited Thomas and Thomas's (1928) 'definition

of the situation' concept (see Chapter 2 above). Goffman argued that
actors do not have complete freedom to negotiate afresh in each situation, as we are constrained by 'frames': the 'principles of organization'
that structure social events. Frames act as a blueprint for social conduct,
by providing a set of shared meanings about what is going on, as well as
understandings of the rules, roles and rituals to be followed. However,
agency is still apparent in the idea that frames have to be interpreted and
applied by actors. Goffman described framing as a 'joint enterprise',
reminiscent of Blumer's (1969) notion of symbolically communicative
joint action.

As a contemporary example, Bishop (2013) used frame analysis
to explore how the idea of a pub 'regular' is constructed, upheld and
managed as both a social identity and a definition of the situation.
Drawing on three ethnographic studies of pubs (Hunt & Satterlee 1986;
Katovitch & Reese 1987; Fox 2004) and supplementing them with
her own observations and interviews in a British pub, she argued that
the perception of customers as 'regulars' or 'non-regulars' (strangers)
is negotiated by patrons as a way of framing the situation. It has the
potential to create either social bonds or symbolic barriers between
those present, and shapes their interaction.

This is tied to the task of identity performance, as patrons seek to
present themselves as regulars through embodied and verbal displays of
insider knowledge and claims to membership – which may or may not
be ratified by the others present. As Hunt and Satterlee (1986: 525) put
it: '. . . the status of a Regular depends not merely on regular attendance
but also on knowledge of the shared rituals and practices of the drinking area.' Those who are perceived as non-regulars are symbolically
excluded from the rituals of friendship (banter, joking, mock arguments
and other playful activities) on which local members rely for their own
role-identities. Bishop observed that regulars were identifiable by their
positions, demeanour and use of space: they were the ones who would
sit at the bar, claimed (and were granted) their own favourite seat and
appeared 'at home' there. Regulars would chat to the bar staff and make
it clear that they were familiar with this environment; when they entered
the bar, they would be greeted by a loud, friendly chorus of recognition
and welcome.

The purpose of FA is to identify the features of talk and other
communicative gestures that indicate how participants are 'framing'
(interpreting and defining) the situation. For example, the 'topic' represents participants' shared understandings of what their conversation is
about, guiding the organization of talk by delineating its focus. Shared
rules govern the introduction and ratification of topics (Ribeiro & de
Souza Pinto 2005), and must be negotiated between interactants. The

speakers themselves and their right to speak also have to be ratified (Hutchby 1999). Actors may use non-verbal gestures to indicate their wish to take the floor, or be invited by others to do so: 'As people speak and perform actions, they signal to each other what they believe they are doing (i.e. what speech act[s] they are performing, what activity they are engaged in) and in what way their words and gestures are to be understood' (Ribeiro & de Souza Pinto 2005: 15).

Goffman introduced a number of conceptual features that can be found using FA. The *primary frame* is the overall definition given to a situation by its participants. These are fairly broad, such as the 'natural frame', where events appear to be unfolding independently of their action, and its converse, the 'social frame', where participants recognize that someone present has influenced the outcome. Within these broader frames, there are narrower ones, referring to the specific content of the encounter: a situation can be recognized as a lesson, party, game, and so on. In this way, frames can be *laminated,* or superimposed upon each other, creating multiple layers of interpretation.

Frames can also be marked, or 'bracketed', as distinct phases of a scene by using *episodic conventions*. These are coded rituals that are rule-governed and highly normative, and so can only be performed by members with insider knowledge. For example, in Bishop's study, the practice of 'buying a round' was important in signifying that a patron had been accepted as a regular and knew how to act in this setting.

*Keying* is the process of moving from one frame to another, often marked by symbolic gestures to signal the transition. Goffman (1974: 43) defined keying as 'the set of conventions by which a given activity, one already meaningful in terms of some primary framework, is transformed into something patterned on this activity but seen by the participants to be something quite else'. Keying is a skilful act that demands an insider's knowledge of the established frame and its normative conventions: one must be able to understand the rules of a game before one is able to change them. Goffman identified a number of basic keys (such as 'make-believe', 'contest' and 'ceremony') which change the meaning of a situation for its participants. For example, housemates may decide to 'break open a bottle' and get drunk together as an expression of affiliation and trust: social drinking is a ritual used to facilitate and deepen social bonds, signalling a transition from formal to more informal and equal relations (Gusfield 1987).

Conversely, in situations that shift from informal to formal, there may be a need to 'warm up' for the main scene and 'attune' everyone to the roles they are about to play (Hutchby 1999). Medical appointments usually start with polite preliminary rituals, such as openings, greetings and small talk, before the official business of the consultation

(Coupland et al. 1994). Verbal markers, such as bridging words ('Now, . . .'), signal the transition from the social to the medical frame, while standard questions cue the patient to take the floor with their symptom reports: 'How are you?' or 'What can I do for you?' (Coupland et al. 1994).

In keying a scene, actors may also shift their *footing*, a term Goffman (1981: 124–61) used to describe each participant's relation to the others present or orientation to the subject matter they are discussing. Goffman identified three positions in the telling of a story: the principal (whose position the talk represents), the author (who scripted the story) and the animator (who speaks the words). Potter (1996) added to this with some further, supporting roles, such as the addressed recipient, overhearer and eavesdropper. Footing may involve the various 'aligning actions' discussed above, through which members display conformity to the group's norms and values: 'A change in footing implies a change in the alignment we take up to ourselves and others present as expressed in the way we manage the production or reception of an utterance. . . . participants over the course of their speaking constantly change their footing, these changes being a persistent feature of natural talk' (Goffman 1981: 128).

Footing can be especially significant when actors want to give an impression of neutrality, presenting themselves as merely the channel through which a message is being transmitted. This happens with news reporting in broadcast media, where it is important that the events being narrated appear to be unbiased (Glasgow University Media Group 1976). Clayman (1992) suggests that newsreaders seek to present themselves as merely the animator of a story, rather than its author, to absolve themselves from any responsibility for its content. Any controversial viewpoints or value-laden terms are clearly attributed to third parties, the principals, through subtle verbal and non-verbal signals. For example, there is the use of the third-person voice ('It is said that . . .' or 'As Dr X said in that report . . .') and of implicit quotation marks (or 'scare quotes') around phrases as grammatical markers, to indicate the newsreader's distance from or scepticism towards the content (Young 1987). Clayman (1992) explains that such displays of footing serve to designate the material as sensitive, emotive or controversial while emphasizing the animator's detachment from it. As a performative display of neutrality, it makes a distinction between the narrated event and the event of narrating (Wortham 1996).

FA can also be useful to examine what is happening when a social encounter does not run smoothly. *Misframing* occurs when an actor misperceives the frame of a situation, or interprets it differently from other participants. This often happens when one is an outsider to a group, approaching it from the position of Simmel's (1908a) 'stranger' who lacks access to their shared stocks of background knowledge (see Chapter 2 above). *Frame disputes* occur when actors explicitly disagree on the definition of the situation because they have different motives, interests or agendas. They will be quite aware that they are making a different interpretation to each other, but are determined to stick to their guns. This can lead to micro-social conflict, ranging from mild tension and strain concealed by polite displays of civility (see Chapter 2), through tight-lipped and frosty exchanges, to heated debate and argument.

Frame disputes are often observed in analyses of institutional talk, where they can indicate power relations, asymmetry and inequality. Medical sociology's studies of doctor–patient relationships in the clinical encounter suggest that these two parties tend to frame the situation in different ways. Mishler (1984) distinguished between the 'medical voice' used by the doctor, with its focus on diagnosis, prescription and scientific authority, and the patient's 'voice of the lifeworld', which focused on personal feelings, social relationships, home and everyday life.

This contrast is particularly stark in the case of psychiatric healthcare, where patients with more severe conditions may find their credibility in dispute. Hamilton (2014) examined the transcripts of ninety-two psychiatric consultations with patients who had been prescribed anti-psychotic medication. A frame dispute often arose here, whereby the doctor would begin by using the 'medical frame' and/or 'interview frame' to question the patient about their compliance with medication and other treatment decisions, but this would be challenged by the patient seeking to introduce matters of the lifeworld, using the 'social frame' and/or 'narrative frame'. For example, in the following excerpt, a patient interprets the doctor's question about how she is coping as a personal inquiry, welcoming the opportunity to tell her rather lengthy version of the story. Note how the doctor interrupts bluntly (albeit unsuccessfully) to silence the lifeworld voice and reassert the medical frame:

> *Patient*: Do you think that – when you asked me how do I cope and I said to you I don't know whether to laugh or not? I don't know whether to laugh, I think it's kind of, incredible that you know me there deteriorating. And at the end of the day, yes weight is a good loss at the end of the day I'm not complaining about that, that's one good factor.
> *Doctor*: Yeah. OK, can we weigh you?
> *Patient*: But you know, erm, you know that I was probably gonna say these things. You know how could I not sit there all that time, nine months, the process that I went through, dumped in a flat and then mixed up

with all my different medications. And then you tell me that take a prescription over the phone. I mean, are you allowed to do that? It's not even acceptable . . .

(Hamilton 2014: 166)

This doctor's interjection demonstrates a final principle of FA. *Regrounding* is an action performed after frame dispute or misframing, which acknowledges that tension has arisen and attempts to restore the situation to 'normal appearances' (Goffman 1969; see Chapter 2 above). This can occur after a momentary hiatus, for example when somebody enters a room by mistake and disturbs a meeting: after they have apologized and left, the Chair might clear her throat and say, 'Now, shall we continue?' Regrounding can also occur after more prolonged deviations. Katovich and Reese (1987: 317) found that pub regulars returning after a period of absence were greeted with elaborate rituals, including melodramatic exclamations like 'We thought you'd died and gone to hell!', and demands for them to give 'truant accounts' of the reasons for their absence. Bishop (2013) suggests that these rituals marked the transition of the regular's status from temporary outsider to reintegrated insider, thereby restoring the disrupted frame.

## Conclusion

This chapter has examined the significance of language, especially conversational talk, in social interaction. Micro-sociological theories like symbolic interactionism and ethnomethodology point to the social construction of 'realities' as perceived and understood by actors. Language is central to this process, for it constitutes the very world(s) it purports merely to describe. It has indexical and reflexive properties that reveal underlying rules and resources, on which actors draw to compose accounts that resonate with their audience's expectations. Aside from using language to define or 'frame' situations, actors accomplish social actions and perform identities through their choice of words and gestures. They may seek to appear honest, credible, neutral or loyal, while being none of these things; cite interests, motives and morals that occlude their true stakes in the encounter; and strategically align themselves with culturally preferred norms and values. Thus talk has a self-presentational function, and can be studied in terms of what it does – what social actions it performs – for people and situations. We have seen how methodological techniques elucidate these processes, from CA's focus on everyday talk-in-interaction, through DA's examination of institutional discourse and rhetoric, to FA's recognition of how power relations and role-based 'footing' allow only certain things to be said, heard or accepted as dominant interpretations. In the following chapter, we take a closer look at Goffman's dramaturgical theory to consider what else actors do to present their self-identities, and how they design and perform roles in everyday encounters.

# 4

# Managing faces

## Roles, performance and self-presentation

This chapter focuses on the dramaturgical theory developed by Erving Goffman, in relation to the design and display of social roles. Here we shall focus on individual identity performances; the next chapter considers the collaborative aspects of group interaction in 'teams'. As we saw in Chapter 1, dramaturgy views social life analogously as being like a theatrical performance, comprised of a series of unfolding scenes enacted by skilled casts of actors. These players present different versions of themselves, like characters, in each situation, tailoring their performances to the script of action and the audience's expectations. Role performances are given in the 'frontstage' region, while 'backstage' spaces allow for actors to relax out of character, rehearsing and reflecting on the drama.

## Performing the self

Goffman's (1959) key concepts of *self-presentation* and *impression management* refer to the ways in which actors constantly monitor and adapt the public display of their identities in order to create a particular image, or desirable impression, upon the audiences they encounter. This involves making careful and strategic decisions about which information to conceal or reveal, and the images one might either 'give' intentionally or 'give off' unintentionally (Goffman 1959). It may then be difficult to ever know the 'true self' behind these personae, the actor behind the character. Goffman (1959: 30) cites the assertion by the Chicago School sociologist Robert Park (1950: 249) that 'everyone is always and everywhere, more or less consciously, playing a role. ... It is in these roles that we know each other; it is in these roles that we know ourselves.'

Audiences are critically evaluative in scrutinizing actors' role performances, and their real or anticipated judgements have the power to refuse or discredit identity claims. Actors take this into account when designing their conduct, using the reflexivity and imaginative perspective-taking that we saw with Mead's (1934) 'I' and 'Me' and Cooley's (1902) Looking Glass Self (see Chapter 1 above). Goffman suggests that the actor's actual qualities are almost irrelevant compared to those that are (rightly or wrongly) attributed to them. A role performance is defined by its reception rather than its inception:

> To *be* a given kind of person, then, is not merely to possess the required attributes, but also to sustain the standards of conduct and appearance that one's social grouping attaches thereto. ... A status, a position, a social place is not a material thing, to be possessed and then displayed; it is a pattern of appropriate conduct, coherent, embellished, and well articulated. (Goffman 1959: 81, emphasis in original)

Goffman (1959: 32) defines performance as 'all of the activity of an individual which occurs during a period marked by his [*sic*] continuous presence before a particular set of observers and which has some influence on the observers'. His idea that roles are performed in a strategic, calculated way, with attention to self-presentation and in pursuit of impression management, presupposes that there is a thinking agent designing this pragmatic action: the actor behind the character. There is a presumption of authenticity, as well as vulnerability, in this 'real' self, who is kept concealed in the backstage region and may be known only to itself: 'Behind many masks and many characters, each performer tends to wear a single look, a naked unsocialized look' (Goffman 1959: 228). However, Goffman was more interested in the mechanics of this process: how and why do actors design their role performances in certain ways, and what attitudes do they have towards the roles that they are playing?

A striking illustration of this comes from Waskul and Lust's (2004) study of fantasy role-playing games, such as Dungeons and Dragons or World of Warcraft. Such activities demand a very consciously contrived role performance as an assumed character, and so make explicit some of the dramaturgical techniques that actors employ in their everyday lives more generally. Waskul and Lust suggest that game players make a distinction between three social statuses: the *self*, the *character* and the *player*. Respectively, these refer to the individual's perception of their 'real self' as a person with other role-identities outside of the game; the fantasy figure they adopt within the game setting, which may build upon aspects of the real self or be a direct contradiction of it; and the game participant, as a social actor behind the character, who is directing and executing this identity performance. This 'player' part of the self is intriguing to contemplate, for it suggests the visible presence and acknowledgement of the 'ghost in the machine', whom we do not normally see. Participating in a fantasy role-play game brings players into proximity with each other in those terms: they encounter each other *as players*, and can engage with these identities independently of their 'selves' or 'character' roles.

## Role-taking or role-making?

Dramaturgy's conception of role performance can be contrasted with the more traditional role theories that preceded it. These models are associated with the classical perspective of structural functionalism, which depicts the 'social system' as an external, macro-level entity; individuals are socialized into this stable order and their action is determined by it (Parsons 1951). Roles are embedded in the institutions of the social system, connected in reciprocal patterns or role sets (Linton 1936), such as teacher–student, server–customer or parent–child. The social role is defined as a relatively stable, pre-existing cluster of rights, duties and obligations associated with a particular position or status (Hewitt 2007). It is fairly standardized in content, prescribed by the culture's norms and values. This allows for little individual agency or variation in the interpretation of roles; it is a model of rather passive role-*taking*.

A famous example of this is Parsons' (1951) sick role. Parsons argued that the social system has to accommodate deviant behaviour to prevent social disorganization. Sickness is a status, provided by the social system, which can be claimed by individuals as a way of legitimating their temporary incapacity to contribute to it. As a role, it is an implicit bargain between self and society, comprising a set of rights for the sick person (exemption from normal role responsibilities, such as work duties; and freedom from blame for the condition) with a corresponding set of obligations (to try to get well; to seek and follow the advice of medical professionals). Sick persons are only entitled to the former if they are prepared to fulfil the latter side of the bargain.

In symbolic interactionism, by contrast, the focus is on role-*making* (Turner 1962). Social roles are depicted non-deterministically as mere resources: loose templates for action that afford the actor great scope for individual interpretation and meaning-making. Roles are not passively taken up but actively made and performed, suggesting agency, creativity and skilful identity work. They are negotiated, emergent and adaptable, as actors navigate a careful path between the demands of the occasion and their own personal agendas of self-presentation.

Goffman (1961b: 75) makes a helpful distinction between the 'role' *per se*, which may be taken on as 'the activity the incumbent would engage in were he [*sic*] to act solely in terms of the normative demands upon someone in his position', and 'role performance' or 'role enactment' as 'the actual conduct of a particular individual while on duty in his position'. In other words, there may be a standard idea of what a role entails, but there are an infinite number of possible ways of performing it, depending on actors' different interpretations.

Goffman also differentiates between 'general roles' that actors carry across situations (such as mother, doctor, vegetarian) and 'situated roles' that they adopt only transiently, within a specific face-to-face encounter: '. . . a bundle of activities visibly performed before a set of others and visibly meshed into the activity these others perform' (1961b: 85). Situated roles might include being a liar, a stranger, a patient or an interviewee. Because they are context-specific, situated roles will often be interconnected in a 'situated activity system', for example a shop assistant, manager and customer.

Within a situation, actors co-ordinate their role performances to accomplish interactional order. Remembering Cooley's (1902) Looking Glass Self and Mead's (1934) dialogic relation between 'I' and 'Me', we can think of role-making as a reflective, strategic activity involving consideration of the anticipated and desired responses of others, with the aim of co-ordinating joint action. Hewitt (2007: 62) defines the role as a *perspective* from which conduct is constructed, guiding smooth interaction. We often seek out encounters with those whom we expect to confirm and ratify our claimed identities. Backman and Secord (1968: 290) suggest that an individual 'may select a role that enables him [*sic*] to interact with those persons who will attribute congruent characteristics to him or who will engage in behavior that validates aspects of self'.

The notion of role-making also implies that each individual will have multiple roles in their repertoire, which they can draw upon and sometimes combine to suit the contingencies of each situation. Performances are tailored to the audience's expectations and normative codes of conduct, and so the individual may present a different face for each occasion they encounter. As James (1890: 295) asserted: '. . . a man [*sic*] has as many different social selves as there are distinct groups of persons about whose opinion he cares.' Although SI retains the idea of a core underlying self who is doing all this work – we are more than just the sum of our performances – it does allow for a more pluralistic, open-ended vision of this entity as being composed of multiple and shifting role-identities (McCall & Simmons 1966) that may be combined in novel and unpredictable ways.

Multiple roles may nevertheless be integrated harmoniously into a stable sense of self (Backman & Secord 1968). We can be aware of playing different roles in different contexts, yet retain a sense of overall self-identity. In his structural branch of SI, Stryker (1968) suggested that social identity was a composite cluster of roles arranged in a pragmatically organized hierarchy. Through a process of *role selection*, we choose to play whichever is most relevant to the demands of the situation. This process has two dimensions: *identity salience* refers to the probability of enacting any particular role rather than others, and thus its prominence within the hierarchy, while *identity commitment* indicates the depth of meaning attached to the role by its incumbent. For example, an actor may have a role set that involves being a woman, professional, black, middle class and a mother, each of which could be salient in different contexts, but across these, the 'mother' role might feel the most important to her.

Roles that involve high personal commitment can be very important to self-identity. Altheide and Pfuhl (1980) showed this in their study of running as a 'serious leisure identity' (Stebbins 1992). The American adults they interviewed explained how, despite initial discomfort and fatigue, they had come to love running and give it new meanings. The solitary, meditative rhythm allowed them to spend 'quality time' alone, while they respected the discipline and commitment required to train regularly. They spoke about their passionate commitment to this role-identity, defining themselves not just as people who went running, but as *runners*: a 'master status' (Hughes 1945) that dominated their self-identities. Social activities, work and even family life sometimes took a backseat to the prioritization of running, and this ritual was the highlight of their day. Running was experienced as a form of total self-accomplishment, encompassing physical, mental and emotional wellbeing and creating an overall sense of authenticity: '[Running] is the most important thing in my life. It's given me the freedom to be myself, to live a life I deemed not worth living. It has freed me from the hang-ups of youth. It has matured me and strengthened me. It is the most important thing I have ever done' (participant cited in Altheide & Pfuhl 1980: 132).

Juggling multiple roles can create dramaturgical dilemmas in managing the consistency between them. Gross and Stone (1964) suggest that a common cause of embarrassment is the discrediting of identity claims, through the failure to fulfil one's role requirements in a situation. This might involve a loss of control over symbolic communicative objects, such as the body, props, speech or physical scenery, which prevents the actor from playing the part they claimed or in the way they intended. Embarrassment feels as if another role-identity (such as 'clumsy person') has come to the fore and is interfering with the impression that we wanted to project.

Consequently, Gross and Stone (1964) make a distinction between the *dominant* role an actor tries to play within a situation, and other subsidiary role-identities that can leak out unintentionally, 'giving off' the wrong impression (Goffman 1959). These include the *adjunct role* (an accompanying activity or characteristic that shapes the way a role is played, such as one's gender, sexuality or disability), *reserve identities* (stable features of a person's identity that they bring with them to a social transaction but which remain in the background as irrelevant, such as their political views or relationship status) and *relic identities* (past identities that have since been abandoned but which threaten to discredit the dominant role performance, such as having been in prison or a psychiatric hospital).

An example of this can be found in Stein's (2011) study of how people construct temporary identities whilst on vacation. Holidays represent 'time off' from the mundane, everyday world and its workaday routines (cf. Zerubavel 1981), and we symbolically express this feeling of escape by taking on a different role, or experimenting with alternative identities. It is as if the events and experiences of the holiday exist in a different realm to that of one's usual routines and duties, providing us with boundaried times and spaces in which to engage in 'licensed carnival' (Bakhtin 1965). Michelle Thomas (2005: 571) found this principle informing young women's accounts of holiday romances: 'What happens in Tenerife, stays in Tenerife.'

Stein's holidaymakers used dramaturgical strategies to achieve role segregation (Goffman 1961b: 73–134; see below) between their identities 'at home' and 'away'. They conducted *rituals of segmentation* before going away, such as packing their suitcase with objects that were symbolically marked as different: clothes suitable for a warmer climate, maps of an unfamiliar terrain or books they had not had time to read. They left behind objects that symbolically represented the roles they were casting off, such as computers and work uniforms. Some people resisted this, performing *rituals of integration*, for example packing their laptop so they could check email while on holiday. In Gross and Stone's (1964) typology, this represents the mobilization of 'relic' and 'adjunct' identities, respectively.

This whole process is reversed when the holidaymaker returns home and must make the transition back into their normal, 'dominant' identity. We perform further rituals to symbolically remove our holiday roles, such as unpacking the suitcase and washing our clothes, and may delay doing this precisely because it represents a return to the dismally mundane. We linger over objects that remind us of our time away and can be brought into the everyday environment, such as a souvenir placed on the office desk or a set of photographs uploaded to a social networking site. Through these various symbolic rituals, we reflexively monitor and regulate the relationship between the plethora of roles in our repertoires.

## Artful strategies

Much of Goffman's dramaturgical analysis is dedicated to cataloguing the various tricks, techniques and strategies actors use to 'make' and perform their roles. These 'arts of impression management' (Goffman 1959: 203) are explained in a core set of his books, including *The Presentation of Self in Everyday Life* (1959), *Encounters* (1961b), *Behavior in Public Places* (1963b), *Strategic Interaction* (1969) and *Relations in Public* (1971), which document many recognizable quirks of human behaviour.

Actors' common concern is to prevent what Goffman (1959) calls 'incidents': unexpected events that disrupt the version of reality fostered by the participants and make the performance grind to an embarrassing halt. These include *unmeant gestures* that leak out of a role performance and give off a contradictory impression, *inopportune intrusions* that occur when an audience member enters the backstage region and catches the performer(s) out of character, faux pas which happen when a performer unthinkingly does something that jeopardizes the image projected by themselves or their team, and actors *causing a scene* by challenging the polite consensus presented by other players.

To prevent such incidents, Goffman (1959: 207) identifies three 'defensive attributes and practices' used in individual role performances. The first is *dramaturgical loyalty*. This refers to the moral obligation between team-mates not to betray their shared secrets (about the staging of their show, its backstage reality and their offstage identities) and the exclusion of those who cannot be trusted in this regard. Goffman gives the examples of parents avoiding talking about family secrets in front of their children in case they disclose them to outsiders, and upper-class householders lowering their voices when servants are present.

Secondly, *dramaturgical discipline* refers to an actor's careful management of their personal front so as to appear nonchalant, while concealing the extensive work they are doing to create this very impression: '. . . while the performer is ostensibly immersed and given over to the activity he [*sic*] is performing, and is apparently engrossed in his actions in a spontaneous, uncalculating way, he must nonetheless be affectively dissociated from his presentation in a way that leaves him free to cope with dramaturgical contingencies as they arise' (1959: 210).

The dramaturgically disciplined performer is one who remembers their own part, while keeping an eye on the show as a whole and ensuring that it runs to plan; if anything goes awry, they have the 'presence of mind' to quickly correct it (Goffman 1959: 210). This involves the careful management of one's facial expression, voice and bodily demeanour so as to give an appropriate affective display. We saw this in my study of the swimming pool (Scott 2009a; see Chapter 2 above), where lap swimmers pretended to be 'away' in their own private reverie, pursuing individual regimes, but were actually keeping a close watch on the scene and monitoring others' behaviour.

Thirdly, *dramaturgical circumspection* refers to the exercise of 'prudence, care and honesty' (Goffman 1959: 212) in the staging of a show, by preparing for likely contingencies and putting measures in place to avoid anticipated disruptions. Circumspection is exercised in the recruitment of team-mates who can be trusted to show dramaturgical loyalty, for example the school teacher who arranges for the inspector to visit when she is teaching her most obedient pupils (Goffman 1959: 220). Actors may limit the size of their performance team to minimize the risk of any member acting improperly, embarrassingly or treacherously. They can also stick to a well-rehearsed script that everyone can be trusted to remember, as shown in Ritzer's (2004) study of a fast-food restaurant. Keeping the performance simple and predictable reduces the risk of any individual fluffing their lines and blowing the team's cover.

Circumspection can also be exercised in selecting an audience who will support one's identity claims. Goffman (1959: 213) gives the example of a married couple excluding visitors from their home about whom they feel differently, fearing that they might not be able to present a united front. Role performances can be tailored to the conditions of the setting, the characteristics of the audience or the information that they are thought to already possess. Actors may be circumspect about which objects they leave out on display in a scene, according to the impression they want to create. Goffman (1959: 50–1) describes a status-conscious housewife serving her guests high-quality food and leaving copies of the *Saturday Evening Post* (a highbrow newspaper) casually strewn across the living-room table, while her actual preferred reading material, the magazine *True Romances,* remains stashed away in her bedroom.

Aside from these defensive practices, Goffman details a number of other techniques used in the execution of a role performance. *Idealization* is the interpretation of a role according to prototypical standards, so that it can be easily recognized by the audience. One might attempt to appear as a 'typical' student or waitress by emphasizing those actions and gestures that are conventionally associated with the role. Goffman explains this as a reflection of the socialization process, arguing that performers idealize their roles in order to demonstrate that they under-stand and conform to cultural norms and values. Today, people posting profiles to online dating sites strive to present an idealized rather than realistic version of themselves, in the hope of creating a desirable image for their imagined audience (Ellison et al. 2006).

Idealization involves maximizing the satisfaction of the audience, who may not be limited to one situational context. Goffman (1959: 57) explains that performers who routinely repeat the same role must nevertheless try to convey to each audience that what they are seeing is a unique performance. Stand-up comedians on tour repeat the same scripted show every night, but adapt some material to refer to the current location or audience members. Shop assistants trained to follow a script of sales patter vary it a little with each customer to create the illusion of spontaneity (Goffman 1959: 57), while a university teacher delivering the same lectures every year must try to sound enthusiastic with each new cohort of students (Scott 2007b). Interestingly, audi-ences can also participate in creating this illusion: Goffman (1959: 58) gives the example that customers who shop around for a service often disguise this fact once they have settled on a retailer, and pretend that they had not considered anywhere else. Mutual flattery between actors and their audience therefore helps to idealize the staging and reception of a role performance.

A related strategy is *dramatic realization*, which involves emphasiz-ing or exaggerating a role performance to ensure the audience both observe it and make the intended character attribution. The aim is to 'dramatically highlight and portray confirmatory facts' (Goffman 1959: 40) about the actor's right to inhabit that role. People waiting on the street to meet someone often feel self-consciously conspicuous, and so make an exaggerated show of gestures to communicate the 'innocent' motive of waiting: checking their watch, looking up and down the road and taking out a mobile phone. Another example is the aesthetic style of camp, whereby homosexual men theatrically exaggerate characteristics stereotypically associated with this status, such as effeminacy, flamboy-ance, frivolity and excess (Sontag 1964). This stylized role performance is given in an ironic, parodic manner, with the political intent of making fun *out of* (rather than making fun *of*) something serious (Isherwood 1954).

Occasionally, however, dramatic realization can lead to the 'dilemma of expression versus action' (Goffman 1959: 43), whereby the actor is so concerned with the aesthetics and technicalities of delivering their performance that they cannot concentrate on the content of the task itself. For example, medical students at a prestigious college who were sitting nervously with their classmates to revise for an exam found that they were so preoccupied with appearing studious and competitively embodying the 'diligent student' role in front of each other that they were unable to take in anything of what they were reading (Becker et al. 1968). Conversely, a dilemma can be experienced when '[t]hose who have the time and talent to perform a task well may not, because of this, have the time or talent to make it apparent that they are performing well' (Goffman 1959: 43). In some organizational settings, these 'expressive' functions of a role performance are assigned to specialists, such as public relations agents, image consultants and personal trainers.

*Mystification* is the strategy of limiting contact between the performers and the audience, so that the latter cannot find out too much about how the show is being staged. One way of doing this is to maintain a barrier between the front- and backstage regions, so that the audience never get a chance to see into the latter. In the home we only allow visitors into certain 'public' rooms (living room, hallway, kitchen) while keeping other backstage regions off-limits (bedroom and bathroom). Mystification therefore helps to hide the 'dirty work' (Hughes 1962) that lies behind the composition of a role performance. For example, Tori McCabe, a 23-year-old British woman, recounts how she felt vulnerable and exposed when not wearing make-up, and went to extreme measures to avoid even her partner seeing her in this state:

> Every morning at 6.30am, I slip out of bed and tiptoe out of the door, careful not to disturb my fiancé, Dean. Locked in the bathroom, I apply a thick coat of foundation to my pale face, then bronzer, mascara, eyeliner and bright pink lipstick.
>
> Afterwards, I climb back into bed for half an hour before Dean and the kids wake up, taking care not to smudge my handiwork on my pillow.
>
> I've carried out this secret morning ritual every day since meeting Dean, 25, five years ago. Why? I can't stand the thought of him seeing me without make-up – he never has in the entire time we've been together. (McCabe 2013)

The final art of impression management is *misrepresentation*: deceiving the audience by presenting a version of oneself that one knows is not genuine. Goffman (1959: 65) suggests that it is easy to get away with this, because audiences tend to take role performances at face value, pragmatically assuming people to be who they say they are. As actors, we can take advantage of this trust and exploit it to our own advantage. To some extent, misrepresentation is a commonplace and inevitable feature of self-presentation: we all tailor our performances to suit the exigencies of the situation, and selectively present or conceal information about ourselves. In Chapter 8, we consider the argument that mild deception of this kind is an inherent, even functional, aspect of social interaction.

## Decorating the stage: scenery and props

The physical setting of a role performance is important in affecting how convincing it will seem. In his concept of the 'front' – those aspects of an actor's self-presentation that are intentionally displayed to fashion a particular impression – Goffman (1959: 32) identifies different types of 'expressive equipment', which are located either permanently or transiently in the frontstage region. 'First, there is the "setting", involving furniture, décor, physical layout and other background items' (Goffman 1959: 32), which provides the scenic aspects of the front. This could mean the rooms of a house, or a university campus. Settings remain fixed in place, so actors have to come to them to take part in the scene. Secondly, there is the 'personal front', which is the mobile items of expressive equipment that actors carry around with them. These can be either fixed in place on the individual (e.g. racial characteristics or body size) or transient signs (e.g. facial expression, clothing or carried objects).

Goffman further divides the personal front into 'appearance', features that identify the actor's status, role or temporary condition (such as a wedding ring, uniform or illness symptoms), and 'manner', which conveys the actor's attitude to these positions, or *how* they are playing the role (e.g. being haughty and aggressive or meek and apologetic). However, because personal fronts are 'sign vehicles', designed to be easily interpreted by audiences, they convey rather abstract, general information and standardized features, allowing the performer to be classified as a certain type of person. Goffman gives the example of the quality of 'professionalism' that service industry employees try to deliver, through expressions of competence, integrity, modernity and cleanliness: 'While in fact these abstract standards have a different significance in different occupational performances, the observer is encouraged to stress the abstract similarities' (1959: 36). This generalization of content is intrinsic to role performances, wherein the role *necessarily* tells audiences more about the character to be perceived than about the actor behind the mask.

Material objects are an important part of the personal front, and can be thought of as dramaturgical stage props. For Goffman (1951), objects are powerful indicators of a person's relative position. *Status symbols* are those that define a person's rank, marking their achievements in a competitive hierarchy (such as medals, trophies and badges), while *esteem symbols* represent success in more general qualities open to everyone, such as being a good friend or lover (e.g. greetings cards left on display, jewellery received as a gift or large numbers of Facebook friends).

Riggins (1990) developed this into a more detailed typology of objects, according to their self-presentational functions. Within the category of status symbols, *occupational objects* confirm one's credentials, such as certificates of qualification. Within the category of esteem symbols, there are *indigenous* and/or *exotic objects,* which display a person's experience as a worldly traveller, and *collective objects,* which represent community ties that transcend hierarchical rank, such as patriotic flags, tattoos and family heirlooms. We might also include football shirts denoting a supported team, and family photographs left on a work desk. In Hurdley's study of home mantelpieces, she found that people often displayed objects that symbolized happy memories and family ties, and these props helped them to perform relational identities. One participant, Sylvia, proudly described a bronze statue given to her by her daughters, alongside an ugly, shapeless doughball her grandson had made: 'It's got a "G" for Grandma on it but I can't see it' (Hurdley 2006: 724).

To these, Riggins adds some further categories. *Stigma objects* are those that highlight a person's sense of difference, or 'spoiled' identity (Goffman 1963a; see also Chapter 6 below). These might be associated with a physical disability (crutches, wheelchairs, walking sticks, syringes) or more morally connotative 'blemishes of character' (Goffman 1963a), such as prison tattoos or psychiatric hospital records. *Disidentifying objects* are used for the purposes of 'deliberate self-misrepresentation' (Riggins 1990: 351), to head off unwanted attributions and replace them with more socially desirable impressions. Riggins gives the examples of fake, reproduction antiques left on display in the home to indicate higher social class, and scholarly-looking glasses worn by the illiterate. *Alien objects* are those used for purposes other than their intended, official use, which are carried to express one's creativity, innovativeness or rebellious attitude. We often find this in fashion, when people dress or accessorize to convey eccentricity. Finally, *social facilitators* are objects used to accompany a role performance that help it to be delivered more smoothly. These would include Goffman's (1963b) 'side involvements': apparently nonchalant, secondary activities (like smoking, holding a drink or fiddling with a mobile phone) that deflect attention from the actor's 'main involvement', if they fear this will be performed clumsily. Goffman makes a similar distinction between 'dominant involvements', which form the official business of a situation, and 'subordinate involvements', which are more devious, private or secretive activities that the actor does alongside this official business: these represent what we can 'get away with' while ostensibly committed to a role performance.

Riggins goes on to outline some additional features that props might have, which can modify their meaning in a social encounter. The examples I give here are my own. *Time indicators* help audiences to judge an artefact's age or locate it in a socio-historical context: for example vintage clothing or antique furniture. They might also symbolize the passing of time, or the owner's patience or perseverance: garden plants carefully nurtured, or hair grown long. An object's *size and proportions* are also important; status can be implied through magnification (e.g. large, ostentatious houses) or minimization (e.g. delicate ornaments or expensive jewellery). Similarly, an artefact's *mode of production* can have connotative meanings that indicate moral qualities of the consumer (e.g. Fair Trade, organic products left out on display, or hand-crafted items indicating a leisurely lifestyle). *Cluttering and dispersing* are used to regulate the amount of space between objects: usually, the greater the space, the higher the wealth or status of the owner (e.g. large, open-plan houses or 'white box' galleries with sparsely dispersed exhibits), but occasionally cluttering can suggest a higher degree of affluence, knowledge or passionate commitment (e.g. the overflowing bookshelves of a professor's study). Actors may also give attention to *display syntax* (which other objects something is placed next to, insofar as this can alter the impression it gives off, e.g. the lavish high quality of groceries on a kitchen shelf being undermined by their juxtaposition to items from a supermarket 'value' range) and the *status consistency* between objects in a collection (e.g. the suite of furniture or decorative theme of a domestic living room). These considerations can be woven into an identity performance as symbolic expressions of a person's claimed 'taste' or class distinction (Bourdieu 1979).

## Lines and moves

Once a scene gets going, actors must perform a 'line' of action. This is the portrayal of a character, with due regard to appearance, manner, personal front, gestures and speech, in such a way that it is consistent with the definition of a situation fostered by the actor and their team-mates. Thus as well as reflecting individual self-presentational motives, lines involve ritualized, symbolic action (Goffman 1967: 4) whose meaning can be interpreted by others and co-ordinated with their own performances.

*Moves* are the set of embodied gestures, movements and expressions that comprise a role performance, helping actors to convey their lines of action. Goffman (1969) identifies some different types of these. *Native moves* are those that appear directly connected to a role in an obvious and logical way, and so are not questioned: a woman breastfeeding her baby or a student poring over books in the library. *Unwitting moves* are those that leak out unintentionally, undermining the character presented. These are the 'impressions given off' that Goffman (1959) distinguished from the carefully designed 'impressions given'. An actor may be discovered by the audience when behaving out of role, for example when they are caught staring or doing something embarrassingly private like picking their nose. Facial and bodily movements are crucial in the 'maintenance of expressive control', Goffman (1959: 59) explains, adding that 'the impression of reality fostered by a performance is a delicate, fragile thing that can be shattered by very minor mishaps' (1959: 63).

*Control moves* are the opposite: these reflect a calculated attempt to manage the impression one is trying to create, usually in such a way as to enhance one's public image. This might include 'make work' (Goffman 1959), the strategy of busying oneself with the official tasks associated with a role and appearing diligently immersed in them, especially when under observation by an authority figure. This is also an example of the art of 'idealization', described above, whereby actors seek to present a perfect, prototypical version of a role to justify their continued occupation of it.

*Uncovering moves* are those that attempt to reveal someone else's suspected motives or 'real', backstage self, in contradiction to the identity they are claiming. This might be motivated simply by *Schadenfreude*, taking pleasure in another person's discomfort, or by feelings of righteous moral indignation, if we feel someone is acting dishonestly and taking advantage of another's trust in their sincerity. For example, if I hear a friend telling someone how hard she has been working all weekend, but yet I saw her sunbathing on the beach, I might decide to interrupt the conversation to pull her up on her lie. Finally, *counter-uncovering moves* are those made by the actor who realizes that they are about to be exposed, and takes pre-emptive measures to prevent this happening. In the above example, my friend might be halfway through her performance of the weary, hardworking scholar when she sees me looking quizzically at her and remembers with a flash of horror that I saw her on the beach that day. She then quickly backtracks and changes her story, perhaps adding in a line about how she took a short break from studying but soon went home and worked late into the night.

## Facework

In a famous essay, 'On facework', Goffman (1967: 5–46) discussed the implications for the social self when a situated identity claim is compromised or discredited, and the mechanisms of interaction are used to repair this. The concept of 'face' can be understood as the publicly respectable image of self that an actor presents in a situation, in line with the norms and values of the group, setting or local culture, which has implications for their status, image and esteem. As Goffman says, it is the positive social value one claims for oneself, regardless of whether or not this claim is accepted. We can think of face as the situational front of a role, which symbolically conveys the characteristics of the person occupying it. Goffman suggests that face is not something that actors carry around with them as part of their personal front, but rather it is located in the flow of events in a social encounter, and therefore only 'on loan . . . from society' (1967: 10); it can be withdrawn if the audience deem the actor unworthy of it.

In social encounters, actors are concerned with being 'in face': projecting an image of themselves that is ratified by the audience, and 'keeping face' throughout the scene. Conversely, to be in the 'wrong face' is to present an inconsistent identity that contradicts the actor's claims and creates another, undesired impression: for example by attending a professional job interview untidily dressed and late. This in turn means 'losing face' by suffering an undignified loss of poise, with feelings of embarrassment or shame. In such scenarios the actor ends up momentarily 'out of face', having failed to create the intended impression. Meanwhile, to 'give face' is to generously respond to another's predicament in this regard, by providing an escape from their embarrassment: we help by 'saving' someone's face or 'sparing their blushes'.

Goffman (1967: 12) defines 'facework' as 'the actions taken by a person to make whatever he [sic] is doing consistent with face'. Its aim is to counteract the 'incidents' outlined above (unmeant gestures, inopportune intrusions and faux pas), whose symbolic implications threaten the official definition of the situation and constitute face threats. Goffman identifies two main kinds of facework: the *avoidance process*, which anticipates and tries to prevent a potential loss of face, and the *corrective process*, which reactively works to repair the damage caused by an actual loss of face. These are overlaid with another important distinction between *defensive* facework (performed to keep or save one's own face) and *protective facework* (saving other people's faces).

Avoidance techniques are often protective: they include *tact and diplomacy* (politely ignoring mistakes or faults, and declining to broach topics that might embarrass the other), *discretion* (neglecting to make

uncovering moves, by leaving challenging facts unstated and maintaining a collusive silence) and *studied non-observance* (pretending not
to notice something discrediting about another's role performance),
but we can also use avoidance techniques defensively: *avoiding contact*
with people who we fear might see through our performances, or using
*go-betweens* to mediate contact with them. Hewitt and Stokes' (1975)
disclaimers (see Chapter 3 above) are an example of this pre-emptive
management of face. Corrective techniques, meanwhile, are mainly
defensive, used by an actor who realizes they have lost face and want
to regain their credibility. These include the other processes of verbal
identity repair work discussed in Chapter 3, such as apologies, excuses
and justifications.

## Students' self-presentation strategies

An empirical study helps to illustrate these various skills of impression management, performance lines and facework strategies. Albas
and Albas (1988) studied the self-presentational techniques used by
Canadian university students after receiving examination grades. They
were interested in whether and to what extent the students chose to disclose their results to one another, given their awareness that they might
have done better or worse than their peers. The researchers were interested in how the students performed their identities in encounters with
one another in such a way as to either (defensively) keep face themselves
or (protectively) show consideration for the faces of others. These were
both avoidant processes, aimed at preventing anticipated face threats.

### Encountering inconsistency

Albas and Albas identified three main categories of students in this
regard: *Aces*, who had scored high grades in the examination, *Bombers*,
who had scored low grades or failed, and *Middle of the Roaders*, who
fared somewhere in between. They were most interested in the encounters that took place between Aces and Bombers, as two extreme,
contrasting role-identities, and they compared these to Ace–Ace and
Bomber–Bomber encounters to show the inconsistencies in students'
lines of self-presentation. Aces were thought to be privately proud of
their accomplishments and Bombers privately ashamed, but they were
only able to indulge these feelings openly in encounters with others
of the same status position: in 'mixed' encounters between Aces and
Bombers, rules of modesty and tact governed each party's decisions
about what information to disclose and which impression to try to

create. This echoes the notion of awareness contexts (Glaser & Strauss 1964), discussed in Chapter 2, whereby the degree of mutual knowledge held by participants about each other and the situation determines what and how much they choose to disclose.

In Ace–Ace encounters, students recognized each other as equally likely to have done well and so risked comparing results; open bragging and friendly rivalry were evident as they talked about how easy the exam had been. Bombers, similarly, felt they did not have to worry about keeping face when in the company of other Bombers. They would honestly 'confess' their low grades, commiserate and engage in backstage camaraderie, licking their wounds in 'orgies of self-pity' (Albas & Albas 1988: 299).

When Aces encountered Bombers, however, they were much more dramaturgically circumspect. Aces tried to gauge how well or badly the other student had done and adapt their face accordingly, playing down their own achievements. If the Bomber seemed disappointed, the Ace would tactfully avoid mentioning their own grade, or modestly attribute it to good luck. This created situational inconsistency in their role performances: whereas one Ace agreed with another Ace that the test had been 'a piece of cake', he was later heard consoling a Bomber that it had been 'unfair' (Albas & Albas 1988: 300).

Bombers, similarly, used defensive facework when they encountered Aces, trying to appear gracious losers by congratulating them on their success. Some used dramaturgical circumspection to work out which classmates had aced the test, so they could tactically avoid them. They would look out for the tell-tale signs and symbolic gestures, such as '"sitting tall" in their desks, displaying "glittering eyes", "broad grins" or a "jaunty walk"' (Albas & Albas 1988: 298). Ace–Bomber encounters involved a sequence of controlling, uncovering and counter-uncovering moves designed to locate one's relative academic status and perform a contextually appropriate role.

Albas and Albas then proceed to document the various strategies of self-presentation used in Ace–Bomber encounters. They divide these into two categories: strategies of revelation (where students sought to reveal their grades) and strategies of concealment (where they sought to hide them).

## Strategies of revelation

Aces' strategies of revelation were designed to let other students know how well they had done without appearing to brag: they were privately proud and wanted recognition for their achievements, but at the same time they were concerned to give an impression of modesty. They therefore developed tricks and techniques that allowed them to reveal their high grades subtly, as if unintentionally, so that they could not be accused of conceit or arrogance. *Accidental revelation* involved students leaving their test paper uppermost on their desk while pretending to be engrossed in other work; anyone passing the desk could glance down and see the grade, but the student could not be accused of having shown it off. Similarly, *passive persuasion* entailed smiling to oneself enigmatically to arouse classmates' curiosity and invite them to ask questions. One participant confessed how this was a strategically designed and calculated performance: '. . . smiling broadly, or giving some positive sign and then saying nothing. Your rather unusual actions raise the curiosity of other students and friends who will ask you how you did. Once asked, it's then OK to crow' (Albas & Albas 1988: 293). Goffman (1981: 105–6) calls this action a 'floor cue' (see Chapter 5 below), designed to summon other actors onto the scene.

The *Question–Answer Chain Rule* entailed asking a fellow student what they had got on the test, so that they would be obliged by the norms of conversational politeness to reciprocate. The first student could then answer and appear modest, as if they were only reluctantly imparting the information out of politeness. The *foot in the door* technique, also found in the patter of door-to-door salespersons, involved asking a fellow student only how they had found a particular question, on the assumption that they would be less resistant to disclosing this smaller piece of information; the shrewd Ace could then follow up with more probing questions about the whole test. Finally, *selective revelation* was a devious tactic in which disclosures were made indirectly. The student would tell their grades to only a few, carefully selected others who were on the same performance team (e.g. parents or best friends), safe in the knowledge that these team-mates would proceed to tell everybody else. The actor could then enjoy the satisfaction of praise and admiration without its usual face-threatening implications of boasting:

I call my mom right away because she tells all of the people she works with. Then when I go home on the weekend and everybody asks 'How are you doing at school?' I respond 'O.K.' In turn, they say 'I heard you were doing really well.' In this way I sound modest and I don't brag because I wouldn't want to say 'Oh, great! I got mostly A's and a couple of B+ 's.' That sounds conceited. (Albas & Albas 1988: 295)

## Strategies of concealment

Strategies of concealment were mostly used by Bombers who were embarrassed about their grades, but also sometimes by Aces, to compassionately play down their achievements. The crudest strategy was lying: students would simply make up a test score that was similar to that of the questioner, to make the prospect of discovery less alluring. Conversely, students could adopt an air of *nonchalance,* implying they did not care about the results. *Absenteeism* meant missing the class or leaving early when the graded papers were returned, so as to avoid being drawn into conversations. These students would use the art of dramatic realization to emphasize the key characteristics of their role (hurriedness), overplaying the performance with exaggerated gestures: 'I quickly gather up my books and depart in a "rushed" manner. This allows me to escape from anyone who might attempt to find out how I fared because it appears as if I'm late for something and can't stay around for idle chatter' (Albas & Albas 1988: 296). *Emphatic concealment* involved using non-verbal gestures indicating clearly one's closedness or inaccessibility to interaction (Goffman 1963b; see Chapter 2 above). Students would assume a rigid posture, angling their shoulders away from the classroom aisles, to discourage their peers from approaching with a question. These contrasted with gestures of *subtle concealment,* which were disguised so as to appear casual and unintended: putting one's elbow over the grade on the paper, or 'just happening' to lay a pile of books down on top of it. Some students preferred this kind of gesture because they wanted to avoid 'causing a scene' that might draw attention to their motives:

> A too obvious 'cover' fails to serve its purpose because others know you're trying to hide something. So, I discreetly cover the grade by draping my arm over it or conceal it by having another sheet of paper over the top of the test paper so the grade is just barely (but completely) hidden. In this way it appears as though my arm or the paper just happens to be there by accident. (Albas & Albas 1988: 297)

## Belief in one's own performance

So far we have seen how actors can be shrewd, instrumental and strategic in the way that they carefully and consciously design their lines of action, rationally calculating the most efficacious way of presenting themselves. But is this always the case? Are we *always* acting, or can we be under the spotlight without contrivance? Can we perform without realizing it, or even be taken in by our own performances?

In his discussion of 'belief in the part one is playing', Goffman (1959: 28–32) acknowledged the different attitudes we can have towards our own role performances. Actors can be *sincere,* genuinely believing in the reality they are upholding and the 'impression fostered by their own performance' (1959: 28). They do not think of themselves as acting a role, and regard what they are doing as an expression of their true self. Alternatively, *cynical* actors see through their own performance as being contrived, not surprisingly because they are the ones who are staging it: '. . . no one is in quite as good an observational position to see through the act as the person who puts it on' (1959: 28). Cynical actors retain a clear awareness of the difference between their 'real' self-identity and the version they are projecting in that situation; the former reflects critically on the latter, like the 'I' and 'Me' phases of Mead's (1934) social self. With an air of 'professional dis-involvement', the actor may delight in wilfully deluding the audience and sneering at their gullibility, 'experiencing a kind of gleeful spiritual aggression from the fact that he [*sic*] can toy at will with something his audience must take seriously' (Goffman 1959: 29).

This resonates with another dramaturgical distinction proposed by Hochschild (1983), between 'surface acting' and 'deep acting'. In her study of flight attendants, who had to perform cheerful goodwill to even the most irksome of passengers, she found that their initial struggles with this contrived role performance (surface acting) waned over time as they became habituated to it. They began to act 'deeply' as the performance became internalized and automatic, and they lost the capacity for critical reflection. This was because the job demanded 'emotional labour' – working hard at being friendly, polite and smiling all the time – which meant they invested a great deal of themselves in the role. To give a convincing performance, they could not act superficially or half-heartedly, but rather had to embrace the role and give it everything. Hochschild critically asserts that such service industries usurp their employees' autonomous selfhood, particularly through the commodification and 'commercialization of feeling'. The flight attendants were forced to hand over control of their private emotions, learning merely to act in line with the 'feeling rules' of the occupational culture.

## Deep acting at Disneyland

Cynical and sincere, or surface and deep, attitudes are not mutually exclusive, but rather actors can move from one to the other over the course of a role performance. This is illustrated by Van Maanen's (1990) ethnography of Disneyland, the self-proclaimed 'happiest place on earth'. Like Hochschild's flight attendants, the staff at Disneyland are in the 'feeling business', their everyday working practices aimed at presenting this public image of the company's identity.

An internal status hierarchy was reflected in the amount of autonomy different employees had over their role interpretation and how much respect they were afforded. Ambassadors and Tour Guides held the highest rank, as they ushered tourists through the park with a guiding commentary that they scripted themselves. Next came the technically skilled labourers, such as the Ride Operators, who drove the trains and the horse-drawn carriages and worked the Monorail. Then came less skilled workers (Assistants, Ticket Collectors, etc.), before the Sweepers, or grounds maintenance staff. Finally came the Food and Concession Workers, whose unskilled and monotonous work tasks put them at the bottom of the status ladder, with a 'Sub-Proletariat' status. They were referred to with derisive nicknames that trivialized their work: 'peanut pushers', 'pancake ladies' and 'Coke blokes'. This hierarchy was symbolically reflected in the uniforms of the park employees, as those at the top wore elaborately designed costumes (e.g. pirates, naval officers and train drivers), while lower-skilled Ride Assistants wore plain overalls or boiler suits, like factory workers.

The recruitment and training of employees involved carefully planned, organizational impression management, to ensure that they presented the desired Disneyland image. Applicants were screened to ensure they were tall, slim, tanned and healthy-looking; they were objectified merely as 'talking statues', 'information signs' and 'pretty props'. Orientation and apprenticeship programmes socialized them into the organizational culture and the specifics of their role requirements. This involved learning the scripts of stock phrases they must cite when speaking to customers, and the techniques of 'line talk' and 'crowd control'. Trainees were also shown 'inspirational' videos produced by the corporation, featuring 'star employees' as exemplars of its ethos, and were given hearty pep talks on the importance of retaining a cheerful countenance at all times.

However, the employees did not respond passively to this expectation of mindless role-taking. Resistance was evident in the way they performed their roles after having been in the job for a while, as they started to critically reflect on the organizational regime and adapt to its demands. This indicates a shift from sincere to cynical attitudes, with actors separating themselves from the characters they played. Using what Goffman (1961a) called 'secondary adjustments' to the institutional rules (see Chapter 7 below), they began to act more pragmatically, doing whatever they could get away with, and devised tricks and strategies to subvert the official rules. For example, staff who were on rotation duties snuck in extra break times by pretending to be walking from one post to another across the park. When backstage in their time off, they would mock and parody their official roles by sarcastically reciting their rehearsed spiels and the recorded messages that they heard all day over the loudspeakers. The staff also took pleasure in exacting revenge on difficult or annoying customers, using tricks that could be disguised as part of their legitimate role performance. Ride Operators delivered the 'seatbelt squeeze' to 'accidentally' belt a customer too tightly into a car so that they would be uncomfortable for the ride, and Drivers administered the 'brake toss' by slamming on the brakes suddenly, making everyone lurch forward in their seats. These gestures of rebellion were small but not trivial, as they reminded the workers that they had some autonomous power to resist the roles imposed on them, and thus to retain their dignity. We explore the notion of 'role distance' (Goffman 1961b: 73–134) later in this chapter.

Nevertheless, this effect was short-lived, as another shift occurred from cynical back to sincere attitudes, or surface to deep acting. Many of the staff lived together in residences close to the park, and so never really left the frontstage region of the setting, nor had a chance to indulge their 'real' selves outwith their occupational roles. Socializing with each other after work, they talked about aspects of the job and helped each other to rehearse their performance lines, which meant they felt permanently in character: 'They are taught, and some come to believe, for a while at least, that they really are "on-stage" at work' (Van Maanen 1990: 67). Sarcastic parodies gave way to sincere repetition of the official party line, as they started unthinkingly to employ euphemistic terminology in their everyday conversations: 'rides' were referred to as 'attractions', Disneyland was not an 'amusement centre' but a 'park', and the 'customers' were to be thought of as 'guests'. It was as if the show they were performing never came to an end.

## Role immersion, embracement and engulfment

Sincere performances involve *role immersion*, whereby the actor focuses so intently on delivering the content (actions, words, gestures, feelings) of their line of action that they forget it is even a performance. This is often a pleasurable experience, associated with non-obligatory roles that we enjoy playing, such as sports and hobbies: we talk of being 'lost' in an activity, 'in the zone' or experiencing 'flow' (Hardie-Bick 2005). Goffman also wrote of *role embracement,* when an actor is attached to, qualified for and engaged in the activity: '[To] embrace a role is to disappear completely into the virtual self available during the situation, to be fully seen in terms of the image, and to confirm expressively one's acceptance of it' (1961b: 94). He points to certain occupational roles that imply a deep level of commitment and dedication, and require intense concentration in the execution of their duties: air traffic controllers and pilots, baseball team managers and professional dancers.

However, if the actor/character line becomes blurred, there is a risk of losing this autonomous potential. Identifying with one's role-identity (McCall & Simmons 1966) is one thing, but over-identification is something else. The performance studies theorist Hayman (1969) makes a conceptual distinction between the actor who can 'find a role in themselves' (learn to play a part, with critical self-reflection) and the actor who 'finds themselves in a role' (developing a new identity from the experience of adopting a character). *Role engulfment* occurs when a performance takes over an actor and changes one's sense of self. Acceptance of the role is so complete that it becomes a new identity, preventing the capacity for role distance (Snow & Anderson 1987). Often this occurs in situations of disempowerment, when actors are forced into a role and lack the resources to resist it. This has been shown in studies of homelessness, whereby the unrelenting stress of living with constant poverty, cold and hunger makes this status feel horribly 'authentic' (Snow & Anderson 1987; Borchard 2011) and the prospect of change unimaginable.

Role engulfment means that even ostensibly pleasurable activities can turn sour in their symbolic meanings. Adler and Adler (1990) found that American college basketball players, who were admired with local celebrity status on campus, developed a 'glorified' sense of self, viewing themselves in the same way and dreaming optimistically of their futures as athletic stars. However, this came at a cost: the 'basketball player' role eventually took over their other role-identities as students, family members and friends, as it became harder to devote as much time to these. By the time the players realized they were engulfed by their athletic identities, it was too late to extricate themselves: they had lost sight of their original, 'true' selves. Similar remarks have been made about the corrosive and alienating effects of celebrity upon a famous person's self-identity (Giles 2000).

## Role conflict

A final form of discomfort arising from the actor's alignment with their character(s) is *role conflict,* sometimes known as *role strain.* This occurs when one is forced to play two or more roles simultaneously that do not fit well together. For example, a university student may have developed a certain persona, whom she presents when socializing with her friends and housemates, but have a different kind of character when at home with her parents. Goffman (1961b: 80) explains that usually this is not a problem because we juggle our multiple roles in such a way as to prevent them coming into contact. This involves two tactical strategies of impression management: *role segregation*, whereby we play only one role at a time, in specific interaction contexts, and *audience segregation*, whereby we keep apart the audiences who witness our different personae, so that neither audience sees the performance (and contradictory impression) that is given to the other.

Role conflict arises when these strategies fail or cannot be mobilized, so two discordant roles clash horribly together in a cacophony of excruciating awkwardness. For example, imagine that this student's parents pay her an unexpected visit and find her playing drunken party games with her housemates. Suddenly she is confronted with both audiences in the same scene, and aware of the discrepancy between the two roles she normally presents to each of them. She cannot perform both roles simultaneously as they are so different, and she cannot persist with one without discrediting her claim to the other, so she is stuck, frozen to the spot and uncertain how to act. Such instances of inconsistent or discredited identity are a major cause of embarrassment, as actors cannot fulfil their role requirements (Gross & Stone 1964) and the action grinds to a halt.

## Role distance

Actors have orientations towards their roles in terms of not only belief (sincere or cynical), but also feeling. In his essay on 'Role distance', Goffman (1961b: 73–134) discusses what happens when an actor finds themselves in a role to which they are relatively uncommitted, and which they may be reluctant to perform. A sense of estrangement arises from a contradiction between the actor's 'current self-in-role' and their 'authentic self' (Chriss 1999). Whereas those who are engaged with their roles can simply *play* them, enjoying an easy symmetry between their performative 'expressions' and their private self-identity (Goffman 1961b: 88), those less committed to their roles can only *play at* them, retaining a self-conscious distance between their 'real' self and their character:

> The individual stands in a double relationship to attributes that are, or might be, imputed to him [*sic*]. Some attributes he will feel are rightfully his, others he will not; some he will be pleased and able to accept as part of his self-definition, others he will not. There is some relationship between these two variables – between what is right and what is pleasing – in that the individual often feels that pleasing imputations regarding himself

are in addition rightful, and unpleasing imputations are, incidentally, undeserved and illegitimate. But this happy relationship between the two variables does not always hold. (Goffman 1961b: 91)

Although role distance may evoke 'euphoric' feelings of liberation and joyful exuberance, more typically it involves negative, 'dysphoric' feelings in the actor (Chriss 1999). These might include resentment (the role has been foisted upon them), embarrassment (they see it as inappropriate), boredom (they have played the role many times before), disengagement (they see it as irrelevant) or dented pride (they see it as demeaning). A familiar example is the employee trapped in a menial job that fails to inspire them: shop assistants mess around and gossip to each other in the back room to pass the time.

We can even engage in what Stebbins (1992) calls 'false role distance', whereby an actor is concerned that the audience may look derisively upon the role that they are playing, despite the actor feeling content with it themselves. They then strive to create the impression of indifference, concealing their positive commitment to the role. For example, the hardworking student in a school whose peer culture is averse to 'swots' may pretend not to care about their schoolwork for fear of being teased. Here we are reminded of Cooley's (1902) Looking Glass Self, as the actor compares an external image from the perspective of the audience with their own idea of their 'true' self, resulting in self-conscious emotions (Tangney & Fisher 1995) such as shame, pride, guilt, embarrassment or shyness.

To illustrate role distance, Goffman gives the symbolic example of a fairground merry-go-round. Younger children ride the horses with sincerity, taking the role seriously and wanting to show their bravery and capability in managing its tasks (the muscular effort of staying on the horse, and the display work of looking like a rider). During the ride they are totally immersed in the role and become attached to it – sometimes literally, screaming when lifted off the horse at the end of the ride (1961b: 86). By contrast, slightly older children of seven or eight want to ride the horses too, but are self-conscious about being watched. Feeling that the role is somewhat beneath them, they express this 'by handling the task with bored, nonchalant competence, a candy bar languidly held in one hand' (1961b: 96).

For those completely uncommitted to their roles, the implications of an inconsistency between expressive action and self-image can be more serious. This constitutes a potential face-threat, 'referring [either] to facts which the individual wishes would not be raised concerning him [sic], [or] implying an unwarranted image of himself that he ought not to have to accept' (1961b: 92). Thus next on the merry-go-round,

Goffman points to teenage boys who ride it ironically, under the guise of 'horsing around' and 'having a laugh' (Scott 2009a; cf. Willis 1977). They perform with an attitude of cynicism, but realize that audiences might misconstrue their actions as being like the serious enjoyment shown by younger children, which would be humiliating. So they enact role distance through an exaggerated performance that mocks and parodies the very idea of being sincerely committed to the role. Leaning forward over the horses as if racing, they kick their heels as if to make them go faster, and brutally rein them in at the end of the ride (Goffman 1961b: 96). Adults, similarly, make ironic meta-statements conveying their occupation of the role as a temporary state that belies their actual status, for example a man makes a joke of fastening an imaginary seatbelt around himself (1961b: 96). Another young couple riding next to their toddler compose their facial expressions carefully to demonstrate that they are not enjoying the merry-go-round as an event in itself, but rather are simply present to take care of their child (1961b: 97).

Role distance therefore involves the *performance of disengagement* from a role, separate from the performance of the role itself. Such displays are given during and alongside the main performance line, as opposed to temporary lapses out of role, retrospective accounts or complete role abandonment (1961b: 96). It is as if the actor 'splits off' (1961b: 93) part of themselves from the role to give a meta-commentary on their relationship to it. Often this involves a claim to be more than just the role or what its ostensible appearance implies: '. . . the individual makes a plea for disqualifying some of the expressive features of the situation as sources of definition of himself [*sic*]' (1961b: 93).

Role-distant actors are at pains to express to any witnesses that they are only playing *at* the role: their real identities are different from and irreducible to it. On the merry-go-round, the symbolic actions of the teenagers and adults screech out pre-emptively, 'Whatever I am, I'm not just someone who can barely manage to stay on a wooden horse' (Goffman 1961b: 95). Chriss (1999) suggests that this implies the construction of a 'negational self', defined by what one is not, or should not be mistaken for. In this meta-commentary of disavowal, the actor is symbolically apologizing (Goffman 1961b: 95), immediately for the demeaning content of the role, but ultimately for its moral implications, in creating a misleading impression of their identity, as someone immature, irresponsible, and so on. As Goffman (1961b: 95) puts it: '. . . the individual is actually denying not the role but the virtual self that is implied in the role for all accepting performers.'

## Discrepant roles

Finally, let us consider a special set of roles that are defined by their position within the social drama. Discrepant roles (Goffman 1959) are those beyond the conventional triad of performer, audience and outsiders, whose incumbents are in a unique position to see what is going on. They have special insight into the 'strategic secrets' – tricks and tactics – used by the performers to stage a scene, and to their backstage processes of rehearsal, deconstruction and review. Goffman calls this 'destructive information', as it has the potential to discredit and embarrass other actors' self-presentation, or disrupt their carefully composed definition of the situation (Thomas & Thomas 1928). Discrepant roles allow people to see both the official appearance of reality fostered by a performance team and the mechanisms used to construct it (Goffman 1959: 144).

Goffman identifies a number of discrepant roles. The *informer* is one who pretends to the performers to be a member of their team, is entrusted with their secrets, but then betrays this confidence to a rival team or outside parties. As well as the most obvious example of the spy who infiltrates political, military or criminal circles, there are more subtle variants, such as the estate agent who gathers information from both buyers and sellers and plays them off against the other.

Secondly, the *shill* is someone who acts as if they are a member of the audience, but in fact is in league with the performance team. They serve as a model for the other audience members, who assume the shill's actions to be what is normatively required, and follow their example. A nervous stand-up comedian places a 'plant' in the audience to start a round of applause and ensure they get a laugh. The proprietor of an impossible fairground game hires a friend to pretend to be a punter, so that bystanders see somebody apparently win a prize and are tempted to buy a ticket. The partner of a dinner party host listens and pretends to be interested while her husband tells an anecdote that she has heard a thousand times before, and feeds him the right lines to support his performance. 'A shill, then, is someone who appears to be just another unsophisticated member of the audience and who uses his [sic] unapparent sophistication in the interests of the performing team' (Goffman 1959: 146).

A variant combining both of the above roles is the informer who is planted in the audience but works to protect their interests, by checking on the quality of the performance. They often have an ethical agenda of maintaining standards, ensuring that the scene presented by the actors matches the reality of their service: for example the 'secret shopper' in the retail industry. However, the informer can also be sympathetic to the plight of the performers and their vulnerability to losing face. They may even hint to the performance team about their real identity, to give them a chance to polish up their show. For example, a hotel inspector might check into the hotel undercover but give a false name ('M. Inspector') that makes it obvious who they are.

Next, we have the *spotter*, who is a similar kind of undercover agent but whose attitude is more ruthless: instead of sympathetically allowing the performers opportunities to present themselves better, the spotter tries deliberately to catch them out, '[giving them] rope with which to hang themselves' (Goffman 1959: 147). This might include the secret shopper who poses as a particularly annoying and difficult customer to see what kind of treatment they receive, or the undercover police officer who goes to buy illegal goods before revealing to the criminals that they have been 'busted'.

The *go-between* or *mediator* is one who learns the secrets of two or more performance teams, giving each the impression that they are on their side, or more loyal to them than the other(s). This can be done with good intentions to reconcile hostile parties, as with the arbitrator of a labour dispute, or a couples therapist. Often the go-between is present with both teams at the same time, and so must carefully manage their impression to convey a position of neutrality. In concealing their bias towards each party from the other, they act as a 'double shill'. Goffman (1959: 149) describes this with rather heartless amusement as 'a wonderful display, not unlike a man desperately trying to play tennis with himself'.

The final discrepant role is the *non-person*. This is someone who is present during the frontstage enactment of a scene but is regarded as invisible, because their thoughts and feelings are viewed as inconsequential. They need make no secret of their presence, even if incongruent with the scene, because it is simply not acknowledged by the performers: the non-person is 'defined . . . as someone who is not there' (Goffman 1959: 150–1). The most obvious example is a domestic servant, who witnesses their host's display of hospitality to guests but is also involved in the backstage preparation of the scene. In other contexts, non-persons can be found in service occupations that involve quietly attending to the staging of a show or busying oneself with actions in the background: cleaners, elevator staff and doormen tend to be politely ignored by those who patronize the scene.

Goffman suggests that despite (or rather because of) their insulting designation of status, non-persons are often trusted with the 'dark secrets' of a performance team, on the assumption that they are too insignificant to worry about. This echoes Simmel's (1908a) remarks about the privileges afforded to the 'stranger' figure, who hovers on the fringes of a group (see Chapter 2 above). Discretion is expected as an absolute requirement of their post, and betrayal is taken to be an equally unquestionable impossibility. Thus the members of a wealthy household may talk openly about private family matters at the dinner table, while being served by their butler and maids. That these non-persons are of course really people, and have the potential to betray their employers' confidence, is an intriguing subtext that puts the servant in a position of power, albeit one that is rarely exploited.

Further discrepant roles can be identified in people who are not present during the scene but who are made privy to potentially destructive information about its staging. The *confidant(e)* is someone to whom an actor tells secrets about themselves and grants access 'behind the scenes' of the formally presented show. This category would include therapists and counsellors, priests, partners and close friends, who assume a role akin to Foucault's (1975) confessor, by listening, sympathizing and imparting advice.

*Service specialists* are those who work towards the 'construction, repair and maintenance of the show their clients maintain before other people' (Goffman 1959: 152). Often these involve technical skills involved in helping actors to get into character and attending to their costume, props or stage set: clothing retailers, interior designers and landscape gardeners are examples. *Training specialists*, similarly, can help an actor prepare in advance of a performance so that they 'look the part' on the day: celebrities may employ personal trainers to get in shape for a film role, while brides- or grooms-to-be may attend weight loss classes in the hope of appearing slimmer in wedding photographs. Like non-persons, service and training specialists are often rendered invisible: car-wash operators, make-up artists and manicurists tend to be ignored while their customers hold conversations with each other.

Finally, *colleagues* are those who 'present the same routine to the same kind of audience but who do not participate together, as team-mates do, at the same time and place before the same particular audience' (Goffman 1959: 158–9). Sharing the same 'community of fate' as the actor, they understand the particular challenges and intricacies of staging that performance, and can sympathize with the difficulties that might be faced. Furthermore, as they experience similar scenarios that the first actor does not attend, they can provide information and advice gleaned from these additional insights. Colleagues develop a sense of backstage solidarity, as comrades who are 'in the know': they compare notes, commiserate on bad performances and help each other rehearse for next time. Most obviously and literally, this would include work colleagues who do the same job in parallel: shop assistants who deal with customers on different work shifts, or university tutors who teach different classes. Colleagues often have a backstage area, officially designated or unofficially appropriated, to which they retreat between performances to lick their wounds: the staff room, theatre dressing room or (wo)men's washrooms. Thus colleagues are sympathetic others who understand the intricacies of staging a particular identity performance, and provide a valued place of solace outside of the theatrical arena.

## Conclusion

This chapter has explored the idea of identity as a role performance (or series of performances), using Goffman's dramaturgical perspective. If social life is a drama, then individuals are social actors, playing different versions of themselves as characters, depending on the demands of each situation and its audience. After performing these multiple roles frontstage, actors periodically retreat to backstage regions to reflect, rehearse and relax out of character. SI emphasizes processes of active role-making rather than passive role-taking. Ontologically, this presumes the existence of an inner, 'true' self who designs the performance: the actor behind the character. We have studied the techniques of self-presentation, or 'arts of impression management', used to this end, such as idealization, dramatic realization, mystification and misrepresentation, as well as the three key skills of dramaturgical loyalty, discipline and circumspection. Facework is important in managing public impressions, and this may be defensive or protective, avoidant or corrective. Actors may believe sincerely in the part that they are playing, remain cynically detached from it or move between the two: following the shift Hochschild observed from surface to deep acting, or vice versa. Cynical performances involve role distance, while sincere beliefs may lead to role immersion or engulfment, whereby this capacity for critical reflection is lost. Finally, 'discrepant roles' are those defined by their position outside of the main drama, which afford opportunities to gain insights into the composition and staging of others' role performances. In the next chapter, we examine how actors co-operate in this endeavour as dramaturgical 'team-mates', presenting scenes and displaying group identities. We shall consider the benefits but also risks of collusive teamwork, examining how loyalty and trust are precariously maintained.

# 5

# Casting members
## Teamwork, collusion and dramaturgical loyalty

In this second chapter on Goffman's dramaturgical theory, we turn our attention from individual actors to 'performance teams', who interact co-operatively to stage a show. As Goffman (1959: 181) put it, we have both 'a need for an audience before which to try out one's vaunted selves, and a need for team-mates with whom to enter into collusive intimacies'. The show presented might be a spontaneously constructed definition of the situation (Thomas & Thomas 1928), or a more enduring display of collective identity. Correspondingly, a team's composition may be either fluid and changeable, defined by the exigencies of the situation, or relatively stable, as in families or friendship groups. Goffman (1959: 85) defines the performance team as 'any set of individuals who co-operate in staging a single routine', and who seek to create an 'emergent team impression'. Meanwhile, the audience to a team's performance is also composed of actors who may be staging their own show, either in direct relation to the first team or for the benefit of another, third party. Teams and audiences can be considered more as perspectives than as groups of fixed membership, and we can move from one position to the other over the course of a situation.

## A loyal cast of players

Teamwork is a micro-political process, demanding trust and solidarity, but also shrewd awareness, between conspiring actors. As we saw in Chapter 4, the practice of *dramaturgical loyalty* (supporting one's team-mates) is one of three main arts of impression management, along with *dramaturgical circumspection* (prudent and selective recruitment of team members) and *dramaturgical discipline* (remaining vigilant over the scene so that one is poised for action).

Dramaturgical loyalty entails two sources of connection between team-mates (Goffman 1959: 88). Firstly, the *bond of reciprocal dependence* means that any member of the performance team has the potential to (intentionally or otherwise) give away its secrets to outsiders, and so they must trust each other not to. Such information might concern the actors' identities, attitudes and motives, or their procedures used to stage the performance – the backstage reality that lies behind and may contradict the impression presented frontstage. Team-mates' mutual knowledge of this 'dirty work' (Hughes 1962) leads to their second tie, the *bond of reciprocal familiarity* (Goffman 1959: 88). This is the idea that, because team-mates strategically collude to present versions of reality, they cannot also maintain that impression before each other: they are too wise to be deceived. Goffman (1959: 88) describes this state of being 'in the know' as one that can engender 'intimacy without warmth': a bond based on the pragmatic need for co-operation rather than any personal sentiment. A team-mate is 'someone whose dramaturgical co-operation one is dependent upon in fostering a given definition of the situation' (1959: 88).

In the interests of practical expediency, a potentially complicated definition of the situation will often be reduced to a simple, 'thin party line' (1959: 91) to which everybody can be expected to adhere, regardless of their private misgivings. Open disagreement between team-mates would undermine the team's integrity and threaten to disrupt the interaction order. Solidarity is especially important between members of a shared rank within a status hierarchy when in the presence of super- or subordinates: for example a school's team of teaching staff will back each other up on matters of discipline when speaking in front of pupils (1959: 95). Individuals may postpone taking a stand until the team's official position has been decided. Sometimes this involves team-mates being briefed by a director overseeing the action (e.g. a mother instructs her children to be on their best behaviour when visitors come to the home), while at other times it is left up to the members themselves to 'get their story straight' (1959: 93). This collusive process can be exploited if one member is excluded from the briefing, which might occur accidentally, or (less often) deliberately, as a practical joke. The actor would then be at a loss as to how to perform, and, through their conspicuous anomalousness, may suffer embarrassment. Goffman (1995: 94) says that '[t]o withhold from a team-mate information about the stand his [*sic*] team is taking is in fact to withhold his character from him.'

Goffman identifies two main sources of power within the staging of a team performance. *Dramatic dominance* is the quality enjoyed by the member of the team who takes a leading role as the protagonist in the drama. As the 'star of the show', they have a certain amount of authority to command fellow actors to play their roles in a particular way, so as to complement and accentuate their own performance. We might think of a bride on her wedding day, who proudly asserts that 'This is *my* day.' Secondly, *directive dominance* is held by the person(s) who direct(s) the show, controlling its timing, pace and co-ordination of roles. The director may be involved in acting out the drama themselves, as a member of the performance team (thus one person may have both dramatic and directive dominance), or they may stand outside of the action and oversee its management, in the role, for example, of a funeral director or company manager. Goffman suggests that as well as being responsible for practical matters like allocating parts and providing props, the director is also concerned with the smooth running of the show at an aesthetic and sentimental level. They may have to perform emotional labour (Hochschild 1983) in 'soothing and sanctioning' (Goffman 1959: 102) performers who become disgruntled and unco-operative, to bring them back into line with the team impression. This might involve motivational pep talks, as we saw with Van Maanen's (1990) study of Disneyland (see Chapter 4 above). The director is responsible for 'sparking the show' to 'stimulate a show of proper affective involvement' (Goffman 1959: 102).

## Harmonious co-operation between team-mates

Recalling his days as a jazz pianist in the Chicago bars of the 1960s, Becker (2000) provides a great example of dramaturgical teamwork. He argues that although jazz improvisation appears to be free-form and spontaneous, it is actually tightly governed by an 'aggressively egalitarian' code of etiquette. The final tune that emerges must be (or appear to be) a collaborative, jointly created product of everybody's skills and input. 'Etiquette is particularly important when people think that everyone involved in some situation *ought* to be equal but really isn't' (2000: 172, emphasis in original). Thus if one band member played four choruses during a solo, the others would all have to do the same: 'To play more would be rude, pushy, self-aggrandizing; to play less hinted that the first player had gone too far and, worse, that the following players who played less had less to say' (2000: 172).

In their performance of equality, the jazz musicians would observe certain tacit codes of conduct. Firstly, they had to 'defer to the developing collective direction' of the music as it emerged. This involved dramaturgical discipline, as they had to remain vigilant, listening carefully for any small gestures that indicated a player's wish to try something different. Secondly, everyone's suggestions were to be listened to and given equal consideration, as there was always the potential that they would lead to something brilliant (even though they usually did not). Thirdly, the audience were to be respected as equals. Many were knowledgeable about jazz and could recognize the rules behind the performance: they could see when the band were 'coasting along' on familiar territory, appreciate when they were being original or taking risks, and give their own performance of this insight by applauding after the trick had been pulled off.

This frontstage performance of 'collective regard' was contradicted by how the band members behaved backstage, when they were rehearsing alone. Here, they still observed the principle of considering everybody's suggestions, but only on aesthetic grounds, rather than as a show of politeness. Players would be impatient, ruthless and brutally honest in dismissing any member's idea that wasn't working; their primary concern was to create the best possible piece of art:

> ... they give no weight to putting on a good show or keeping up appearances. ... Whenever anyone does something clearly better, everyone else drops their own ideas and immediately joins in working on that better idea. People do not move gingerly, gradually converging on some sort of amalgam of hints and implications, thus respecting the fiction of equality. ... Likewise, people must have a real shared interest in getting the job done, an interest powerful enough to overcome divisive selfish interests. (Becker 2000: 174–5)

This is a reminder of how important it is that actors have backstage regions to retreat to, where they can remove their masks and slip out of character. For performance teams, this allows them the opportunity to review and rehearse their show as a collaborative venture, but also to 'be themselves' as a collective unit. Becker's study shows how it was in these private backstage moments that the real creative work of band musicianship was done, and when they most genuinely collaborated.

## Team collusion and pseudomutuality

However, teamwork is not always so harmonious and generous-spirited. Sometimes the bonds of reciprocal familiarity and dependence extend only between certain members of a performance team, leaving others dangerously excluded. Actors can also switch loyalties over the course of an encounter, forming alliances and coalitions in unexpected combinations.

In her discourse analysis of ninety-two transcribed psychiatric consultations, Hamilton (2014; see Chapter 3 above) considers how the presence of a third party, such as a family member, affected the interaction dynamics of the doctor–patient encounter. Sometimes the patient and third party colluded to present a rehearsed account to the psychiatrist, in order to influence the outcome of the treatment decision, such as reducing medication or going into hospital. To make this show convincing, they co-operatively 'worked up' (McKinlay & Dunnett 1998) the patient's identity as an obedient, sensible person who listens to advice. This enactment of the 'good patient' character is an example of 'dramatic realization' and 'idealization', two techniques of self-presentation used in individual actors' role performances (Goffman 1959; see Chapter 4 above), but it was also supported by the third party's dramaturgical loyalty. The patient might call on their family member to confirm what they were saying, using the technique known as 'active voicing' (Wooffitt 1992): knowing that their own credibility may be doubted, they strategically added weight to it by drawing on the authority of someone else, whose rationality could not be questioned. Thus in this extract, a patient contemplates aloud the prospect of trying some medication, discussing it with her sister (as team-mate) in front of the doctor (as audience):

> *Patient*: Shall I go on them?
> *Sister*: I think you should give it a go. No harm in that.
> *Patient*: I have to stay in hospital did you say?
> *Doctor*: You'd probably be in for a few days.
> . . .
> *Sister*: Do you want to try it or not? It's up to you I'm not saying for you.
> *Patient*: So will it make me better then?
> *Sister*: Well, we don't know do we until you try it
> *Patient*: I don't want this tablet no more do I?
>
> (Hamilton 2014: 252)

In other cases, however, it was the psychiatrist and family member who formed an alliance, as they tacitly agreed to define the patient as irrational and obviate the need to listen to their views. Smith (1978: 27–8) calls this the 'cutting out operation', as it undermines the patient's identity claims to credibility and trustworthiness as a witness to their own condition. Hamilton found that sometimes the psychiatrist would ask the patient a question but then verify it with their accompanying carer, or even address it directly to the third party, bypassing the patient altogether. Sometimes the same alliance would be initiated by the family member, who would interrupt the patient's account to contradict, correct, 'speak for' or 'speak over' them:

> *Doctor*: I think it might make sense if we give it a little bit longer at (unclear) maybe just taking the (unclear) on a regular basis (unclear) doesn't even start, just nips it in the bud. That might be the (unclear)

*Mother*: Can I just say
*Doctor*: yep
*Mother*: she's alright now, she's sitting here, but when she's at home you know you said like that constant movement, there is that, it is a continuous thing.

(Hamilton 2014: 244)

A third form of devious collusion concerns the display of 'pseudomutuality' (Wynne et al. 1958), which occurs when team-mates present a united front or party line of dubious veracity. Their motives are to convince each other, as much as the audience, that what they believe is true. This was illustrated by a series of studies by the anti-psychiatry movement of the 1960s and 1970s, which pointed to the family aetiology of severe mental illness. The radical proponents of this view argued that 'madness' was just a label applied to socially deviant behaviour that challenged other people's ideas of what was 'normal'. Schizophrenia, particularly, involved thoughts and feelings that appeared bizarre and nonsensical, but which made absolute sense if understood within the context of the 'schizophrenogenic' home environment, where communication dynamics were distorted (Laing & Esterson 1964; Cooper 1978). Family members deflected attention away from this source of the problem by focusing on the individual as a scapegoat, whilst emphasizing their own rationality and sanity. The show of agreement and solidarity they presented to the psychiatrist served as a smokescreen for the conflict, anger and resentment that actually existed between them.

Laing and Esterson (1964) presented eleven case studies, based on transcribed family interviews. They made a convincing case that it was the family members, not the patient, who displayed odd behaviour and whose ideas sounded delusional. Mr and Mrs Abbott, for example, believed that their daughter Maya had 'exceptional mental powers, so much so that they convinced themselves *that she could read their thoughts*' (1964: 21, emphasis in original). Listening to these accusations, Maya appears relatively sane as she calmly points out errors in her parents' version of events. 'Their response to this blow was interesting' (1964: 21), the researchers drily observe, for in defending themselves the parents revealed more strange behaviour of their own. They confessed to having devised a set of coded non-verbal gestures (removing spectacles, blinking, frowning and nose-rubbing), which they used to symbolically communicate in front of their daughter, 'testing' and 'experimenting' to try to catch her out:

*FATHER*: If I was downstairs and somebody came in and asked how

Maya was, if I immediately went upstairs, Maya would say to me, 'What have you been saying about me?' I said, 'Nothing.' She said, 'Oh yes you have, I heard you.' Now it was so extraordinary that unknown to Maya I experimented myself with her, you see, and then when I'd proved it I thought 'Well, I'll take Mrs Abbott into my confidence,' so I told her . . . one Sunday I said – it was winter – I said, 'Now Maya will sit in the usual chair, and she'll be reading a book. Now you pick up a paper and I'll pick up a paper, and I'll give you the word and er. . .' – Maya was busy reading the paper, and er – I nodded to my wife, then I concentrated on Maya behind the paper. She picked up the paper – her em – magazine or whatever it was and went to the front room. And her mother said, 'Maya, where are you going? I haven't put the fire on.' Maya said, 'I can't understand –' no, 'I can't get to the depth of Dad's brain. Can't get to the depth of Dad's mind.'

(Laing & Esterson, 1964: 22)

Not surprisingly, Maya became suspicious: 'She could not really believe that what she thought she saw going on was going on' (1964: 25). Laing and Esterson (1964: 23) conclude that the 'ideas of influence' Maya displayed were not psychotic symptoms but in fact accurate perceptions of what was really happening: her parents *were* trying to influence her thoughts. In this extraordinary case, we see how dramaturgical team-mates can sow the seeds of their own destruction, undermining the show they have worked hard to present.

## Symbolic displays of membership

Team membership can be not only the basis from which social action springs, but also the focal point of the action itself. Team-mates perform their collective or group identity through symbolic communicative gestures (Blumer 1969) aimed towards each other or rival performance teams. As Williams (2000) argues, identity is relational, as we define ourselves through comparison to reference groups, in terms of similarities, differences, insider/outsider status and status divisions.

This can be seen in empirical studies of sports, hobbies and popular fandom. The pursuit of a serious leisure identity (Stebbins 1992) is often mediated by team relations, particularly when the activity is a niche interest with a small but loyal following; group participation provides a sense of cohesiveness and insularity. Shamir (1992) argued that sports team members express their commitment not only to the activity but also to the group; this collective identity develops through relations of loyalty, reliance and mutual responsibility. As Patrick and Bignall (1987: 207) put it,

We become racquetball players, golfers, bridge-players, and mountain climbers both for the satisfaction we derive from these activities and for the social interactions based on them and the identities that are created by competent performance of them. When we claim competency in a particular area of endeavour, we also establish an identity as one of them.

Group alliances can be expressed through clothing, equipment and other prop-like objects that form members' personal fronts (Goffman 1959) – those aspects of their self-presentation that they carry around with them between social scenes. For example, Kane and Zink's (2004) study of kayakers noted the symbolic value of a sporting kit, particularly that which bears a logo or slogan, in communicating one's insider status. Football team strips and other sporting uniforms demonstrate the kind of 'neo-tribal' solidarity that Maffesoli (1996) described, formed through local subcultural networks and reasserting bonds of friendship and community. Group practices (adjunct to the focal physical activity) can also be used as tools of collective identity performance. These might involve sports tourism (Stebbins 1992), whereby team members travel around together on tours or holidays, investing a great deal of time, emotion and money in sharing memorable experiences (Green & Jones 2005).

Symbolic displays like this make fandom a group identity performance (Sandvoss 2005). Hodkinson's (2002) ethnography of the goth subculture pointed first to the distinctive style of dress, as a symbolic display of resistance (cf. Hebdige 1979). Black clothes, heavy make-up and dyed hair symbolized the members' perceived exclusion from mainstream culture but also their newfound acceptance by this marginalized group. Secondly, there were participatory rituals of collective consumption through which the goths toured their subcultural scene. The Whitby Goth Weekend is an annual convention that brings goths together from all over the UK, to gather at one site and socialize, listen to goth music, buy special clothing and jewellery, and so on. Hodkinson writes about how the goths would arrive in their droves, taking over the 'goth-infested' small town and for once being in a powerful majority, with a strong visual presence. He talks about the excitement of 'getting gothed up' for the first evening's events and the gleeful practice of 'goth-spotting' through car windows as they hurtled up the motorway. Remembering Durkheim's (1912) theory of religion, what was most important here was not the material content of the subculture, but rather the fact that it was consumed collectively, in an effervescent spirit of solidarity.

On the other hand, fan cultures and subcultures are also prone to internal divisions and conflict (Hills 2002). There is often a status hierarchy of members, in terms of their claims to 'subcultural capital' (knowledge of the field, access to revered people or places, greater experience and social visibility [Fiske 1992]), which in turn generates 'fan social capital' (Hills 2002): connectedness within social networks. These hierarchical strata range from the more established, long-term 'expert', 'executive' or 'super-' fans down to the more casual, occasional or newcomer 'proto-fans' (Hills 2002). Thus Hodkinson describes an emergent competitive spirit, wryly acknowledged by members as the 'Gother-Than-Thou Syndrome'. The older generation of 'first wave' (1980s) goths, who self-identified ideologically through values of sensitivity, melancholy and Romantic intellectualism, looked down upon the younger 'trendies' or 'baby goths', whom they saw as superficially preoccupied with fashion: '. . . like the baby goths. I think that's probably Marilyn Manson's fault. . . . They've got short hair, and they've just got a little bit of eyeliner, a little bit of lipstick and they think "oh, I'm a goth"' (participant cited in Hodkinson 2002: 79). The goths tailored the standard 'uniform' to express personal tastes, for example with different coloured hair or elaborate costumes. However, there was an irony in that every member was trying to do this same thing, with the same motives: they were united in their bid for uniqueness. As one participant laughingly admitted: '. . . you're all individuals but everyone's got the same boots on!' (Hodkinson 2002: 67).

## Facilitative rituals

As well as material objects, team-mates use verbal and non-verbal symbolic gestures (Blumer 1969) to express their collective identity. These are communicated through the ordinary, routine situations that occur when actors encounter each other in everyday life, and form part of the wider societal 'conversation of gestures' (Mead 1934) that is constantly unfolding. Within situations, as social scenes, these gestures are exchanged through interaction rituals (Goffman 1967; see Chapter 2 above), holding a symbolic meaning that is tacitly understood by both performers and audiences.

### Tie signs

Beginning with non-verbal symbolic gestures, Goffman (1971) identified a category called *tie signs*. These are effectively relationship markers: acts, moves, objects or arrangements that signal a connection between two or more people. Often these are physical items worn about the body, constituting part of the personal front that an actor carries around with them, for example a wedding ring worn on the recognized 'ring finger'. Goffman calls these 'anchoring mechanisms', as they communicate an individual's place within a collectivity, and have connotative meanings of home, belonging and familiarity. Tie signs form part of the 'ritual idiom' of symbolic gestures that are universally recognized and understood by all members of a society.

Tie signs are indices of intimacy, as they imply that the actors share the same private, even secret, lifeworld, from which others are excluded (cf. Simmel 1908b). This other, special realm exists elsewhere: in a different place (e.g. sharing a regional dialect: the two 'northerners' who bond because they find themselves in a sea of 'southerners'), at a different time (e.g. old school-mates who reunite and swap nostalgic stories) or at a different level of intimacy (e.g. the respect afforded to a bereaved next-of-kin in making funeral arrangements). By signalling their tie as a pre-existing bond, actors demonstrate its legitimacy, which can be used pre-emptively as a non-verbal justification (Scott & Lyman 1968) for conduct that might otherwise be questionable. For example, a newly married couple canoodling in public may be looked upon more fondly and tolerantly if they are wearing shiny new wedding rings. '[Tie signs] make it possible for individuals in public to engage in encounters without too much fear that their innocence will be misunderstood and that compromising will occur' (Goffman 1971: 279).

Tie signs often involve symbolic actions that imply the right to share a social space or access the same private territory, which would otherwise be seen as invasive: holding hands, pushing someone else's wheelchair or a baby's pushchair. People also make private declarations or reference private information in public settings, knowing that others will witness it and not understand: for example friends exchanging esoteric comments and in-jokes on social networking sites. Despite seeming to be private, personal exchanges, these are highly visible displays aimed deliberately towards an audience: they serve to accentuate the difference between those 'inside' and 'outside' a closed circle. As Bailey (2000) argues, there may be separate spheres of 'public intimacy' in this regard.

### Remedial interchanges: induced collusion and obligatory reciprocity

There are two main types of verbal ritual that facilitate teamwork: remedial and supportive interchanges (Goffman 1971). We encountered the former in Chapter 3 with performative utterances: spoken lines that 'do things', or accomplish social actions. Remedial interchanges perform the rejection, repudiation and disavowal of deviant conduct, whether actually committed or merely anticipated as a 'virtual' offence

(Goffman 1971). Moreover, as aligning actions (Stokes & Hewitt 1976), they demonstrate an awareness of normative conventions and situational proprieties (the 'right' way of behaving), reassuring others of our usual reliability as team-mates. As we saw in Chapter 3, this category of utterances includes accounts (excuses and justifications), apologies, requests and disclaimers.

These rituals are called 'interchanges' because they evoke a response from the addressed recipient, who is thereby transformed from audience member to performer, and generate a conversational sequence. An individual act of self-presentation becomes a joint social action (Blumer 1969) between team-mates. This involves two speaking roles, or turns: the 'virtual offender', who has made or might make the faux pas, and the 'virtual claimant', who stands to be offended by their feelings being hurt, rights infringed or face threatened. For example, in Chapter 3, we saw Goffman's (1967) analysis of the apology as a sequential interaction ritual, comprising the four stages of challenge, offering, acceptance and thanks.

This induced collusion is easiest to see in the case of requests, insofar as these are phrased as questions that explicitly demand a response. Furthermore, this response is one of reassurance to the virtual offender that their actions are not damaging, and so the virtual claimant is drawn (we could even say manipulated) into aligning themselves with the first speaker as a team-mate. This reciprocity obligation works because of the politeness norms that underlie the ritualized sequence, which are unthinkingly and automatically obeyed before we have time to consider our private opinions.

A request may be made in a deliberately vague and open-ended way that makes it difficult for the addressee to refuse, or at least obliges them to keep listening: 'Can I just ask you something?' or 'Do you have a minute?' Goffman explains that if the recipient were told the full story from the beginning, they would probably not want to get involved, but being denied this information disarms and wrong-foots them. This tactic is often used pre-emptively by people who routinely impinge upon others' territories and know they will be perceived as annoying. For example, 'chuggers' – charity collectors who stop people on the street and ask for donations – seek to distance themselves from their bad reputation by prefacing their request with a personal or friendly gesture: 'How are you today, Madam? Will you be the first kind person to stop and talk to me?'

Fascinatingly, Goffman (1971) points out how the polite phrasing of a request can be such that it invokes the claimant to give permission for the violation to occur – even to positively invite it. For example, asking 'Do you mind if I sit here?' or 'Would you mind letting me go first?' tends to make the recipient respond immediately with 'No, of course not,' even though they actually mind very much! In the service industries, staff often *ask* rather than *tell* customers to do things that are mildly inconvenient, such as 'Would you mind filling in this form, please?' or 'Would you like to take a seat and wait?' in order to elicit their willing acquiescence. This kind of politeness ritual immunizes the virtual offender against accusations of intrusiveness because it turns the tables to make the claimant take joint responsibility for the action: they are made complicit in their own subjugation. As Goffman (1971: 145) puts it: '. . . when a violation is invited by he [*sic*] who would ordinarily be its victim, it ceases to be a violation and becomes instead a gesture of regard performed by this person.' Clever work indeed.

## Supportive interchanges

The second set of verbal rituals are ways in which team-mates express their fellow-feeling, through shows of concern for each other's welfare, status or social face. Goffman (1971) calls these 'supportive interchanges', and emphasizes that, as with remedial interchanges, their ultimate function is to let team-mates demonstrate to one another that they remain as such and can be relied upon to offer dramaturgical loyalty.

Firstly, there are *access rituals*, such as greetings, leave-takings and farewells, which occur when actors enter or leave each other's company. These provide reassurance that the actors recognize and will continue to observe a more enduring tie between them. The content of these rituals (the actual words that are said) is not as important as the sentiment they convey. Access rituals are effectively just 'grooming gestures', expressing a more generalized attitude of mutual regard. As indexical utterances (Garfinkel 1967), they make a symbolic nod towards this broader context of cohesive social bonds, referencing a set of shared interpretive meanings about what is 'really' going on. In particular, access rituals accomplish what Goffman (1971) calls the 'ritualization of identificatory sympathy' by communicating feelings of empathy, care and solidarity.

For example, greetings often include displays of concern about another actor's situation, such as enquiries about their welfare ('How are you?'), but these are not meant literally. Instead they generate a conversational sequence of recognized turns that is performed in a ritualized, automatic manner. As Garfinkel's (1967) ethnomethodological breaching experiments showed, to deviate from these normative expectations (answering 'How are you?' with a literal description of one's health) would evoke reactions of bemusement, irritation and moral indignation.

When taking leave at the end of an encounter, actors often prime each other with verbal or non-verbal signals that preface the action ('Well, I must be going') and warn their team-mates it is about to take place, giving them time to prepare their own performance line of regret and sorrow ('Oh really? What a shame'). Often these prefaces offer an apologetic reason for leaving – a prior engagement, or pressing deadline – which tactfully deflects the alternative interpretation that they simply do not want to talk to the other person any longer. Similarly, when saying goodbye, team-mates often go through the ritual of reassuring each other that they will reconnect ('See you again soon') and urging them to 'Take care.' Sometimes these are spoken insincerely, as when friends say 'We must meet up for coffee soon!' or 'I'll call you!' and heartily agree, even though they both know this is unlikely.

Secondly, actors extend *courtesies and small offerings* (such as 'Would you like a cup of tea?'), which function more as symbolic gestures of hospitality than pragmatic, instrumental actions. There may be no expectation of the offering being accepted or reciprocated, as the intended meaning behind it is enough. These rituals include the *tactful avoidance of open exclusion*, as when a pair of friends is joined by another who only knows one of them: that person must then introduce them so that neither party feels snubbed in favour of the other. Even though the two strangers do not care about each other and will probably never meet again, they pretend to show an interest. The three team-mates collaborate in the performance of a polite fiction (Burns 1992) for the sake of upholding the interaction order (see Chapter 2 above).

Finally, we have *rituals of ratification*. These are the 'little strokings' of reassurance given to people who have recently undergone a status change, to confirm their continued membership of the performance team (Goffman 1971). Following a relationship break-up, the friends of one partner might extend gestures of friendliness to the other (e.g. inviting them to socialize), to reassure them that they are still welcome in the broader group's company. If a sports player suffers a career-ending accident, fellow players rally round to talk about how they might re-join the team in a different capacity (Sparkes 2002). Subtler versions of these rituals take place in everyday life following more mundane changes of status. Someone who appears one day sporting a new haircut or outfit will often be complimented that 'It suits you!', in recognition of the fact that they might be feeling self-conscious and in need of reassurance. Again, the literal content of these utterances may not be sincerely meant, for what matters is their form and sentiment. Rituals of ratification reassure a vulnerable actor that despite their change of status, they can still rely upon their team-mates' dramaturgical loyalty.

## Protective and collective facework

This last point about dramaturgical loyalty brings us back to the concept of facework (Goffman 1967: 5–46), discussed in Chapter 4: the techniques actors use to rescue lines of self-presentation that are in danger of embarrassment. Actors strive to 'keep face' or stay 'in face' but are vulnerable to 'losing face' through mishaps that discredit their identity claims. To 'save face' in these situations, actors can perform either defensive or protective facework, for their own or someone else's face, respectively. The latter category therefore applies to the dynamics of teamwork.

### Tact

Goffman (1959: 222) identifies 'tact' as a set of 'protective practices' that 'help the performers save their own show'. For example, while individual actors (defensively) control who has access to their front and back regions, out of respect for this, team-mates (protectively) stay away from regions into which they have not been invited (1959: 223). When circumstances require that we do encroach on another's territory, we give warning signals (knocking on doors, coughing, making appointments) to alert them to our presence and give them time to compose themselves, get into character and be poised for the encounter. Goffman (1959: 223) says these gestures give the 'addressee' a chance 'to decide what kind of greeting the individual is going to receive, and time to assemble the expressive manner appropriate to such a greeting'.

When physical barriers like walls and doors are absent, we tactfully pretend not to see or hear one another, so that other actors' performances can unfold smoothly. This happens even – or especially – when their action threatens to disrupt the interaction order: as Goffman (1959) said, we avoid confronting 'incidents' that would 'cause a scene' (see Chapter 4 above). Strangers sitting at adjacent tables in a restaurant feign obliviousness to each other's conversations (even arguments) to afford them privacy, and we politely disattend to crying babies out of sympathetic respect for their parents. If somebody on the train starts a loud mobile phone conversation, we pretend not to hear, let alone to be eavesdropping. Goffman (1959: 223) calls this *tactful inattention* and it is similar to his concepts of 'studied non-observance' and 'civil inattention' (Goffman 1963b; see Chapter 2 above). Paradoxically, strangers making a show of ignoring one other in this way are actually behaving co-operatively as team-mates, giving a joint performance.

It is interesting to consider under what circumstances this norm might be broken. When something out of the ordinary occurs, actors are jolted out of their habitual customs and routines, and may acknowledge each other to address the situation. For example, I was recently walking down a quiet residential street with just one other person approaching in the other direction; we both automatically put on our blank 'city' faces and used civil inattention to ignore each other. However, just as we were about to pass, there was an almighty retching noise coming from the upstairs window of a nearby house, and somebody began vomiting onto the pavement. The situation was so bizarre and unexpected that the stranger and I made eye contact, first with surprised expressions and then with laughter, and exchanged a few sarcastic words: 'Nice!' / 'Yes, that's a nice welcome, isn't it!' The unusualness of the situation demanded that we come together to give an impromptu team performance to manage its disruptive effects, before resuming our positions as lone actors.

*Audience tact* is the courteous way in which people respond if they witness (rather than act within) a frontstage performance and want to make its reception successful. Here Goffman identifies various gestures of politeness, such as showing due interest and attention in what the other is saying (even if secretly bored), holding in one's own performance so as not to steal the limelight, and being careful not to offer any information that might contradict the impression the person is trying to create. A dinner party host may listen to her spouse drone on to their guests with an anecdote that she privately regards as tedious, feigning interest and laughing at the right points to cue the others to join in. This also reminds us how actors can shift positions during an encounter, in this case from audience members to team-mates, as third parties enter and leave the scene.

Actors show *sympathetic tact* for one other when a team-mate makes an embarrassing mistake, particularly when they are known to be a 'beginner' at the activity. They feel sorry for their fellow actor, appreciate how difficult the task is for them, and make special allowances or show extra consideration to tolerate flaws that might otherwise annoy them. Hairdressers' clients who are served by a nervous junior trainee reassure them that they are happy with the result. Parents watching a primary school play are patient with small children messing up their lines, prop and costume faults and out-of-tune singing, and feel only proud of them. In these situations we make sympathetic adjustments of the standards we expect, taking into account the actor's novice status.

An illustrative example of tact comes from a study some colleagues and I conducted of shyness in contemporary art galleries (Scott et al. 2013). This was based on two multi-method case studies of UK exhibitions: at Fabrica, a small, local, contemporary art gallery in Brighton, and the V&A (Victoria and Albert), a large traditional museum in London. In an effort to facilitate public engagement, such galleries and museums are increasingly housing digitally interactive exhibitions involving 'hands-on' creativity, fun and play (Heath & vom Lehn 2008). The 'Visitor Self-Discovery' model leads to the restriction of information and instructional signs, on the principle that visitors should be free to interpret the artwork in whatever way they wish. However, we argued critically that this assumes a certain level of competence, both technical and performative, in visitors, in terms of their willingness to interact with exhibits that may appear intimidatingly complex, mysterious and ambiguous. This scenario has the propensity to evoke shyness, through dramaturgical concerns about 'not knowing the rules' and having to improvise a performance before a potentially judgemental audience (cf. Scott 2007a).

Nevertheless, we found that visitors responded adaptively to this dramaturgical dilemma. In the absence of a formally provided social script to guide the situation, they looked elsewhere to find a replacement, and here they used each other as a resource. Fellow visitors – both accompanying friends and family, and strangers – were enlisted as dramaturgical team-mates to co-create a new set of rules and meanings, for example a different way of interacting 'playfully' with an ambiguously designed exhibit. This supported shy actors' faces through the principle of 'safety in numbers' or 'following the herd': whatever they did, it could not be 'wrong' because it was what everybody else was doing, and thus normatively appropriate for the situation. The cohesiveness of the team formed a protective shell around the actor, shielding them from the potentially scrutinizing judgements of outsiders.

For example, one exhibit at the V&A, 'Videogrid', invited people to make a short film of themselves, which was then projected onto a large screen alongside others in a grid pattern. Visitors appeared to be more confident when they approached it in groups than when they were alone:

> [Videogrid] Young couple from earlier. Seem very confident and keen to have a go. Watch impatiently from the side, trying to peek around people. Within one minute she says 'Shall we record one?' and he says 'Yeah!' They do a silly film together, pulling faces, then immediately go round to the other side of the screen to see the results. I follow them: they are taking photos of each other standing next to their square on the grid, pointing to themselves in the video and grinning. (Scott fieldnotes, V&A, 27.02.2010) (Scott et al. 2013: 15)

## Tact regarding tact

While audiences and team-mates offer assistance to keep other performers in face, the latter are often aware of this and adapt their lines of action so as to 'make the rendering of this assistance possible' (Goffman

1959: 227). For example, to allow bystanders to give the impression of not overhearing their private conversation, a group might try to keep their voices down. This 'tact regarding tact' requires two strategies. Firstly, the performer must be 'sensitive to hints and ready to take them' (1959: 227): that is, they must notice signals from the audience that their show is not convincing or their face is under threat, and that they need to modify it.

Secondly, if the performers plan to be misleading in their self-presentation, they must do so in a way that leaves opportunities for backtracking and saving face, lest they get caught. They must 'use a method which allows of an innocent excuse' (1959: 228) and provides a believable pretext for the state of affairs. Moreover, this pretext should be easily understandable by the other actors present, so that they can quickly grasp what is going on and lend tactful support to save the person's face. For example, a bald man may wear a hat indoors to cover up the attribute he is embarrassed about, but if 'caught out' in doing so, he could nonchalantly pretend that he had merely been feeling cold (Goffman 1959: 228). His friends might realize what the truth was, but can play along with his cover story to spare his blushes. This is an example of a pretence awareness context (Glaser & Strauss 1964; see Chapter 2 above), whereby all interactants know what is really the case, but collusively uphold another account. Had the man worn a wig instead, Goffman notes, there would be no ambiguity of meaning and thus no opportunity for renegotiating the definition of the situation. The label of 'impostor' applies in these latter cases, where an actor is not especially malevolent in their deception, but simply 'makes it impossible for his [sic] audience to be tactful about observed misrepresentation' (Goffman 1959: 228). It is the responsibility of the first actor, then, to decide on a line of self-presentation that allows their team-mates to exercise tact and provide protective facework.

## Collective facework

Defensive or protective facework is performed by individual actors to save an individual's face (their own or someone else's, respectively). But what if the social face that is compromised belongs not to an individual but to a group? A colleague and I suggested that there could be a third category of *collective facework*, which occurs when the members of a group perceive a threat to their shared face – the common identity they wish to present – and use tacitly agreed-upon strategies to avert this danger (Rossing & Scott 2014). For example, Lee (2009) described how rap bands dealt with the embarrassment of singers 'falling off the beat' by stepping in together to cover up the mistake. This 'collateral face-saving' was delivered not to spare the individual's blushes but to protect the dignity of the group as a whole and smooth over the cracks in the performance.

Rossing and I found evidence of collective facework in her ethnographic study of a workplace-based exercise group in Norway. This had been set up as part of an initiative led by the Norwegian government to improve health and fitness levels in certain sectors of the population who were unaccustomed to exercise. The company Rossing studied (using participant observation, interviews and logbook diaries) was a social research organization, whose employees had sedentary, office-based jobs and were deemed to be relatively unfit. They were invited to sign up to a beginners' aerobics class, held during their working hours over a course of several weeks. Rossing was intrigued by the role conflict (see Chapter 4 above) this scenario produced between the employees' working identities, as competent professionals, and their newly created exercise identities, as members of the humiliatingly named 'low-ability' aerobics group.

We explored the strategies used to manage this role conflict and avoid feelings of stigmatization, shame and embarrassment. Aside from the defensive and protective facework participants used to spare their individual blushes, collective facework was required as a team performance, to manage the way in which their 'groupness' was perceived. In fact, they presented themselves *not* as a group, feigning unawareness of both their shared background as co-workers and their current designated status as 'low-ability' exercisers. Instead, they performed as if they were mere 'familiar strangers' (Milgram 1977; see Chapter 2 above) – people who encounter each other regularly but do not have any bonds of mutual obligation. This denial of group ties involved seeking only 'non-binding relationships' through 'minimal interaction'.

Defensive strategies included individual actors *regulating the spatial distribution of their bodies* across the room, to avoid any physical contact that would require them to acknowledge each other's presence, and *body gloss* (Goffman 1971), the use of exaggerated gestures to cover up any mistakes they had made when executing a dance step (e.g. pretending to be taking a break and stepping out of the circle for a moment to recover their composure). Protective strategies included *sympathetic identification*, when one member would notice another looking embarrassed by their incompetence and stepped in to spare their blushes (e.g. claiming that they too found the moves hard), and *externalizing failure*, by blaming a fellow member's poor performance on factors other than their personal ability, such as the difficulty of the dance moves or the hot temperature of the room.

Collective facework, meanwhile, occurred when the exercising colleagues perceived a threat to their claimed identity as familiar strangers and worried that they were being viewed as a ('low-ability') group. These strategies included, firstly, Goffman's (1963b) *civil inattention*, whereby actors glanced briefly at but then away from each other, as strangers would, to avoid being drawn into any focused encounters that would draw attention to their common status (see Chapter 2 above). In the aerobics sessions, colleagues stared straight ahead at the instructor rather than at each other, and in the locker rooms they got changed in deafening silence. As one participant recorded in her logbook,

> I tend to get a little disturbed when we are standing in a circle. You have to be careful not to stare at somebody, [but] at the same time it is impossible to avoid it. If you randomly happen to meet the gaze of someone, it feels embarrassing: have you been observing the other person? Should you smile or something? (Haley, logbook, winter 2010) (Rossing & Scott 2014: 180)

Secondly, the actors occasionally resorted to silence, or *muteness*, by failing to respond to questions and instructions from the instructor. We thought that this must be because she was addressing them as a group, thereby invoking their collective identity as low-ability exercisers. Had they replied, it would have indicated acquiescence to this definition.

> Every class the instructor addresses the class with different comments, cheers and questions like: 'Is everybody doing well today?' 'Give a little bit extra now, this is the last of it!' 'Do you want me to show you one more time?', 'Is the music loud enough?', 'You are looking amazing today. Good job!' These attempts to interact were left completely unattended and unanswered. The participants kept staring straight ahead, as if they were not being addressed. (Rossing fieldnotes, 19.10.2009) (Rossing & Scott 2014: 182)

This study demonstrates the resilience of performance team dynamics despite the odds. Even when attempting to deny their collective status, these actors ended up co-operating on a different line of joint action, to create the team impression of being mere familiar strangers. Ironically, in striving to distance themselves from one unwanted group identity, they invoked another, strengthening the bonds between themselves and betraying a tacit understanding of their common dramaturgical fate.

## Directorial procedures

In dramaturgical terms we can think of social scenes being choreographed by an unseen director, whose hand guides the actors' role performances. Usually, of course, there is no actual director figure, but rather team-mates direct their own performances, by skilfully co-ordinating their lines of action and navigating the theatrical space. As we saw earlier, an actor can enjoy both 'directive dominance' and 'dramatic dominance', although the two are technically separate. In designing their individual moves, they anticipate those of their team-mates, and cue them with verbal or non-verbal symbolic gestures to take the floor.

## Response cries

A fantastic essay in Goffman's *Forms of Talk* discusses the notion of 'response cries'. These are the short utterances people emit while performing an action, which seem ostensibly to be instinctive and private 'self-talk' (1981: 79), but actually serve a communicative function. Response cries are interactive, public statements, which claim something about the actor's present condition or orientation to the scene. Often they influence the surrounding actors, by invoking their co-operation as team-mates and prompting them to respond supportively.

The *transition display* is a sound we make when entering or leaving a physically uncomfortable environment, to expressively externalize an inner state. When going outside into the cold, we say 'Brr!', and when coming back into the warm indoors we say 'Ahh!' or 'Phew!' Goffman (1981: 100) explains that this gives us a moment of composure to 'orient ourselves to the new climatic circumstances and fall into cadence with the others' already present. In the case of escaping discomfort, the utterances express a sense of relief from the concentration of holding ourselves in, which gets 'released with a flourish' (1981: 100).

Next, we have the *spill cry*. These are the words like 'Oops!' and 'Whoops!' that we make when we drop, spill or otherwise lose control of something in our immediate environment. This can be a material prop object, a part of the body or a movement connecting the person to the setting (e.g. catching one's clothing on a door handle). We might wonder why someone who makes such a mistake would want to point it out and accentuate its impact, as gestural markers do. Goffman explains that these sounds make the claim that the mistake was unintentional and out of character for the individual, who is expressing surprise that the mistake happened: it 'defines the event as a mere accident, shows we know it has happened, and hopefully insulates it from the rest of our behavior' (1981: 101). By implication, the actor is reassuring their team-mates that they are usually reliable and can otherwise be trusted to show dramaturgical loyalty.

The spill cry can be thought of as a remedial action (see above) that performs repair work on a fractured situation. Like the apology, it effects a splitting of the self between the part that made the blunder and the other part that has critically observed it. The latter is presented as the dominant, typical part of the self, and implies 'some presence of mind. A part of us proves to be organized and standing watch over the part of us that apparently isn't watchful' (1981: 101). This gesture emphasizes a virtual offender's alignment with their team's shared norms and values, smoothing over temporary disruptions so that the show can continue running smoothly.

The *threat startle* is an exclamation of fear and surprise, such as 'Eek!' when we see a spider, or 'Yikes!' when we narrowly avoid falling down some stairs. Crucially, however, these are not immediate, instinctive reactions, but rather studied expressions that are designed as part of our impression management. Threat startles communicate not that the actor *is* afraid, but that they *were* momentarily startled and are now back in control of the situation. They may be overplayed through exaggeration or parody, to emphasize this reflective self-distancing. Additionally, they are often given a moment *after* the event has occurred, 'as we survey what might have been our doom, but from a position of support we have had ample time to secure' (1981: 102). Threat startles are expressions of reassurance to team-mates that there is nothing to be concerned about and that the emergency is over: they are a 'warning*like* signal in dangerous*like* circumstances' (1981: 102; emphasis in original).

*Revulsion sounds* are those like 'Ugh!', 'Yuck!' or 'Eeew!' that are uttered when a person comes into contact with something that they perceive as physically or symbolically contaminating, such as dirt (Douglas 1966). These gestures express an attitude of role distance (see Chapter 4 above), as the actor is at pains to communicate to onlookers that they did not want or expect to be infected. As well as rejecting the association between themselves and the contaminating matter, the actor again creates a division within their social self, as the contaminated part is split off and viewed with disgust by the witnessing part, which is aligned with the audience. By implication, this suggests that the actor is a clean, respectable person with the same moral values as everyone else. This can be particularly helpful when the actor is trapped within an occupational role that necessitates doing 'dirty work' (Hughes 1962), such as cleaning, plumbing or refuse collecting. Here, revulsion sounds 'show that indelicate, dirty work need not define the person who is besmeared by it' (Goffman 1981: 102).

*Floor cues* directly implicate the presence of team-mates and enlist their co-operation, turning an individual line of action into a joint team performance. These are statements actors make about an event or situation, which are designed to attract others' attention and evoke (or cue) a response. The response desired is usually a question or request for further information that will enable the actor to elaborate on what has happened and how they feel about it. For example, a man reading a newspaper 'suddenly brays out a laugh', causing his wife to turn around and ask, 'What's so funny?' (Goffman 1981: 105). Floor cues are cleverly designed tactics, as they lend the appearance of being just unselfconscious manifestations of a private state, which gives a false impression of modesty. The actor does not explicitly say 'Hey, look at this!' but rather makes the team-mate do the work of showing interest and feeding them their next line:

> Wanting to avoid being thought, for example, self-centered, intrusive, garrulous, or whatever, and in consequence feeling uneasy about making an open request for a hearing in the particular circumstances, we act so as to encourage our putative listeners to make the initial move, inviting us to let them in on what we are experiencing. (Goffman 1981: 105–6)

We saw an example of this in Chapter 4, with Albas and Albas's (1988) study of students' self-presentation after receiving their exam results. 'Aces' who did not want to openly brag about their high scores would affect an air of nonchalance, leaving their test paper casually out on the desk for passers-by to comment on, or emitting a dreamy smile that invoked them to ask, 'How did you do?'

## Communication out of character

The second set of self-directing strategies that team-mates use involves what Goffman (1959) called 'communication out of character'. He begins with the premise that actors can be aware of multiple, co-existing definitions of reality, which may be contradictory. The show presented is not a spontaneous response to the situation, but rather 'something the team members can stand back from, back far enough to imagine or play out simultaneously other kinds of performances attesting to other kinds of realities' (1959: 202).

In other words, team-mates may co-operate on presenting one social scene to an audience – the official version of events – while making surreptitious allusions to other, contradictory interpretations of what is really going on. The action unfolds on two levels simultaneously, one making a meta-commentary on the other by acknowledging its performativity and declaring it as fake: 'We all know this is just a sham!' This resonates with the 'polite fictions' discussed in Chapter 2, but here actors are colluding to deceive the audience rather than themselves, and can therefore make reference to the contradictory subtext, rather than pretending to ignore it and remaining at the surface level. These

communications typically occur as subtly encoded messages, undermining the events that are ostensibly taking place. As Goffman (1959:
168) puts it, they 'convey information incompatible with the impression
officially maintained during interaction'.

Actors may slip out of character, dropping the line of self-presentation
that they had been projecting. This can happen accidentally, when an
unexpected shock causes a 'crisis' that prevents the show from unfolding as planned: '. . . a portrayed character can momentarily crumble
while the performer behind the character "forgets himself" and blurts
out a relatively unperformed exclamation' (Goffman 1959: 167), such
as 'My God!'

More commonly, however, this happens as a strategic ploy, taking
place within the scripted action. Audiences are oblivious to what is
going on, while performers enjoy pulling the wool over their eyes.
Communication out of character is therefore a risky but thrilling
venture in which team-mates dare to acknowledge to each other that
the scene they are presenting is contrived, not real: the performance is
*only a performance*.

However, this is a dangerously fateful gamble, because should their
cover be blown, the cast's performance would grind to an embarrassing halt. As well as contradicting their own individual lines of
self-presentation, they are undermining the presented reality (Scheff
1968) of the scene. In theatrical terms, they are 'breaking the fourth
wall' between themselves and the audience by acknowledging that the
events unfolding are not real. Lyman and Scott (1968) refer to this
'disruption of the dramatic frame' as a potential hazard that threatens
to unravel the smooth running of the show, causing an anxiety akin to
stage fright. Juggling two contradictory versions of reality simultaneously demands complex skills of impression management, as well as
unwavering dramaturgical loyalty from team-mates.

Goffman identifies four ways in which team-mates may deliberately
communicate out of character. The first of these is *treatment of the
absent*. This occurs when cast members retreat backstage between
performances and talk about the audience in a derogatory way that
contradicts the positive regard they had afforded them frontstage; this
might include ridiculing, mockery, caricature and criticism. Such 'ritual
profanation of the front region as well as of the audience' (1959: 170)
brings relief to those normally obliged by status differences to treat the
audience respectfully. Goffman observes a Machiavellian tendency for
actors to treat each other 'relatively well to their faces and relatively
badly behind their backs' (1959: 173). Restaurant staff in the Shetland
Hotel would serve the guests courteously and deferentially, but once
backstage in the kitchen would make fun of them with 'belittling code

names' and imitations of their 'speech, tone and mannerisms' (1959: 173). Similarly, Wulff (1998) describes how members of a ballet company enjoyed 'cutting the audience down to size' by mocking their ignorance of the art.

*Staging talk* refers to the pragmatic planning discussions team-mates have about how they are going to stage a performance: their costume, props, scripts, lines and moves. By anticipating possible disruptions and exploring solutions, team-mates reduce the likelihood of embarrassment: they are effectively running a dress rehearsal, to ensure that the performance runs smoothly 'on the night'. The staff of a school that is about to undergo an inspection carefully select which classes will be observed and which pupils the inspector will meet, to ensure they give the best possible impression. Staging talk can also occur retrospectively, through 'post-mortem talk' after an event, where performers discuss what went wrong, lick their wounds and gather morale ready for the next occasion (Goffman 1959: 174). We can imagine such a scene unfolding in the staffroom after the inspector leaves.

*Team collusion* is secret communication between team-mates that takes place alongside the manifest performance, involving coded words or gestures. Unlike staging talk, which occurs before or after the show, team collusion occurs while it is going on, frontstage and right under the audience's noses, without threatening the impression of reality that is fostered for them (Goffman 1959: 175). It allows the performers to discuss aspects of the scene as it unfolds, and even talk about the audience in front of them, acknowledging their 'cynical' orientation to the roles that they are playing (see Chapter 4 above). For example, Goffman describes a system of manoeuvres used by workers in a shoe store observed by Geller (1934: 285). If a customer asked to try a shoe in a larger size that was out of stock, the shop assistant would call out to his colleague in the back room to 'stretch the shoes on the thirty-four last' – a code term for 'wrap them up as they are and leave them under the counter for a while' (cited in Goffman 1959: 176). Team collusion may involve 'staging cues' to supporting actors elsewhere on the set. For example, a business executive trapped in a difficult meeting may pre-arrange with their secretary to interrupt with a pretend 'important matter' that requires their urgent attention (1959: 176).

A subtype of this, 'derisive collusion' (1959: 183), involves actors indicating to themselves or others that they refute the version of events they are obliged to present. Individually, this is a form of role distance (Goffman 1961c; see Chapter 4 above), while, collaboratively, it is a gesture of mutual sympathy that helps team-mates endure a common predicament. For example, a couple whose annoying neighbour has popped round may hold a polite conversation with him whilst looking

over his head to exchange knowing 'pain grimaces' and roll their eyes in
tacit understanding of what they both really think.

Echoing Simmel (1908b), Goffman writes of the satisfaction of colluding in secret communication, which can affirm the bonds of solidarity
between team-mates. They may perform their roles in an exaggerated
or distorted way for the amusement of their bystanding team-mates,
sometimes drawing in a 'side-kick' victim from the audience (such as
a customer) to bear the brunt of their mischief (Goffman 1959: 185).
There may be internal divisions within the team as members collude
against each other: in the Shetland Hotel, the cook would politely
respond to a guest at the kitchen door while behind him 'the maids,
straight-faced, would secretly but persistently goose him' (1959: 185).
Sharing a private joke at another's expense is an important way of
building cohesion while bolstering personal dignity: 'By mocking the
audience or teasing a team-mate, the performer can show not only that
he is not bound by the official interaction but also that he has this interaction so much under control that he can toy with it at will' (1959: 185).

The final type of communication out of character is what Goffman
calls *realigning actions* (not to be confused with the discursive techniques
discussed in Chapter 3). This involves the use of particular 'safe' channels for expressing dissent from the working consensus, because they do
not openly threaten the integrity of the team or its members. Although
team-mates may 'strain at the leash' (Goffman 1959: 188) to dispense
with the official script, it is risky to do so until they can be sure that
their fellow actors feel the same way. Instead, they take advantage of the
ambiguity embedded in certain tentative expressions that allows them
to be interpreted in multiple ways, so that should they prove offensive,
it would be difficult to prove definitively that a particular meaning had
been intended. An unofficial line of communication accompanies the
official line as a subtext, but it can easily be retracted if the situation
becomes sticky, and the actors can resort to the manifest script as if that
was all that had been present all along.

This tactic is used in humorous exchanges, when a speaker is unsure
how the audience will take the joke: Goffman (1959: 187) gives the
examples of innuendo, mimicked accents and expressive overtones
('nudge nudge, wink wink'), all of which are subtle and ambiguous
enough to be denied if necessary. 'Double talk' is a related technique of
using coded terms to refer to things that it would be dangerous to spell
out explicitly, for example in the communications between criminal
gang members negotiating a deal, or a lawyer advising their client how
to present their story (1959: 191–2). Sarcasm is another example, as
this allows team-mates to exchange insults and criticisms about third
parties that can be retracted if the sentiment turns out not to be shared.

As Goffman (1959: 187) puts it, one team can put another in an unfavourable light 'under the cover of verbal courtesies and compliments that point in the other direction'.

Realigning actions can also be used to defensively save an actor's face in situations where they are making themselves vulnerable: rather than give an overt statement, actors will proceed cautiously with veiled hints and guarded self-disclosures. Coming out about one's sexuality may involve first 'testing the water' by tentatively 'putting out feelers' (Goffman 1959: 188) as to how a particular audience will react. Flirting is another example, as it relies on the tentative exchange of subtle or ambiguous gestures that build up only if both parties pursue the unofficial line together. If one party is not keen and refuses to take the cue, the suitor can hastily fall into cadence with this official definition of the situation, hiding their humiliation at the rebuff. At any step in the trajectory of the conversation, its progress in one direction can be halted and it can be dispatched onto another track. Realigning actions demonstrate the aforementioned practices of 'tact' and 'tact regarding tact', as they demand the co-operation of team-mates in a dance of mutually negotiated, unstable and emergent meaning-making.

## Conclusion

In this chapter, we have explored those aspects of Goffman's dramaturgical theory that pertain to group rather than individual identity performances. Using his notion of the performance team, we have seen how actors come together in social situations to stage routines, present team impressions or convey versions of reality, before audiences who may be more or less discerning. Team-mates demand trust and dramaturgical loyalty, relying on each other to uphold their official 'party line'. However, the 'bonds of reciprocal dependence' that unite them also leave them vulnerable to betrayal, and so circumspection is exercised when casting members. Team-mates often co-operate harmoniously to negotiate the presentation of a scene, but collusion can have a darker side, as alliances form, loyalties shift and internal divisions occur. Collective identities are performed through symbolic displays such as clothing, prop objects, demeanour and gestures, as well as through verbal and non-verbal interaction rituals. Tie signs communicate intimacy privileges, supportive interchanges allow actors to access or leave each other's company without causing offence, and remedial interchanges (such as apologies and requests) repair any such damage that may occur. Tact and regard for fellow actors' faces is central to teamwork, and in the discussion of protective and collective facework, we considered the intricacies of this as a shared endeavour. The rituals of sympathetic tact, audience tact and tact regarding tact are all interactive processes of joint social action, whereby actors work hard to keep each other (and the group as a whole) 'in face'. Finally, we considered the tactics that team-mates can use to direct the drama and influence each other's actions, so as to support their own performance lines. Response cries summon fellow actors to validate a situational identity claim, while communication out of character allows team-mates collusively to stage different, contradictory versions of a scene before the audience and between themselves. Teamwork is a complex and multifaceted process of micro-social interaction, which allows actors variously to claim, support, collude with and undermine each other in their mutually shaped identity performances.

## 6

# Spoiling careers

### Deviance, stigma and moral trajectories

This chapter explores the micro-social processes through which identities change over the life course. Symbolic interactionism imagines this through the concept of the *career*: a sequence of roles or status positions that unfolds successively and cumulatively to create an emergent sense of self. We can study each stage as an interaction context wherein meanings are negotiated, through situated encounters and social relations with significant others. Identities are processes of *becoming*, rather than simply *being*, certain types of person (Becker 1963), which are interactionally contingent, open-ended and perpetually unfinished. A second term, *trajectory*, describes the temporal pattern of an identity career, sometimes punctuated by salient experiences, key events and turning points.

Careers have a *moral* dimension when they involve normative judgements about the person's character or actions; they are additionally *deviant* when these judgements express social disapproval. Such labels and attributions may be internalized by the individual, changing their view of themselves. *Stigmatization* occurs when a person's career trajectory is disrupted by a pivotally negative experience that radically alters the way others view them. Identities can be threatened, discredited or 'spoiled' by such moments, making them 'fateful' for future social relations. In the final part of the chapter, we consider whether it is possible to step off a trajectory that is moving in an unwanted direction, and exit a moral career.

### Identity as career

The conceptualization of social identity as an interactionally mediated career can be attributed to Strauss (1969), although it also resonates with ideas from Goffman and earlier figures in the symbolic interaction-ist tradition. Strauss disputed the psychological theories that presumed the self developed through a fixed, universal sequence of maturational stages, culminating in an end point, such as ego integrity (Erikson 1968). Instead, he argued for a more open-ended, exploratory process of identity formation that took place through negotiations of meaning in social relations. Careers were individually specific, socially contingent and diverse in form, making infinitely different trajectory patterns over the life course.

Strauss (1969) defined the career as a series of movements through social positions, which had two sides: the objective (events that happen to a person and can be externally observed, such as changes of occu-pational status, ageing and transitions into different family roles) and the subjective (changes in self-image, private feelings and emotional experiences that lead to a rethinking of one's own identity). Similarly, Goffman (1961a) suggested the career had a threefold nature, combin-ing objective movements through social status positions, subjective experiences of these and the resultant, reflectively redefined self.

Interactionists study how actors navigate their way through different settings, their routes mediated and constrained by others, and how this creates transformations of the self (Atkinson & Housley 2003). This was first theorized in organizational settings, such as workplaces, where status transitions are often formalized by mobility between hierarchical ranks. Becker (1952: 470) suggested that the career reflected a tension between 'movement and fate' – or agency and structure – and described it as a 'patterned series of adjustments made by the individual' to their placement and positioning by others. This could be 'typically consid-ered in terms of movement up or down between positions differentiated by their rank in some formal or informal hierarchy of prestige, influence and income'. Beyond organizational settings, Cohen and Taylor (1995) broadened the concept to include leisure careers, subcultural careers, sexual careers, and so on. Goffman (1961a: 119) gave a similarly gen-eralized definition of the career as 'any social strand of any person's course through life'.

Some component features of careers are identified by Lindesmith et al. (1999). Firstly, careers can be *multiple*, as we pursue several different goals in our lives. My occupational career may be developing in one direction while I simultaneously pursue a leisure career and a family career. We can examine the relationship between an individual's various careers: ideologically, do they complement each other harmoniously or clash, with a conflict of interests? Chronologically, do they begin and end simultaneously (e.g. entry and exit from prison being paralleled by movements in and out of the employment market), consecutively (e.g. leaving the parental home to begin an independent residential life) or in overlapping periods (e.g. periods of intermittent mental illness coinciding with changing personal relationships)? Secondly, there is career *visibility*. How important is any given career to the individual in the context of their life as a whole? Some careers, such as those defining one's health or relationship status, turn out to be central to self-identity, and fateful (Goffman 1967: 149–270) for future interactions, while others may be less significant. This reminds us of Stryker's (1968) idea of 'identity salience' within hierarchical role sets. Thirdly, *career others* are the people with whom we interact at each stage of a trajectory, affecting whether, when and how we progress to the next. These might be friends, family, leisure group members, colleagues, enemies and people in authority. Finally, there are variations in the amount of *control* or agency individuals have over the direction, pace and reversibility of the path(s) they pursue. Did they embark on this journey voluntarily or did someone else (or cultural norms) lead them there? Do they have the potential to disembark?

One example of an identity career is that of 'serious leisure'. Stebbins (1992) distinguished this from more 'casual' involvement in an activity by its features of systematic pursuit, the acquisition of specialist skills and knowledge, and a deeper level of commitment. This trajectory involves gradual progression through stages of learning, interim goals, turning points and markers of incremental improvement. Other features of serious leisure are an attitude of perseverance despite obstacles (danger, embarrassment or low motivation), personal effort (training, investing time and energy), durable benefits (lasting effects, such as pleasure and physical fitness) and an associated culture with a distinct ethos. The latter implies regular interaction with fellow enthusiasts who function as 'career others', as evidenced by studies of surfing, skateboarding and kayaking (Kane & Zink 2004) and wheelchair runners (Patrick & Bignall 1987). Levine and Moreland (2006) identified four stages of identity negotiation in such contexts: pre-socialization (gathering information), socialization (learning the practical skills but also the norms, values and subtler etiquette of the sporting culture), acceptance (of membership claims) and consolidation (branching off into specialist subgroups formed around niche interests).

## Making sense of ourselves

Retrospectively, we try to make sense of these changes, performing *identity work* (Snow & Anderson 1987) as we reflect upon key events and experiences and interpret their significance in relation to our life as a whole. We may try to convince ourselves that certain occurrences had a symbolic meaning or were building towards some ultimate purpose, by saying things like, 'If [x] and [y] hadn't happened, I wouldn't have done [z]]', or 'Those experiences were tough but they made me who I am today.' Strauss (1969) suggested that because we like to imagine we have agency, we tend to use the first-person and the active voice to assume responsibility: 'I did [x]' rather than '[X] happened to me.' However, if the event in question was undesirable, tragic or inexplicable, we may use the passive voice to present ourselves as victims of circumstance.

Narrative sociologists have argued that we perform *biographical identity work* (Holstein & Gubrium 2000) upon the self as an object of reflection. We compose personal myths and stories of the self (McAdams 1993) to create a sense of meaning, explanation and order (Bruner 1991). New experiences are incorporated into these self-narratives, which can be modified to accommodate anomalous or unexpected happenings. Treating our selves as 'projects' to be worked upon, we contemplate existential questions about who we are, what we want to achieve and how we can live more authentically (Giddens 1991). Drawing on wider cultural norms and discourse, we may also perform *social problems work* (Holstein & Miller 1993), managing identities that we know are considered deviant.

These narratives are not definitive but, rather, provisional and open-ended, subject to constant revision. As Lindesmith et al. (1999) point out, although they appear to tell the story of the person's whole life, they are only snapshot tales, constructed in specific times, places or situations. We might construct several self-narratives over the life course, or employ multiple narratives simultaneously to explain our various career trajectories: '. . . an individual will most likely develop a story that is specific to each ongoing career as well as a master story that accounts for all of them' (Lindesmith et al. 1999: 319).

## Trajectories

The trajectory of a career is the pattern of movement that it makes over the life course. We can study the component stages, their articulation and arrangement, and mechanisms of progression. Sometimes there are clear 'bookend' stages of entry and exit, but often these are quite nebulous. Careers may unfold as simple, linear sequences (e.g. job promotions through an occupational hierarchy), while sometimes they are messier circles of disruption and indeterminacy (e.g. a journey through intermittently poor mental health). Thus one important variable is *career flow* (Lindesmith et al. 1999), or the degree to which trajectories unfold smoothly and easily.

There are also some common types of trajectory in terms of their shape and format. *Gradual realization* (Strauss 1969) involves subtle and insidious changes of which the individual may not at first be aware. Lindesmith et al. (1999) suggest five stages in this protracted process: fragmentation of one's prior sense of self; provisionality in trying out alternative 'possible selves' (Markus & Nurius 1986); praxis, or subjecting the chosen new self to tests of verification, such as seeing whether it would be accepted by significant others; consolidation of the new identity into one's self-image; and (sometimes) segregation: removing oneself from previous associations.

*Alternation and conversion* (Travisano 1967) describe identity transitions in terms of their alignment with cultural values. Alternation refers to identity changes that are socially sanctioned, even positively approved, for example the heteronormative script of falling in romantic love, getting married and having children (Jackson & Scott 2010). Conversion, on the other hand, refers to negatively evaluated changes of identity that invite disapproval, hostility or stigmatization, such as acquiring a criminal record. The latter is more difficult to incorporate into one's existing identity and may lead to social rejection.

*Coming out* is a process of revealing erstwhile private information about oneself to a public audience. Most obviously, this can mean disclosing a non-normative sexuality, and the interaction sequences this engenders. Coming-out stories follow a distinct narrative structure, with moments of discovery, reflection and revelation (Plummer 1995). Carrigan (2011) suggests the same pattern appears in asexual people's stories, too, insofar as this identity is regarded as culturally deviant. He suggests that 'becoming asexual' involves a self-reflexive awareness of several trajectory stages: feelings of difference, self-questioning, assumed pathology, self-clarification, biographical narrativizing and communal identity (Carrigan 2011: 471).

*Sudden or dramatic change* refers to experiences of identity transformation, in which one feels that one's life has been fundamentally and irrevocably changed; this evokes intense introspection and a radical reorganization of identity (Athens 1995). Medical sociologists have studied the impact of severe injury, illness or disability as a moment of 'biographical disruption' (Bury 1982). Those affected realize their life can no longer follow the trajectory they had expected, and so they must reconsider aspects of their everyday routines, social relationships and future plans.

For example, Smith and Sparkes (2008) present a case study of a young man, Jamie, who suffered a spinal cord injury (SCI) that left him paralysed and unable to continue his career as a rugby player. He underwent a dramatic transformation from having a 'quite remarkable body . . . able and strong' (2008: 221) to losing the athletic ability that had defined his identity: 'My life was sport. . . . The body I had was lost. Now what?' (2008: 221–2). Being trapped in this new, alien body was extremely emotionally painful for Jamie, as he was constantly aware of its contrast to his previous able-bodied state, and the life that could have been. SCIs are 'embedded in time. The body becomes a perpetual memorial to the split second of time in which the spinal cord was severed' (Seymour 2002: 138). The radical change to Jamie's identity was not limited to his sporting career but also extended to his gender identity as a father and an economically self-sufficient man, as he was no longer able to work and to provide for his family.

Jamie's account of this transformation also reveals the social reactions he encountered. Recovery narratives can conform more or less to culturally preferred templates, and have greater or lesser qualities of 'tellability', or acceptability to their audiences (Smith and Sparkes 2008). Some stories are more tellable than others because their format and morality are recognizably conventional. What Frank (1995) calls 'restitution narratives', which focus optimistically on the heroic power of medicine and the prospect of recovery, are preferred over 'chaos' narratives, which are more pessimistic and emotionally conflicted, with a fragmented structure that defies the audience's expectations. Thus when Jamie tried to voice his feelings of devastation and despair ('The whole thing, just completely shattering . . . life's been beaten out of me. . . . My life is a mess now. I can't remember when I was happy last' [Smith & Sparkes 2008: 223]), he found that others were reluctant to listen and got frustrated with him for not 'fighting' harder. Jamie felt as if not only was his story invalidated, but also he was dismissed as an 'unreliable narrator', depriving him of the only source of identity that he had left.

## Critical junctures

### Epiphanies and turning points

As well as looking at the overall pattern of the career trajectory, we can examine some key moments within it. Firstly, there may be salient and memorable experiences that the individual regards as pivotal to their identity development: critical moments in defining who they are or have become. Sometimes these are experienced as dramatic at the time, but often they are redefined as such retrospectively, as they search for biographical meaning. Strauss (1969) called these 'turning points', or 'moments of epiphany', which force people to challenge, question and redefine their self-identities. They signify a moment of transition between two different versions of ourselves: we divide our lives into the times 'before' and 'after' the event happened. DeGloma (2010) studied narratives of autobiographical 'awakening', whereby people discovered revelatory truths about moral, political or personal matters, for example becoming a born-again Christian, or recovering memories of childhood sexual abuse.

Strauss (1969) identified several types of turning point that can trigger an identity transformation. *Forecasting* occurs when an external authority figure decides that an individual has met a required standard needed to progress to the next level: for example, an examiner decides that a candidate should gain their qualifications. A variant of this is *meeting the challenges of an institution*, for example when a psychiatrist decides that a patient is well enough to be discharged from inpatient care. Thirdly, there are *private proclamations to a public audience*, such as coming out about one's sexuality. Fourthly, epiphanies can arise from the experience of *playing a strange, unexpected or new role successfully*. Those who find themselves in an emergency situation and act in ways defined by others as brave or heroic may change their view of themselves: an example of Cooley's (1902) Looking Glass Self evoking feelings of pride (see Chapter 1 above). More commonplace but no less transformative of self-identity, there are moments that mark a transition from one life course stage to another: leaving the parental home to go to college (Karp et al. 1998) or becoming a mother (Thomson et al. 2009), for example. Finally, discovering acts of *betrayal* can radically disturb our trust in others and our ontological security (Laing 1960). Women negotiating post-divorce relationships report adopting a different attitude 'after' than 'before', exercising greater caution and prudence in choosing a new partner (Smart 2004).

## *Status passage*

Socially mediated processes can mark transitions between the stages of a trajectory. The term *status passage* (Strauss 1969; Glaser & Strauss 1971) was first used to describe patterns of occupational mobility within business organizations. As Weber (1922) argued, meritocratic bureaucracies have a formal structure of offices, arranged in a hierarchical rank order. Statuses are positions built into this structure as 'resting places', existing independently of the individuals who occupy them. As people are constantly entering and leaving offices, there has to be an efficient process for managing the overall dynamic system. Status passages are therefore socially regulated, standardized and formalized mechanisms for moving people up or down the hierarchy, often involving prescribed rituals and ceremonies.

Glaser and Strauss focused on the subjective meanings that status passages hold for role incumbents. This depends on several factors, such as *centrality* to one's life (e.g. being promoted to company director, compared to a minor probationary upgrade), *reversibility* (e.g. marriage carries the possibility of divorce, whereas becoming a parent is a permanent change), *inevitability* (e.g. the physical ageing process compared to the decision to have cosmetic surgery), *voluntariness* (e.g. choosing to enter a therapeutic institution versus being put into one) and *sociability* (e.g. travelling by oneself or as part of a group).

Strauss (1969) identified some 'regularized status passages' as triggers of identity change. Firstly, *coaching* is an arrangement that involves one person helping another to move along a sequence of stages towards a mutually agreed goal, such as physical fitness. This is a unique relationship of trust and risk-taking: the coach puts the learner into progressively more challenging situations, repeatedly testing their limits and encouraging perseverance. As Adler and Adler (1978) argue, 'momentum' in sport is not merely a matter of individual psychology but, rather, a precarious quality negotiated through the interactions between instructors and players. Perceived failure in sport, from the smallest setbacks to the starkest ending of a career, can have enormous emotional effects upon a player's self-esteem (Harris & Eitzen 1978). Remembering that identities are relational, coaches themselves follow a career trajectory as they follow their clients' progression and invest much time and energy in this, sometimes involving geographical and social mobility (Sage & Loy 1978).

Secondly, a role incumbent can *disidentify* with their current status and seek to escape from it. Strauss (1969) pointed to the difficult process of extricating oneself from oppressive or intensely insular organizations, such as totalitarian regimes or religious cults. Scaramanga (2013) writes about his decision to leave an Accelerated Christian Education school, following growing disenchantment with its value-laden curriculum. Once a fervent believer, he came to regard it as a dangerously biased form of indoctrination, and now tours the public speaking circuit advocating tighter regulation of independent religious schools.

Thirdly, people undergo *temporary shifts* when circumstances require suspension from an otherwise habitual role. The social system needs to accommodate those who temporarily cannot fulfil their role requirements, by removing and/or replacing them, but there is a tacit expectation that the individual will re-enter after a period. Status passages guide exit out of and re-entry into erstwhile status positions and ensure social (re)integration. Strauss (1969) pointed towards religious observances such as Ramadan, which involve 'moratorium', or periods of social withdrawal and self-reflection. In Chapter 4, we saw how Parsons' (1951) 'sick role' involved a balance of rights and responsibilities that allow the individual to be excused from, but also to resume, their social duties. The same process happens with the social regulation of the 'sleep role' (Schwartz 1970), as the rituals of bedtime and waking provide temporally bounded zones in which to take off and put on our social faces (Goffman 1959). Bereavement, too, means that an actor will be out of circulation for a while, and so the process of mourning has to be socially managed. Psychologist Kübler-Ross (1969) outlined five sequential and universal stages of grieving (denial, anger, bargaining, depression and acceptance), although such models have been criticized for being too culturally normative and rigidly prescriptive. Craib (1998) argued that mourning was a messier and more complicated process, involving movements back and forth between stages rather than linear progression, and emotionally ambivalent feelings towards the object of loss.

## Rites of passage

Status passages are often marked by ceremonial events that have a ritualized character. The purpose of these *rites of passage* is to formally acknowledge, legitimate and celebrate the identity transition. These are publicly staged, collective events that bring people together as witnesses to the performance, ratifying its acceptability in accordance with their group or cultural norms. Thus the content of the rituals is not as important as what they symbolically represent. This echoes Durkheim's (1912) theory of religion as serving a social function of generating cohesion and solidarity: what matters is not so much *what* is worshipped as *how* worship occurs, collectively. Participation in ritual ceremonies ultimately affirms members' commitment to shared norms, beliefs and values, as the society's 'morality'.

The term 'rites of passage' originated from the anthropologist Van Gennep (1909) to describe the rituals marking an individual's transition from one stage to another in the life course, especially from childhood to adulthood. The term is now used more broadly to describe any transitional 'milestone' moments in the life course that change a person's status as a member of a social group: for example religious baptisms, confirmations, Bar and Bat Mitzvahs, 'coming of age', leaving home, marriage and even death.

Van Gennep suggested that rites of passage have three distinct stages, which may be marked by separate rituals or compressed into one prolonged ritual. First is *separation,* when the person is physically or symbolically detached from their previous associations. Second is the *liminal* stage, when they are suspended between the old and new status positions, not belonging to either. They hover on the threshold between two symbolic worlds, having left the first one but not yet entered the next. Turner (1967) described liminality as an ambiguous position 'betwixt and between' two others, when people lack a clear role, status or social identity. He called such people 'neophytes', or identities in potential, conjuring up an image of a butterfly in a chrysalis: they are just waiting for the next stage of their lives to start happening. This can create feelings of alienation and uncertainty: for example, in the summer between leaving school and going to college, students may feel as if their lives are being held 'in limbo', and they are 'drifting' without any direction (Karp et al. 1998). The long-term unemployed may similarly experience a sense of 'identitylessness' and normlessness as they find themselves suspended between occupational roles and routines, and this lack of purpose can be a cause of depression (Jahoda 1982).

The third stage is *reintegration,* when the individual is accepted into the new group or culture and can claim the new identity. This is often marked by celebratory rituals to confirm and consolidate the status and create a feeling of belonging: for example, freshers' welcome events at university that bestow the student role upon participants. Traditionally, symbolic artefacts would be presented to the new recruits as gifts, especially items of adornment such as rings, belts and crowns. Contemporary equivalents would include wedding rings, army medals, scout badges, karate belts and graduation gowns.

## Degradation ceremonies

Some rites of passage mark an individual's demotion in status, loss of role or rejection from a social group; these often involve rituals of humiliation and public shaming. Garfinkel's (1956: 402) concept of the *degradation ceremony* describes a process whereby 'the public identity of the actor is transformed into something looked on as lower in the local scheme of social types.' This occurs as a collective response to perceived deviant behaviour, expressing a community attitude of moral indignation. The participants include two principal parties – the 'denounced', who stands accused as a perpetrator of deviance, and the 'denouncer', who makes this accusation – and an audience of witnesses. The most obvious example of this is a court trial, but there are some less formal equivalents, as we shall see.

Identities are changed in degradation ceremonies through 'communicative work directed to . . . the destruction of one social object and the constitution of another' (Garfinkel 1956: 421). A person is first deprived of their former roles, responsibilities and dignity, before being given a replacement set symbolizing a lower status. 'The other person becomes in the eyes of his [*sic*] condemners literally a different and new person. . . . He is not changed, he is reconstituted' (1956: 421).

One example of this is Goffman's (1961a) discussion of admission to 'total institutions', such as prisons, hospitals and boarding schools. (We explore this concept fully in Chapter 7 below.) In the psychiatric hospital he studied, Goffman said that patients underwent a humiliating process that he called the 'mortification of the self'. Their previous identities were stripped away from them via symbolic rituals, such as the removal or confiscation of their personal possessions and the imposition of a standardized hospital uniform (pyjamas), placement (a designated bed space on a ward) and routine (the hospital's daily schedule). There was a violation of the patient's 'informational preserve', as private details about their medical history and home background were made available to the staff, as well as invasions of their privacy and 'territories of the self' (Goffman 1963b) through sharing general ward space and facilities. Inmates were subjected to 'contaminating exposure' to objects, places and people with whom they would not normally choose to associate, further insulting their dignity and independence. Finally, through the imposition of timetabled schedules, inmates lost control over their 'personal economy of action': they could not choose which activities to do, when, where and with whom; and had to ask permission to access resources they would normally take for granted. In having their lines of action opened up to scrutiny, challenge and intervention, the inmate was humiliatingly disempowered.

Garfinkel (1956) identified eight sequential stages to this interaction ritual, through which 'successful' degradation was accomplished. Firstly, both the offensive 'event' and the perpetrator must be removed from the everyday realm and designated as unusual. They are 'typed', or treated as an example of a social category with negative symbolic meanings, such as 'cheat', 'addict' or 'traitor'. Secondly, a preference is stated for a different type of behaviour; the two counterparts are presented in a 'scheme of preferences' to the audience. Thirdly, the denouncer must identify themselves as a public figure, acting within the capacity of a role, rather than making a personal confrontation. Fourthly, the audience are reminded that a social or moral value is at stake, which they have a shared responsibility to sanction. Fifth and sixth, the denouncer asserts the right to speak as a defender of these shared values, and this claim is accepted by the audience. Seventh, both the denouncer and the witnesses remove themselves from the perpetrator, through physical or symbolic gestures of withdrawal. Finally, the denounced person is left standing outside the group, in the position of the stranger (Simmel 1908a).

The public enactment and witnessing of the subject's denunciation is important here. Echoing Durkheim's (1898, 1912) remarks about social solidarity, Garfinkel (1956) suggested that the ultimate function of the degradation ceremony was to unite the viewing audience through their shared disapproval of the deviance. They performatively enact their own conformity to the shared values this has offended, and consequently their immunity to status loss. Despite its focus on an individual scapegoat, therefore, ritual shaming serves to strengthen social solidarity and cohesiveness, and is a hallmark of Durkheimian social morality. It is only in societies that are 'completely demoralized' (Garfinkel 1956: 420) or 'anomic' (Durkheim 1898) that this mechanism of social control would be lacking.

### Rites of recovery: Alcoholics Anonymous

One example of a rite of passage, involving degradation but also resurrection, is Denzin's (1987) study of the Alcoholics Anonymous (AA) support group. We shall examine the interaction dynamics of these 'Twelve Step' therapeutic programmes further in Chapter 7. Denzin suggests that just as 'becoming an alcoholic' is a career trajectory, so is the journey of recovery, as a socially mediated status passage. Becoming a 'recovering alcoholic' demands movement along the sequential trajectory of the Twelve Steps, each symbolizing progressively deeper commitments to an alcohol-free life. During this period, members are suspended in a liminal state (Turner 1967) between addiction and recovery. Thus the 'recovering self' that eventually emerges is a socially negotiated identity, constructed through the encounters between AA members in their regular meetings. Reaching the status of 'recovered' requires validation of this identity claim by the audience of peers, who witness the transformation: recovery is not just a personal project but also a collective accomplishment.

AA meetings are characterized by a ritualized sequence of joint action in which all members participate (cf. Hoffmann 2006). Firstly, there are recitations from the equivalent of a sacred text: the Big Yellow Book, or AA manual, contains inspirational readings, such as the Serenity Prayer, which are solemnly recited in unison. The group leader then recaps on the Twelve Steps of recovery, and asks the group whether anyone has a 'sobriety birthday' to celebrate. The main part of the meeting unfolds through the 'two minute check-in' as the leader goes round the circle, asking everybody to declare their name, current stage of recovery (the infamous '"My name's [X] and I'm an alcoholic') and a summary of how their past week has been. This confessional ritual, which reduces the members down to one humiliating label, suggests an element of ritual shaming (Hayes 2000). However, through this public denunciation of the unwanted identity, members ultimately demonstrate their stronger commitment to the future of recovery, and to the new identity that awaits them. The meeting closes with a collective recital of the Lord's Prayer whilst holding hands in a circle, symbolizing the members' unity, equality and commitment to mutual support.

## Moral careers

The *moral career*, outlined by Goffman in his books *Asylums* (1961a) and *Stigma* (1963a), describes those identity trajectories that have a moral dimension: where social reactions to a person's actions involve normative judgements expressing attitudes of distaste, disapproval, impatience or intolerance. These attributions are especially 'fateful' for long-term identity as they encompass the individual's whole character, with one 'master status' (Hughes 1945) assuming dominance over all other aspects and clouding perceptions of the person in future encounters. The designated problematic attribute is often contrasted with a more desirable, morally approved identity, which the individual is assumed either to have given up or to have the potential to acquire. Current and future selves are defined in terms of success and failure, competence and incompetence, membership and exclusion (Goffman 1961a). The depth and pervasiveness of these external attributions make it easy for them to be internalized as subjectively meaningful, with powerful effects upon the actor's sense of self. Thus Goffman (1961a: 119) defined the moral career as a 'regular sequence of stages that career entails in the person's self and in his [*sic*] framework of imagery for judging himself and others'.

In *Asylums* (discussed more in Chapter 7), Goffman wrote critically about the 'extrusory' effects of involuntary institutionalization, in progressively eroding the inmate's autonomy and independence. They underwent a status transition from civilian to inmate, a 'civil death' of their prior identity and everything that had given them a sense of personal selfhood. Possessions, autonomy, freedom and dignity were taken away from them, leaving a void into which the new, replacement self could be fitted. We have already seen how the 'mortification of the self' was enacted through degrading admission procedures, but this was just one occasion in a more protracted career involving three stages: prepatient, inpatient and ex-patient. Goffman (1961a: 130) saw this as an abusive, immoral act of symbolic violence: '. . . the prepatient starts out with at least a portion of the rights, liberties, and satisfactions of the civilian and ends up on a psychiatric ward stripped of almost everything.'

The *prepatient phase* was the period before the person was hospitalized, when others around them began to notice that something was 'wrong' and took steps towards professional intervention, such as calling a doctor. They might trick or persuade the person to go into hospital 'for a rest', without any mention of diagnosis or treatment. Goffman writes of the 'circuit of agents' involved in this process as an 'alienative coalition': family, friends and medical professionals colluded with each other against the individual. To the extent that inmates experienced this as betrayal, they resisted the threat to their identities in the accounts (see Chapter 3 above) they gave of hospitalization. 'Apologias' were defensive assertions of one's normality ('I got here by mistake because of a diabetes diagnosis, and I'll leave in a couple of days. [The patient had been in seven weeks.]' [1961a: 141]), while 'sad tales' accepted the status designation but blamed external circumstances ('I was going to night school to get an MA degree, and holding down a job in addition, and the load got too much for me' [1961a: 141]). These stories reflected a 'self-respecting tendency' through which the inpatients struggled to keep their civilian identities alive.

The *inpatient phase* was the period of time spent in the hospital, beginning with the degrading admission procedures described above, and continuing through a series of experiences that incrementally committed the inmate to their role. They began by learning the official rules of the institution (primary adjustments), then the unofficial rules of what they could get away with (secondary adjustments), through informal socialization with their fellow inmates in the 'underlife' subculture. Meanwhile, staff monitored the inmates' progress towards recovery as a sequential journey, documenting their behaviour in a 'case record' file. However, Goffman cynically argued that 'progress' merely meant compliance with the hospital regime: staff argued tautologically that a compliant patient was in better health while a disruptive patient was simply acting out their symptoms. Deviance and rule infractions were seen as evidence of the patient's deterioration rather than as wilful, agentic resistance (cf. Rosenhan 1973). Obedient and disobedient conduct was duly sanctioned by rewards and punishments, such as promotion up or demotion down the hierarchical 'ward system' or the granting and refusal of privileges. The whole self was implicated, as the patient's position on this trajectory was read as an index of their moral worth and status.

Upon release, the moral career did not end but rather entered a new stage, the *ex-patient phase*. This was when the person attempted to reintegrate into community life but found their efforts compromised by the way that their past came back to haunt them: making friends, finding housing and seeking employment were all more difficult because their identities were tainted by the identity of having been a 'mental patient'. We shall return to this concept of *stigma* shortly.

## Becoming a skydiver

Hardie-Bick (2005) applied the moral career concept in his ethnographic study of skydiving. Following Goffman's model, this career had aspects that were objective (the sequential stages of training) and subjective (the experience of undergoing this, and processes of identity change, consolidation and commitment), which culminated in ontological transformations of the self. The meanings attached to skydiving changed over time, from initial fear through curiosity, adventurousness and exhilaration, to pleasure, enjoyment and, eventually, the experiential state of 'flow', or total immersion in the activity (Csikszentmihalyi 2002).

Those who progressively committed (Becker 1963) to this trajectory regarded it as a serious leisure identity (Stebbins 1992) and distinguished themselves from others who were more casual in attitude, such as those doing a one-off jump for charity. They also performed identity work by talking disparagingly about 'hedonistic consumers' (Hardie-Bick 2005: 123) who did not take skydiving seriously, such as the 'laddish' types whose air of bravado gave way to quaking with fear when they got up in the air (2005: 124). However, many of those who had reached 'serious' status had themselves begun as casual hobbyists (Stebbins 1992) and unintentionally become hooked on the activity. Furthermore, their movement along the trajectory had been propelled and mediated by interactions with others in the skydiving community, who served as aspirational role models. As one participant, Emily, reflected,

> . . . when I did the training I didn't think about [progressing in the activity] at all. It was just to do it for the first one jump and I thought I was going to be happy with that really. But on the first day somebody . . . during the feedback that they gave us there were more experienced people who were better and had done more jumps and that encouraged me because it made me think, ah, you can move on, you can get better. I think that's the key to why I want to progress. (Hardie-Bick 2005: 153)

The transition from novice to expert skydiver was a socially negotiated status passage, whose trajectory was formalized through an instructional training course. Leaving behind those who made only 'tandem jumps' strapped to an instructor, the 'serious' students enrolled on a course called the Ram Air Progression System (RAPS). This took them through eight sequential categories of progressively more difficult manoeuvres in the air. In the earlier stages, the student jumped with a 'static line', a cord attached to the aeroplane, which automatically opened their parachute as they fell. They did this in groups, jumping one after the other, giving the whole procedure a routinized anonymity. Karl described this derisively as just being a 'dope on a rope' (Hardie-Bick 2005: 156). Later on, they learned to climb out of the plane, holding on to the wing strut and balancing precariously on one leg before jumping off, and to become responsible for checking and opening their own canopies. Other stages along the way included practising with 'dummy pulls' (a device for manually opening the reserve canopy, should the main one fail); five-, ten-, fifteen- or thirty-second 'delays' (waiting before opening the parachute so that the fall is faster); the 'unstable exit' (making the conditions for the jump more challenging by falling in a deliberately unco-ordinated manner); and 'free-falling' (diving and then adopting a horizontal position, to prolong the experience and incorporate manoeuvres; this can be done in group formation as a competitive sport). Upon reaching this final 'Category eight', the student became a licensed skydiver, and so the first free-fall jump was a rite of passage, celebrated by staff and fellow students as a momentous transitional event – in Strauss's (1969) terms, a turning point of identity transformation:

> Everyone makes such a big deal about it when you've done your first free fall. The instructors and skydivers have so much admiration 'cos you've got to that level. 'Cos they say that if you haven't done a free fall you're not a skydiver, you're a parachutist. It's the fact that you've jumped out of the plane and opened your own parachute, and that's what it's all about. You've done it all yourself. I was buzzing afterwards. I don't think I came down from about 10,000 ft until about Wednesday. I was on a high for days. (Karl, participant cited in Hardie-Bick 2005: 155)

The moral aspect of this career was embedded in the idea of 'learning to be serious'. The trainees underwent a period of intense safety training beforehand, which focused on what could go wrong during a jump and the checks they must carry out to deal with this. Multiple disastrous scenarios were presented, including a 'bad canopy' that does not open, getting entangled in a malfunctioning canopy, and a 'static line hang-up' whereby one stays hanging, suspended below the plane. The instructors emphasized how important it was to take these risks seriously, and taught the students a number of safety drills to memorize until they could be executed automatically, should the need arise.

The training sessions had a ritualistic aspect as the students performed their seriousness, solemnly reciting mantras such as 'Look, locate, peel, punch, pull, arch, check canopy' (the procedure for manually opening a reserve parachute) and corporeally acting out manoeuvres. The atmosphere was tense as they were tested by on-the-spot questions and chastised if they got them wrong: 'The instructor allows the student to finish before casually informing him that he has just killed himself. Not only has he killed himself, but he has killed everyone else in the plane' (Hardie-Bick 2005: 134).

Paradoxically, humour was used to convey the notion of seriousness; however, its use was carefully regulated and contingent upon status. While it was acceptable for an experienced skydiver to mess around, playing with equipment and parodying the safety drills, novices who tried to have fun were frowned upon for not taking things seriously enough. A woman asking to repeat one of the practice escape manoeuvres explained apologetically, 'I just don't want to die', which made everyone laugh; however, the instructor sternly admonished them by pointing out that this was an actual risk, so they would do well to follow her example (Hardie-Bick 2005: 127). The student's serious commitment to safety was thereby redefined from a laughably neurotic over-reaction to a sensible, proportionate appreciation of the weightiness of the task.

## Stigma

Moral careers can stretch into the future, having long-term effects on a person's identity. Goffman's (1961a) ex-patient stage, the third in the asylum inmate's trajectory, described what happened after the dramatic events of the previous two stages, when merely having had such a status in the past could negatively affect current social relations. In *Stigma* (1963a), Goffman explored this idea further, pointing to the 'blemishes of character' that can 'spoil' one's identity in the eyes of others. Here, he was not suggesting that any such attributes were inherently undesirable, but rather that definitions of stigma emerged out of social encounters, affecting participants' views of each other.

Goffman begins with a distinction between two versions of the self that actors might present in everyday life (see Chapter 4 above). The 'actual' social identity is the set of characteristics that a person 'in fact' possesses, while the 'virtual' social identity is the image they hope to project in a situation, or impression they hope to create; these are characterizations 'in effect' only, which may not be communicated successfully. Stigma arises from a discrepancy between these two identities, when the former contradicts or undermines the claims made by the latter, 'spoiling' its effects. Stigma is an attribute of character that is 'deeply discrediting' (Goffman 1963a: 13) of the person's virtual identity; it is 'obtrusive', to the extent that it interferes with their social relations.

By contrast, Goffman posits the existence of another group, the 'normals'. Here again, he is not implying that there is anything inherently normal or better about the characters of these people, but rather that they perceive themselves as such compared to the stigmatized individual because they do not possess the fateful attribute. No one is essentially normal or abnormal, but we often make these attributions of each other, and this drastically affects the way we interact. The normal and the stigmatized are not essential but relational identities (Williams 2000), each defined by contrast to the other. It is the disjuncture between normative expectations and perceived difference that creates the perception of stigma in others. Social reactions, ranging from fascination to pity, disgust and discrimination, imply a fear of contamination, which may lead to social rejection of the individual: 'He [sic] is thus reduced in our minds from a whole and usual person to a tainted, discounted one' (Goffman 1963a: 12).

Normals, who assume their view of the attribute is a common-sense truth, hold a tacit expectation that the person will feel ashamed, try to minimize its impact so as not to make them feel uncomfortable, and cheerfully get on with their lives. This assumed strategy of 'good adjustment' carries moral connotations of how one ought to behave to fit in with the demands of 'normal' society. Where this is not possible, the stigmatized are expected to quietly withdraw and not 'make a fuss'. In return, normals express an attitude of acceptance, although this may be a mere façade.

This empty gesture of 'phantom acceptance' allows normals to maintain the polite fiction (see Chapter 2 above) that they are being tolerant without actually having to change their attitudes. Disability rights activists such as Smith (2014) have written critically about the UK media coverage of the 2012 Paralympic Games as embodying this pseudo-liberal attitude of inclusivity through its self-congratulatory and patronizing narrative tone. Marvelling at individuals as 'special' made able-bodied people feel good about themselves while dangerously distracting them from wider political issues of institutional discrimination. This constituted 'inspiration porn':

> . . . a brilliant distancing tactic that allows people to abstract themselves from serious structural issues. If you turn a disabled athlete into an object to goggle at, you can sidestep ableism, you can sidestep harmful social

attitudes, you can sidestep the actual issues faced by disabled athletes. It becomes a narrative of overcoming the disability, rather than overcoming the society that makes being disabled so difficult. (Smith 2014)

Goffman identified two main types of stigmatizing attribute: the discrediting and the discreditable. Discrediting stigmas are those that are immediately visible and undeniable, evidenced on the body or in publicly accessible information: for example, facial disfigurement, or a scandalous media report of a celebrity's behaviour. As the individual cannot prevent this 'knownaboutness', all they can do is try to manage other people's reactions to it. They might present a demeanour of shame or regret to show their alignment with 'normal' values, or, conversely, emphasize the feature to express a defiant pride. Here we may recall how when the musician George Michael was caught 'cottaging' for sex in public toilets, he made a pop video satirizing the whole affair. In terms of physical disability, 'corrective equipment' (Goffman 1963a: 115) may be made more visible, turning it into a dramaturgical prop to convey symbolic meanings: for example, decorating a walking stick or having a customized wheelchair in bright colours and a fashionable design. A third strategy is 'covering', whereby the individual softens the effect of an attribute to reduce shocked or discomfited reactions, for example when blind people wear dark glasses (Goffman 1963a: 125). In averting embarrassment, this is also a gesture of tact (see Chapter 5 above), saving the face of the other as much as oneself.

Discreditable stigmas, on the other hand, are those that might be regarded as deviant if they were known about, but can be hidden, such as having a criminal record, a non-normative sexuality or a mental health condition. This invisibility is a double-edged sword: on the one hand, it offers the possibility of 'passing' as a normal and avoiding suffering obtrusive effects upon social relations. Goffman gives the example of psychiatric patients applying for jobs and giving the hospital address in the form of a street name and number, to 'pass' as a non-patient civilian. On the other hand, the person lives with the constant fear of the attribute being discovered, with potentially disruptive effects upon interaction: the applicant may get the job but then worry that the firm will ask to check their medical records. Self-presentation then becomes concerned with trying to conceal the attribute and prevent its inadvertent revelation. 'Information control' describes the range of strategies involved in such impression management, as actors decide what and how much to reveal to whom, selectively disclosing different versions of themselves to different audiences.

Goffman identified two social groups of sympathetic others from whom the stigmatized individual may find support. The *own* are people who share the same attribute and so understand the concerns and predicaments that must be faced in everyday life. They provide a backstage haven for the individual: 'a circle of lament to which he [*sic*] can withdraw for moral support and for the comfort of feeling at home' (Goffman 1963a: 32). For example, those who have a particular physical disability may commiserate with each other on the common prejudicial attitudes they encounter. The *wise* are those who do not share the attribute but are nonetheless knowledgeable about it and familiar with its implications: for example, those with a friend or relative who shares the same condition. The wise belong to the category of 'normals' but have a special set of circumstances that has allowed them honorary membership of the stigmatized group, and are entrusted with their secrets.

The stigmatized develop a moral career in learning about the kind of social reactions they will typically encounter and how best to deal with these. This entails a process of socialization into the views of the generalized other (Mead 1934), or the 'standpoint of the normal' (Goffman 1963a: 45), towards oneself. Goffman suggests four common trajectories for this career. Firstly, those with an inborn stigma, such as a birth defect, learn from early childhood how they are 'different' and how pragmatically to navigate their way around norms and expectations. Secondly, a child may be shielded from ignorance and prejudice by a 'protective capsule' (1963a: 46), such as parents who decide which other children they can play with. Inevitably, there comes a time when the young person encounters less benign reactions, such as bullying at school, and is ill equipped to deal with this. They feel shocked as they undergo a sudden 'realization of the situation' (1963a: 47), and this moment of disillusionment becomes a pivotal turning point (Strauss 1969) in their biography. Thirdly, those who become stigmatized later in life, or who learn relatively late that they have always been discreditable (e.g. finding out that they have been adopted), may undergo a 'radical reorganization of [their] lives' (Goffman 1963a: 47), involving re-identification of themselves and sometimes shame or disapproval towards the virtual self that they had previously claimed. Feelings of self-estrangement may result from this fragmentation of identity, as the person questions who they are or now can be, and the authenticity of the life that passed before. Goffman cites a respondent in Linduska's study, who had developed the illness polio with sudden onset:

> I woke up one morning, and found that I could not stand. ... The education, the lectures, and the parental training which I had received for twenty-four years didn't seem to make me the person who could do anything for me now. I was like everyone else – normal, quarrelsome, gay,

full of plans, and all of a sudden something happened! . . . I was a greater stranger to myself than to anyone. . . . I suddenly had the very confusing mental and emotional conflict of a lady leading a double life. It was unreal and it puzzled me, and I could not help dwelling on it. (Linduska 1947: 177, cited in Goffman 1963a: 48–9)

Fourthly, there are those who have been socialized into an 'alien community' with alternative norms and values, but choose to leave it and reintegrate with the mainstream: for example, those who abandon a religious sect (Barker 1989). This requires a process of resocialization into 'normal' modes of conduct and a shaking off of previous associations. In such careers there is a gradual shift from feelings of uneasiness about new associates (post-stigma acquaintances) to a fresh insight of uneasiness towards one's old associates (pre-stigma acquaintances).

Increasing association with the 'own' group who share the stigma can alter the individual's self-conception. There may be well-established communities with long-standing customs and traditions (Goffman 1963a: 52), into which the person must delicately negotiate entry and wait to be accepted. Frequent and regular interaction with these groups effects a peer-mediated, informal socialization into the different meanings that they give to the stigmatizing attribute, altering the individual's view both of it and of themselves. Feeling that they now have less in common with the 'normal' outside world, they may reduce their contact with it, reconfiguring their identity as a member of the new reference group. This can evoke deeply conflicted feelings of emotional ambivalence. Goffman gives the example of a newly blind woman leaving the hospital and enrolling at a specialist institution:

I was expected to join this world. To give up my profession and to earn my living making mops. The Lighthouse would be happy to teach me to make mops. I was to spend the rest of my life making mops with other blind people, eating with other blind people, dancing with other blind people. I became nauseated with fear, as the picture grew in my mind. Never had I come upon such destructive segregation. (Keitlen & Lobsenz 1962: 10, cited in Goffman 1963a: 51)

## Encountering stigma

Social encounters between the stigmatized and the 'normal' depend partly on what kind of attribute the individual possesses. A selection of empirical studies illustrate this in relation to stigmas that are visible (discrediting), hidden (discreditable) or belong to third parties (courtesy).

## Discrediting stigmas

Davis (1961) studied interactions between able-bodied people and those with physical disabilities who were wheelchair users. This is an example of Goffman's discrediting stigma that is visible and immediately 'known about', inevitably affecting the interaction. As Levitin (1975) argues, some physical impairments challenge normative expectations and evoke defensive reactions; they transgress the 'expressive boundaries' of what others are comfortable with seeing. Davis suggested that these reactions include fear, pity, disgust and embarrassment. This discomfort is revealed by 'signs of stickiness', such as guarded references to the impairment, compulsive loquaciousness (talking too much about other things) and a fixed stare elsewhere.

By taking the role of the other (Mead 1934) in social encounters, Davis's participants imagined how 'normals' perceived them and anticipated embarrassing awkwardness, or 'strained interaction'. Able-bodied people might perceive the disability as an 'ambiguous predictor of joint activity', worrying whether they would be able to find things in common to talk about, or that they might cause offence by suggesting something that the disabled person could not do. The latter tried to avoid this by *disavowing* their stigma: for example, emphasizing the 'normal' activities that they could do, such as sports, shopping or dating. Levitin (1975) similarly found that temporarily disabled people downplayed the impact of this upon friendships, by *disavowing* it as an enduring state and positively *avowing* all the 'normal' things they intended to do once they had recovered. Davis's participants also used protective facework (Goffman 1967: 5–46; see Chapter 5 above) to spare their interaction partners' blushes, by pretending not to notice and joining in with 'artificial levity'. This illustrates the strategy of studied non-observance chalance or 'acting natural' to maintain a 'polite fiction' that the scene presented is one of 'normal appearances' – a definition of the situation that everyone knows is not really true (see Chapter 2 above).

## Discreditable stigmas

Studies of epilepsy (Scambler 2005; Schneider 2009) show this to be an invisible condition that usually does not affect a person's daily activities. However, when a seizure does occur, it is sudden and unexpected, and this unpredictability creates concerns about potential embarrassment. Living with epilepsy creates dilemmas of self-presentation, demanding strategies of concealment, passing and information control. Scambler and Hopkins (1986) made a distinction between *enacted stigma*, which involves actual prejudice or discriminatory treatment, and *felt stigma*, where these occurrences are only anticipated, but nonetheless feared. As Gray (2002: 737) explains, felt stigma stems from the dreaded prospect of a 'public showdown', and sufferers experience living with the 'daily risk of exposure': 'The experience of felt stigma ... refers to an individual's fear of failing to enact a normal appearing round of life, and reflects the essential precariousness of maintaining a normal identity in the face of a possible failure of interaction.'

Schneider and Conrad (1981) identified four 'modes of adaptation' to this discreditable (felt) stigma, divided into three *adjusted* strategies and one *unadjusted*. The latter was a relatively passive feeling of helplessness and debilitation, as sufferers felt overwhelmed by the epilepsy's unpredictability. The former category included the majority of people who gradually came to terms with their condition and found ways of managing felt stigma in their everyday lives. Firstly, the *pragmatic* were those who employed the strategy of selective disclosure, telling only certain people about their epilepsy if they thought there was a risk they might have a seizure in their presence, for example college tutors and friends. The *secret* stigmatized were those who tried to conceal the condition from everyone, in order to 'pass' and be accepted into mainstream activities. The *quasi-liberated* were those who proudly and openly told anyone about their condition in the hope of demystifying it, using humour to diffuse any tension and getting involved in awareness-raising activism.

## Courtesy stigmas

A third experience concerns what Goffman calls 'courtesy stigmas': attributes possessed by other people associated with us, which affect our own identity by proxy. The first example comes from Gray's (2002) study of children with autism, a developmental condition involving social and communicational difficulties. Gray explains that because this is manifest in behavioural rather than physically embodied symptoms, it is often mistaken for mere 'naughtiness'. Gray was interested in how the *parents* of such children managed the condition as a discreditable courtesy stigma: when out in public with their child, they were always aware of the potential for them to 'cause a scene' (Goffman 1959), and for those around them to misinterpret this as bad behaviour. Moreover, because the child was a dependant of theirs, the parents thought they would be blamed and held responsible for this rulebreaking action. 'Scenes' threatened to disturb the 'normal appearing round of family life' (Birenbaum 1970) as well as the interaction order of public places (see Chapter 2 above). This caused feelings of shame and embarrassment, as well as frustration at the misunderstanding. For example, this mother described an occasion when her son's behaviour evoked a reaction of moral disapproval:

> We went for a walk [and a] bike rider was going through . . . and [my son] got this plastic bag and just threw it at this lady. And he was standing right here in front of her. Oh, and she said, 'How dare you do that. Can't you keep control of your kids?' (Gray 2002: 745)

In response to this recurrent predicament, parents devised strategies for managing social encounters. Some, anticipating intolerant reactions, avoided public places (cf. Voysey 2002), restricting their socializing to essential outings and meetings with those who were 'wise', or 'in the know' (Birenbaum 1970). Some tried to 'pass' as a 'normal' family, entering the same situations as everyone else and just hoping that their child would not cause a scene (Gray 2002). Others engaged in selective disclosure (West 1986) as information control, telling onlookers about their child's condition if they seemed sympathetic, or indeed were parents of autistic children themselves and so constituted 'own' group members. A final strategy was the defiant refusal to feel ashamed or apologize for their child's behaviour, and instead to turn the tables on the critics, by challenging and educating them about their prejudice. This mother proudly reported,

> I never make excuses for him because . . . I want him to think he's normal. And if he mucks up, I don't just [say] to a group of people, 'Oh, forgive me for the way he behaves. He's autistic. Please excuse him'. . . . I only bring it up if people . . . start talking about him. I just happen to say to them, 'He has high functioning autism'. And . . . straight away I'll get a . . . sympathetic response. . . . [However,] I get people [who] will turn around and say, 'Oh, there's nothing wrong with him. . . . He just needs a good kick in the backside', you know. And I just end up saying, 'You need a smack in the mouth'. (Gray 2002: 741)

Another example of courtesy stigma comes from Johnson and Best's (2012) study of heterosexual parents of young gay and lesbian people. They argued that, just like their children, the *parents* also followed a moral career trajectory on the basis of this identity. They went through various stages in accepting, coming to terms with and in some cases proudly advocating for their child's sexuality, through the support group PFLAG (Parents, Families and Friends of Lesbians and Gays). The interaction context of this peer group mediated their development of a collective, self-attributed identity as 'Radical Normals', and consolidated their commitment to the trajectory:

'It's a journey,' says Roxy. 'It really is, it's a process,' quickly follows Deb. 'And we have lots of literature for you to read,' Mary chimes in. 'I don't want to read any of that stuff, I don't like seeing stuff I don't agree with in my mind, but I do want to change, I'm just not ready to read that stuff.' 'Well, then just come back,' Mary advises, 'We really hope you come back. Because we've all been there.' (Johnson & Best 2012: 331)

As well as building new relationships with their children, these parents learned to negotiate social encounters with other adults, including fellow PFLAG members (Goffman's 'own' group) and prejudicial outsiders ('normals'). Some parents experienced their child's sexuality as a discreditable stigma – one that could be hidden – and so used strategies of information control: deciding whether to 'come out' to other family members or try to 'pass' by pretending the young person was heterosexual. Coming out was itself a long-term, interactive process of gaining confidence from positive reactions, and gradually widening the circle of people who were 'in the know' (Goffman 1963a). As these three mothers discussed:

> *Mary*: . . . I started with people who were gay and accept and moved on to closer friends, and I also, I mean, these were people I worked with, I mean, they had accepted all the gay people at work, too. So.
> *Kate*: You kind of start with the safe people.
> *Mary*: Yea.
> *Lacy*: And you move on from there.
> *Kate*: Yea, yea, and then you, kind of, if you don't tell people, like I had a hard time telling my father, and my brother told him, then you worry, well, if he finds out, so you have to tell all the right people.
> (Johnson & Best 2012: 329)

## Deviant careers

Nor only are some career trajectories evaluated in moral terms, but they also produce identities that are regarded as deviant. Here we draw upon the symbolic interactionist labelling theory of deviance, which shifted the focus away from individual people or acts to the social reactions and processes through which they are defined as such (Kitsuse 1962; Erikson 1964; Schur 1971). Becker proposed a relativist approach that considered the transactions between more and less powerful groups, asking 'Deviant for whom?' and 'From which values?' He famously argued that 'social groups create deviance by making the rules whose infraction constitutes deviance, and by applying those rules to particular people and labeling them as outsiders. . . . The deviant is one to whom that label has been successfully applied; deviant behavior is behavior that people so label' (Becker 1963: 9).

Paradoxically, labelling theories suggest that deviance is normal: most people drift (Matza 1964) in and out of rule-breaking action throughout their lives, but only some get caught and publicly identified. Often the acts are inconsequential because they go undetected, are seen but ignored or are *normalized*: accepted, condoned and attributed to unusual circumstances. Lemert (1967) made a distinction between *primary deviance*, the initial rule-breaking acts that may or may not be noticed, and *secondary deviance*, the longer-term effects upon those who have been labelled. Actors may drift into this further rule-breaking behaviour as a 'means of defense, attack or adaptation to the overt and covert problems created by the societal reaction to primary deviation' (Lemert 1967: 17). Disapproval, punishment and marginalization are social reactions with moral significance; some people fatalistically live up to these expectations and internalize the label. Secondary deviance therefore involves a 'symbolic reorganization of the self' and a radical change in identity. Eventually it becomes difficult to act or be recognized in any other terms: the attribute becomes a 'master status', dominating one's social identity (Hughes 1945).

Becker (1963) argued that the process of *becoming deviant* is a socially negotiated career trajectory, through which interactions lead individuals to alter their perceptions, dispositions and motivations towards the relevant activity. It is a status passage of sequential stages, taking the individual from primary to secondary deviance, as they become 'progressively committed' to the new identity. Authority figures may intervene as 'moral entrepreneurs' to admonish the behaviour or the group associated with it, bringing it to public attention. For example, Cohen (1972) showed how police, politicians and journalists led a 'moral crusade' against the Mods and Rockers subculture in the 1960s, using the mass media to fuel a 'moral panic' that seeped into public consciousness. Peer interaction is also important in determining whether or not the label becomes subjectively real to the actor. They may seek out the company of others similarly identified, finding solace in their shared fate; once integrated into such a community, new loyalties develop and the identity becomes more firmly entrenched.

This was illustrated by Becker's (1953) study of 'becoming a marihuana user' through the interactional processes of socialization, status passage and career mediation. Regular encounters with a subcultural peer group changed the way new recruits experienced the activity, the meanings they associated with it, and ultimately their view of themselves. Becker pointed to three key stages in this career trajectory. Firstly, *learning the technique* meant smoking the drug in such a way that would produce the desired effects of light-headedness, relaxation, feeling 'spaced out', and so on. Secondly, the actor must *learn to perceive the effects* as signs of being 'high' rather than just as physical symptoms, attributing new meanings to their bodily sensations. Thirdly, they must *learn to enjoy the effects*, by making new symbolic associations between the physical feelings of being 'high' and the social meanings of having fun and belonging to a group. Thus deviant identities emerge through ongoing negotiations of meaning with significant others.

## Shyness as a deviant career

Deviant careers occur not only with law-breaking behaviour but also with more everyday experiences. My research into shyness (Scott 2007a) explored how this identity could be reconceptualized from a symbolic interactionist perspective. Shyness can be understood not as an inherent individual pathology (such as a personality trait or innate temperament) that only a minority of people have, but rather as a situational state into which anyone can drift, and which is therefore normal and commonplace. Shyness does involve private thoughts and feelings (inhibition resulting from a sense of one's own perceived relative social incompetence), but these are defined in relation to the other actors present in a particular encounter. An individual may feel shy in some situations but not in others, and experience it occasionally without self-identifying as a 'shy person' in general. Whether or not they become committed to a shy identity depends on the patterns of interaction they experience over the life course.

One contingent factor affecting this is the social reactions that shyness evokes from others who regard it as deviant, insofar as these indicate cultural attitudes, norms and values. Shyness involves occasions of interactional rule-breaking, such as quietness, verbal clumsiness, avoiding eye contact, retreating to the margins of social encounters and 'failing' to take one's turn in conversation. Sometimes these actions are normalized, with reference to the actor's age (shy children are often seen as endearingly 'cute'), gender (shy women may be tolerated more because they fit the stereotype of 'feminine' behaviour) or external circumstances (a situation may be identified as one that would make 'anyone' feel shy, such as a job interview). Often, however, shy behaviour breaches the audience's normative expectations about the fundamental, 'residual rules' (Scheff 1966) of interaction, evoking reactions of puzzlement, impatient frustration and moral indignation. The actor's motives are misinterpreted as rudeness, aloofness or snobbery, a cruel irony given their actual concern with wanting to be accepted. One respondent, Etta, recounted a memorable occasion:

... when I travelled by bus, I'd avoid sitting near anyone I knew might start a conversation and the whole bus could listen in. One particular lady with a loud voice shouted one day at me, down the length of the bus, 'Who do you think you are tossing your head at? You think you are too good to sit near me.' I was mortified, as all I'd done was scuttle past her, pretending not to see her! (Scott 2007a: 134)

Those who repeatedly experience such reactions may come to be recognized in such terms. As Georgia put it, being shy 'almost defines what you are, I suppose. It's like just saying that someone's a positive person or a negative person ... it's definitely labelling, isn't it? So you kind of box people into how you see them' (Scott 2007a: 145).

The 'shy' label has other connotative meanings, which may lead to compound labelling. Both Nook and Johnboy said that they had been labelled 'weird' for being shy boys at school, while Natalie voiced her frustration at being labelled 'quiet and sensible' and, by implication, 'boring'. Some found that these social reactions escalated into teasing and bullying, leaving them feeling hopelessly typecast. Etta remembered a difficult childhood:

My parents always called me 'the shy one of the family'. .... [My uncle] would always ask me, 'How's my shy girl?' He'd say it as if he took some enjoyment in watching me cringe. He knew I was shy and would pursue it to no end. My [other] uncle would also give me a certain look with a smile on his face. He would just stare at me until he could get me to put that shy look on my face. We all know the 'shy look', I think. I would turn beet red as I silently died inside. .... The more I showed I was shy, the more they would taunt me. (Scott 2007a: 146–7)

Over time, shyness can become a 'master status' (Hughes 1945), an over-riding definition of social selfhood based on one salient characteristic. As those labelled 'shy' internalize the image other people have of them, they come to see themselves in the same terms. This can become a self-fulfilling prophecy: it is easier to fatalistically live up to others' expectations than to challenge them and assert a new social identity. Georgia commented that 'once you start being quiet, it's easy just to get quieter and quieter, and get less and less noticed.' Anna also reflected,

I think it's who I am now, cos after so many years of being like that, I think I am [shy]. And I think quite a few times, some people have said, 'Oh, Anna's the quiet one'. . . it kind of stuck with me, I suppose . . . if people expect you to act a certain way, then yeah, I think sometimes you tend to . . . if people say 'Oh, you're nice and quiet, you are' and then you just think, 'Well, why say anything then? Why really speak up?' (Scott 2007a: 147–8)

Drifting *out* of the shy role again can be difficult, because such inconsistency further confounds others' expectations, attracting more unwanted attention. As Ruby explained, on the occasions when she did feel brave enough to be more sociable, she was restricted by a drama- turgical dilemma. Taking the role of the other towards herself (Mead 1934), she realized that she risked being seen as doubly deviant: firstly committing the norm-breaking acts of shyness, and then defying the expectations attached to the label:

> ... once you're classified as a shy person, you can't do anything that's not shy, cos if you do that, then it's like there's something wrong with you. You can't do something just, like, drastic or outrageous, cos they'd say 'Oh, what's wrong with you? Are you sick?' ... I can't switch from being Little Miss Quiet in the corner and then to be Little Miss Loud, cos it's like – people just look at you funny. (Scott 2007a: 149)

The gradual realization that one is effectively trapped in the shy role means that it becomes subjectively real for the individual, and so by the end of the trajectory some people do self-define as shy. The frustration and isolation this engenders may be why many also experience it as a problem – not in itself, as others do (primary deviance), but rather through its consequences for interaction (secondary deviance). Anna explained:

> ... the problem is that eventually, when you start to feel more comfortable with people, and you want to start talking to them more, etc., you feel like you're stuck in a rut. Either that or they've given up on you and decided you're not worth the effort because you don't reciprocate. Then it's really hard to break out of that trap. If you suddenly 'came out of your shell', some people might be surprised or shocked and that would draw even more attention to you, so you'd retreat back into your shell again. It's all a vicious circle that I find very frustrating. (Scott 2007a: 150)

## Career exit

This leads us to a final question about what happens at the far end of an identity trajectory, in terms of possibilities for career exit. Are status transitions irreversible? Once one has started to pursue a different iden- tity, is forward velocity inevitable or is it possible to step off this path?

Lindesmith et al. (1999) suggest three ways in which an identity that has been acquired may subsequently be rejected, discarded or lost. *Emergent self-loss* involves private feelings of discomfort about a role, which build gradually towards a desire to be free of it. For example, an athlete who has trained for years in their sport may decide to leave it and pursue a different career. Although such decisions are voluntary, the loss of a role that had been a centrally defining aspect of identity can evoke a radical reorganization of the self (cf. Athens 1995). *Pre-planned exclusion* is an externally initiated (even enforced) removal of a person's social status, often involving dramatic interventions to 'rescue' them from dangerous influences: for example, religious cult members who are 'deprogrammed' after suspected 'brainwashing', or substance users who are faced with an 'intervention' and taken away to a detoxification centre. *Emergent exclusion* refers to a more gradual process of ostracisim: studies of the process of becoming mentally ill (Scheff 1966) have highlighted the interactional processes through which actors are alienated and excluded (Lemert 1962) from their social circles, which Smith (1978: 27–8) calls the 'cutting out operation' (see Chapter 5 above).

Illustrating the first of these routes is Ebaugh's (1988) study of the moral career of an ex-nun. Ebaugh argues that losing an identity is not a wholly negational experience, for it is simultaneously a 'process of becoming' something else; the discarding of one status leads to the search for another to replace it. With the exception of death (at least for those with no belief in an afterlife or reincarnation), every ending is a new beginning. The 'ex' status is therefore both an identity in itself, and something that opens up the possibility of a new identity. Similarly, the *role exit* process, or 'becoming an ex', is both a career in itself and the generator of another, subsequent trajectory. Both of these periods of readjustment are socially negotiated through patterns of interaction with significant others. The role exit process could apply to the loss of any aspect of identity that carries with it the potential for alternative, imagined futures. Comparable experiences are becoming an ex-addict by undergoing rehabilitation, an ex-offender by doing time in prison or an ex-partner by surviving a relationship breakdown.

Ebaugh identifies six phases in the trajectory of becoming an ex-nun. Firstly, the woman experiences doubt as to whether the Church is meeting her personal needs and therefore whether she still belongs in it. Secondly, she realizes that she has the autonomy to decide whether to stay with or leave the religious order. Thirdly, she experiments with alternative futures, imagining different pathways forward into new roles or possible selves (Markus & Nurius 1986). Fourthly, she may reach the 'vacuum' stage: a period of moratorium in which no action occurs but the potential for change gathers intensity. Suspended in a liminal zone 'betwixt and between' (Turner 1967) the statuses of nun and ex-nun, the woman belongs to neither category and lacks a distinct social identity. This is a position of omniscience, as she can view both roles with an outsider's perspective and compare them somewhat objectively. She might imagine her life going in either direction: back to the convent or onwards to a new life. Fifthly, the nun reaches a *turning point* (Strauss 1969), a critical juncture between the past and future when she makes a definitive decision to leave, knowing that she cannot turn back. In other cases, career exit is reversible: for example, leaving prison or a detox centre does not preclude the possibility of 're-offending' and consequent re-entry. Finally, there is the stage after leaving, when the woman must consolidate and adjust to her ex-nun status, while putting into action her plans to forge a new identity. Becoming an ex, like any other career identity, is a perpetually unfinished, socially negotiated process.

## Conclusion

This chapter has examined how social identities change over time, through the concept of the career trajectory. This sequence of status positions is interactively mediated, encounters with significant others shaping the way that we see ourselves and understand our biographical development. Careers can be moral and/or deviant when they involve others' normative judgements about one's character or action. They can also be stigmatizing, when a discrepancy between virtual and actual identities leads to strained interaction with self-proclaimed 'normals'; however, actors adaptively devise strategies for managing the effects of these discrediting, discreditable and courtesy stigmas. Relating to more sympathetic 'own and wise' others is important, both in providing solace and in consolidating the new identity. Associating with people in similar positions, while feeling excluded by those differently defined, can affect the extent to which we internalize labels and attributes as subjectively real, and become progressively committed to them as role-identities. Career trajectories can take many forms, some unfolding slowly and imperceptibly and others punctuated by critical junctures, epiphanies and turning points. Status passages manage the transformation of one identity into another, while rites of passage ceremoniously mark these events. Ceremony does not equate to celebration, however, as we saw with rituals of degradation: a previous self can be ruthlessly 'mortified' and coercively replaced. In the next chapter, we shall explore this idea further, examining the ways in which institutional life can radically alter a member's identity, with variable proportions of control and voluntarism.

# 7

## Reinventing futures

*Organizations, power and institutionalized identities*

The focus of this chapter is on how social organizations and institutions shape the identities of their members, by working on and transforming social selfhood. These changes indicate power relations, operating at the micro level through interaction contexts and social processes of negotiated order. Revisiting Goffman's classic model of the total institution (TI), I consider whether and to what extent these power relations have changed from being relatively coercive to more voluntaristic. I present my own model of the contemporary reinventive institution (RI), to which people willingly admit themselves in pursuit of self-improvement, and to which they attach more positive symbolic meanings. We shall look in detail at three types of RI: spiritual communities, military camps and rehabilitative clinics. This leads us to revisit theoretical debates about the ontology of selfhood and the contested terrain of agency, authorship and institutional inscription.

### Negotiating institutional order

Social *organizations* can be thought of as structures in which particular activities are carried out in a regular, rule-governed way towards a collective goal. They operate as social systems, involving hierarchies of roles (Turner 1962), formally prescribed rules (Albrow 1970) and rational administrative procedures, such as those of a bureaucracy (Weber 1922). As such, organizations are associated with modernity, Fordism and the Japanese model (Clegg 1990), although social change has led to the rise of alternative forms, such as the aesthetic or performative, postmodern organization (Linstead & Höpfl 2000) and the social democratic Scandinavian model (Booth 2014). Organizations are often physically bounded spaces, which can be relatively closed or open in terms of interaction with other social systems, non-members and the wider society.

Social *institutions*, meanwhile, involve established practices, relations or culturally normative routines of interaction that may or may not take place within a bounded site (Fulcher & Scott 2007). In functionalist terms, a social institution addresses the 'system needs' of a group or society, such as those for order, stability and the (re)integration of its members (Parsons 1951). This may take the form of an abstract ideal, such as the family, or a more tangible structure, such as the university.

SI encourages a conflation of these terms. Just as social structures are viewed not as abstract, external entities but as comprised of individuals interacting in regular, patterned ways (Scott 2009b), so too can organizations be thought of as constructed through their institutional fabric: the everyday relations and practices of their members. Goffman (1961a) used the term 'institutional arrangements' to refer to these micro-level structures, arguing that organizational power was exercised through face-to-face encounters during the 'daily round' of institutional life. In Clegg's (1989) 'circuits of power' theory, this micro-level agency represents the 'episodic circuit' of day-to-day communication, conflict and resistance, which operates within the macro-level 'dispositional circuit' of rules and structural authority and the 'facilitative circuit' of technology, design and environmental infrastructure.

Negotiated order theory (Strauss et al. 1963; Strauss 1978) reflects this micro-level, symbolic interactionist approach, focusing on the ways in which rules are interpreted and enacted on the ground. Rules are not static, inflexible forces upon behaviour but, rather, emergent products of interaction, which are subject to continual revision. Power is not held by those in certain roles or positions, but rather is fluid and dynamic: different interest groups compete and bargain with each other to gain access to resources. The snapshot of social order we observe in a specific organizational setting is a collective accomplishment, contingent upon the various factors of the 'negotiation context', such as the number of actors, their experiences, skills and knowledge, the sequence and frequency of interactions, the number and complexity of issues under discussion and the visibility of the negotiations to other parties (Strauss 1978). These negotiations can occur vertically, across levels of the role hierarchy, or horizontally, within the same organizational stratum.

Negotiated order theory emphasizes actors' agency, through their constant adaptation to the structures in which they are embedded (Fine 1984). Rules can be selectively applied, stretched or 'fudged' in accordance with the particular interests of actors, and we can detect a 'revolutionary potential' in the perspective (Day & Day 1977: 131).

This was exemplified by Gouldner's (1954, 1955) studies of industrial conflict within workplace organizations, where the hierarchical divisions between employees and their line managers created competing interest groups. Gouldner (1954) argued that the rules could be enforced in three main ways: through a punishment-centred bureaucracy (with open hostility and resentment between the two parties), a representative bureaucracy (with workers contributing to the formation of the rules and agreeing to comply with them) or a mock bureaucracy (whereby there was a tacit understanding that the rules would not be enforced, creating solidarity between the two parties). In the latter case, an 'indulgency pattern' (Gouldner 1955) operated, whereby managers and workers turned a blind eye to each other's rule infractions. However, when a new employer chose instead to enforce the regulations, the employees rebelled by 'working to rule', eventually resulting in strike action.

## Total institutions

The concept of the total institution (hereafter 'TI') was introduced in Erving Goffman's influential text *Asylums* (1961a), an ethnographic case study of St Elizabeths psychiatric hospital in Washington, DC. Although this study is often located within the anti-psychiatry movement (Laing 1960; Szasz 1961; Scheff 1966), Goffman's aim was rather to demonstrate how the self was socially reshaped by patterns of interaction, which were crystallized in the rules and practices of institutional settings. He defined the TI as 'a place of residence and work where a large number of like-situated individuals, cut off from the wider society for an appreciable period of time, together lead an enclosed, formally administered round of life' (Goffman 1961a: 11). TIs are therefore places to which people are confined around the clock, immersed in a 'totally' encompassing environment – members eat, sleep, work, and so on, all together in the same site. These include not only hospitals but also institutions such as army barracks, boarding schools, and prisons, in which disorderly groups are segregated, reformed and ultimately 'improved' (Wallace 1971). Goffman identified five types of TI by their function: to care for the disabled, 'incapable' and harmless; to contain those with infectious diseases; to protect the community from 'dangerous' people; to enable the collective pursuit of an educational or work task; and to provide sanctuary for those who have voluntarily retreated from society. Focusing on the first three types, which he regarded as coercive, he examined what happened when members were institutionalized against their will.

The four key features of Goffman's TI were: the unfolding of the daily round in the same place and under the same authority; batch living, or being treated alike as one anonymous mass; the rigid timetabling and scheduling of activities, imposed by a formal system of rules and a body of officials; and the orientation of these activities towards a single rational plan or institutional goal, namely that of resocialization. The overall effect was one of 'collective regimentation', as TIs broke down some barriers – between spheres of activity (work, sleep and recreation) and between individual inmates (who were treated *en masse*) – while creating others – between the inside and outside worlds and between staff and inmates.

A central theme of *Asylums* is of the self under threat: any environment that so 'totally' encloses its members – physically, spatially, temporally and culturally – has the power to rewrite their identities without challenge. Goffman used polemical language and violent imagery to convey his disquietude at the ways in which TI inmates were debased, degraded and deprived of their human rights and civil liberties, effecting a systematic erosion of their prior selves. Power lies at the heart of these institutional arrangements. As Clegg (2006: 144) argues, TIs render the self 'pliable and plastic' for extreme transformation, often against the inmate's will. He continues: 'Organizations exert power over their members by making them do things that they would not otherwise do and take on identities that they would not otherwise have assumed' (Clegg 2006: 149).

Taking an anti-psychiatric stance, Goffman argued that the medical model was an inappropriate and misleading metaphor for psychiatric treatment. He criticized the psychiatric profession's image as a personal service occupation, in which clients request the assistance of a technical expert and enter into a voluntary, contractual agreement. Instead, he declared, '[m]ental hospitals institutionalize a kind of grotesque of the service relationship' (Goffman 1961a: 321), disguising an abuse of power as an act of benevolent professionalism. Drawing an analogy with the car repair industry, he describes a process by which customers bring a damaged possession to the servicer, leave it at the workshop and return to collect it. This is an impersonal relationship, because the client's self remains separate from the object under repair, and the servicer is only interested in 'tinkering' with that detached part. In the asylum, by contrast, patients are committed involuntarily, having no choice about whether and how they are treated. The person must remain within the hospital while their civilian life grinds to a halt. Treatments are not simply technical but moral, and socially 'fateful': the patient's whole self is deemed to be faulty, not just one part, and so any 'correction' will significantly alter their identity.

## Mortification and moral careers

As we saw in Chapter 6, Goffman imagined the process of becoming a psychiatric patient as an identity trajectory or 'moral career', comprised of three sequential stages: prepatient, inpatient and ex-patient. The prepatient stage occurred when those around them formed an 'alienative coalition' or 'betrayal funnel' that led to their admission. Entry was marked by a symbolic degradation ceremony (Garfinkel 1956), through which the person was stripped of their previous identity and 'disculturated' from their home world. Goffman called this a 'mortification ritual' as it represented the death of the inmate's civilian self (see Chapter 6 above). The actor lost control of their self-presentation, as personal possessions were confiscated and replaced with standard institutional issue (pyjamas, toothbrush, comb). There was a violation of their 'informational preserve' (private details about their bodies, eating and sleeping routines and behaviour were made available for scrutiny by staff), 'personal economy of action' (control over their time and choice about activities) and 'territories of the self' (invasions of personal space and privacy), all of which resulted in a humiliating loss of dignity.

The inpatient phase represented the time spent in the TI: the routinized daily round of institutional practices, through which the inmate's identity was systematically replaced. Progress along the moral career trajectory was represented by a 'privilege system' of rules, rewards and punishments for more or less desirable behaviour, such as promotion or demotion through the graded hierarchy of the 'ward system'. Behaviour was documented in a 'case record', with incidents being 'looped' self-referentially to justify diagnosis and treatment decisions, while contrary evidence was overlooked. Staff therefore wielded considerable coercive power in being able to rewrite the inmate's self-identity.

## Institutionalization

The cultural milieu of the 'inmate world', as Goffman called it, involved a distinct interaction context that mediated its members' experiences. Dunham and Weinberg (1960) emphasized the solidarity and friendship that developed between patients, bolstered by their subordinate relationship to the staff. However, many studies were critical of the effects that hospital ward life had upon patients, who became socialized into the role of the docile, compliant inmate. Concerns were raised about patients becoming 'institutionalized' (Wing 1962), with an attitude of fatalistic passivity as they grew so accustomed to life within the asylum walls that they lost the motivation to return home. Braginsky et al. (1973) observed that many long-stay, chronic patients came to see the hospital as their new home, in contrast to the acute patients, who remained focused on discharge. Roth's (1966) study of Farewell Hospital, a chronic care home, bemoaned the 'slow motion' pace of life, which fostered social and economic dependence on the institution: '. . . many hospitals are not so much medical facilities as huge boarding houses for the damaged and derelict of our society' (1966: 25). Soon afterwards, Rosenhan (1973) famously demonstrated how difficult it was, once labelled mentally ill, to negotiate release. His team of researchers faked schizophrenia to gain admission to psychiatric wards, but found that when they ceased to display the symptoms, their 'normal' behaviours were interpreted in the light of the diagnostic label and their protests dismissed as 'acting out'.

However, it is important not to exaggerate this picture of passivity and dependency. Denzin (1968) argued against the inevitability of institutionalization: in the hospital he studied, patients were reluctant to elect a leader or establish an informal code of rules, for fear of getting too comfortable and feeling settled and 'at home'. Wulbert (1965) and Karmel (1969) also found that asylum inmates saw their identities as merely temporary, using role-distancing strategies in their verbal accounts. Interviewees in Wulbert's study made defensive justifications, akin to Goffman's 'apologias' or 'sad tales' (see Chapter 6), that emphasized their intentions to resume civilian roles upon release. 'Well right now I'm not seeing much of [my friends] . . . .'

## Resistance, rebellion and inmate underlife

Elsewhere, we find a more optimistic picture of TI inmates demonstrating agency and resistance against institutional authority. Clegg (2006: 145) suggests that 'Goffman documents the tenacity of the self to be what it is and resist being prescribed as that it should be.' Goffman (1961a) identified various 'lines' of action the asylum inmate could take, reflecting different levels of commitment to the official rhetoric and compliance with its regimes. *Withdrawal* (rendering oneself incommunicative or inaccessible) and *intransigence* (refusing to co-operate) suggested that the patient retained a sense of their own agency and struggled to protect the boundaries of the self. *Conversion*, meanwhile, suggested a genuine transformation, whereby the inmate believed in the benefits of reinvention and was fully immersed in the role of the mental patient. Most commonly, inmates learned to *play it cool* with a combination of these techniques, vacillating between different levels of commitment.

Some patients were more calculatingly devious in presenting displays of docility. These were 'cynical' performances (see Chapter 4), whereby actors offered the responses they thought the staff wanted to hear but did not 'sincerely' believe in the parts they were playing. The well-socialized inmate recognized that in order to be deemed eligible for release, they must play along with the rules and pretend to have changed. As Goffman (1961a: 143) sardonically remarked, '[T]he patient must "insightfully" come to take, or affect to take, the hospital's view of himself.' This indicated a sense of 'moral loosening' or fatigue, as patients ceased to care about defending their previous identities, and resignedly did whatever it took to get out, playing a 'shameless game' of 'civic apathy' (Goffman 1961a: 151). In a more recent example, Hornbacher confesses to having invented a story about childhood sexual abuse in order to convince staff at an eating disorders hospital that she was engaging with her 'real', deeper issues and therefore eligible for release: 'The remainder of my time in Lowe House was spent dealing with this non-issue. . . . I lobbed a firebomb to the right, and while everyone was chasing the firebomb, I disappeared stage left. Absolved. I created a straw man and he took all of the blame' (Hornbacher 1998: 212).

These individual gestures of resistance can become established in the institution as an alternative value system. What Goffman called the 'underlife' of a TI was its subculture of resistance, through which inmates socialized each other into an unofficial code of conduct. Once they had made their 'primary adjustments' to the official regulations, they learned another set of 'secondary adjustments' to the reality of what they could get away with, to make life in the TI more bearable. They devised subtle tricks and strategies to 'work the system', 'fudge' the rules (Day & Day 1977) and defy authority. Secondary adjustments involved either taking an unauthorized means to a legitimate end (e.g. sneaking extra food from the canteen) or taking legitimate means to an unauthorized end (e.g. using a day pass to buy contraband items in the town). 'Make do's were artefacts reworked for a new purpose, such as spoons carved into knives, or rolled-up newspapers used to cushion hard seats. Spatial territories could be subverted, as inmates retreated to private areas (toilet cubicles or phone booths) to indulge in forbidden activities like smoking, or pilfered goods from a shared resource like the kitchen.

Fraternization with fellow inmates was crucial to the transmission of this value system. Established inmates mentored new recruits and 'showed them the ropes', while a buddying system operated as inmates paired up. Patients also devised trading systems to circumvent the official rationing of supplies, by exchanging contraband possessions, bargaining, bartering and gambling with substitute currencies, such as cigarettes. Nevertheless, Goffman argued that the inmates remained primarily self-interested and focused on their individual fate: while

resentful of the TI's coercive structure, they failed to mobilize collectively against it, so their protests remained small and ultimately
ineffectual.

## Reinventive institutions

Although TIs still exist, in the form of hospitals, prisons, and so on, we
can detect the emergence of a new institutional form that holds different
– positive – meanings for its members. Entry to these settings is voluntary, and they are designed to have beneficial effects on self-identity, to
be empowering, liberating and transformative. In *Total Institutions and
Reinvented Identities*, I proposed the concept of the reinventive institution (RI), which I defined as

> a material, discursive or symbolic structure in which voluntary members
> actively seek to cultivate a new social identity, role or status. This is
> interpreted positively as a process of reinvention, self-improvement or
> transformation. It is achieved not only through formal instruction in an
> institutional rhetoric, but also through the mechanisms of performative
> regulation in the interaction context of an inmate culture. (Scott 2011: 3)

I have identified six different types of RI (Scott 2011), although there
may be more: religious and spiritual communities, military camps,
secret societies and fraternities, therapeutic clinics, academic hothouses
and virtual institutions. Later in this chapter we shall look at three of
these types in more detail.

The rise of the RI can be understood within the context of contemporary Western culture, with its neoliberal values of achievement,
competitiveness and individualism. Cultural critics have observed
trends towards narcissistic self-absorption (Lasch 1979), anxiety and
suffering (Wilkinson 2001, 2004), risk awareness (Beck 1992), fear and
paranoia (Furedi 2001, 2002) about whether we are good enough to
meet the increasing social demands of late modernity. Detraditionalist
theorists such as Beck, Giddens and Bauman point to the decline of
traditional structures, such as family, community and religion, which
leads us to turn inwards to focus on the self. Beck and Beck-Gernsheim
(2002) describe a process of individualization, whereby the late modern
actor seeks to plan and control their life, through constant reflection and
rational choice: the 'DIY biography'. There is an anxious preoccupation with the self as unfinished business (Furedi 2004), a collection of
loose ends waiting to be tied up. We have become more introspective
and self-vigilant, treating our identities as projects (Giddens 1991) to

be reflexively monitored, worked on, even perfected – although this promise may turn out to be a 'disappointing' myth (Craib 1994).

RIs have arisen to both create and meet this demand, defining the obligation to self-actualize as an individual problem, while signposting solutions to it. They offer to process, reshape and reform by trimming away negative emotional experiences, replacing them with a new, improved identity. This may be presented as an opportunity for self-actualization and unlocking potential – seemingly altruistic motives that suggest a journey made under one's own volition. At the same time, RIs encourage trust in the authority of inspirational leaders and guides. This 'faith in the counsellors' (Halmos 1965) has intensified with the rise of the 'psy' disciplines and experts (Rose 1990), the secular priests who promise to save us from ourselves. Foucault (1976) argued that confessional rituals, such as psychotherapy, offer symbolic purification, for acknowledging one's shortcomings and requesting guidance relieves the burden of individual responsibility. Simultaneously, they legitimize an exercise of power, as expertise is vested in the confessor to 'judge, punish, forgive, console and reconcile' (1976: 61–2).

However, individuals do not enjoy complete autonomy in the authorship of these new selves: they can only choose from the limited array of identity templates available from cultural scripts and discourses. Gubrium and Holstein (2001) suggest that the very private troubles of contemporary selfhood are understood and accounted for by publicly available narratives, which can be bought over the counter at institutional outlets. A 'panorama of discursive environments' (2001: 12) surrounds the individual, providing an array of convenient identity templates: not only for the troubled selves we might have been in the past, but also for the ideal, possible selves we might become. Each of these is 'in the business of structuring and reconfiguring personal identity' (2001: 2) in accordance with the 'going concerns' of particular institutions (Hughes 1957). This reflects a wider cultural process that Gubrium and Holstein call the deprivatization of the self, whereby personal troubles are opened up to scrutiny and public consumption. Clients perform identity work by selecting from these templates and fitting themselves into them, accounting for their troubles with standardized discursive frames.

## Performative regulation

The mode of power that operates within the RI can be understood as what I call performative regulation: a form of disciplinary power (Foucault 1975) that operates pervasively through the dramaturgical interaction context of the inmate culture. Foucault's claim that disciplinary power is pervasive and impersonal encourages us to move away from conspiratorial ideas of coercion towards a subtler process of legitimation, whereby beliefs and practices come to be taken for granted as normal, natural and inevitable. However, in the RI, disciplinary power is exercised not only vertically, through the penetration of authoritative knowledge down into individual consciousness, nor even bi-directionally, as Rose (1989) suggests, with individuals willingly submitting themselves to the gaze, but multi-dimensionally, surveillance being dispersed through the reticulated network of the negotiation context. This resonates with Clegg's (1989) idea of the episodic circuit of organizational power, operating through micro-level interactions. It also evokes the 'third dimension' of power that Lukes (2005) identifies, whereby those in authority secure their subjects' will to be governed. RIs are 'institutions without walls' where members are ostensibly free to leave but choose not to, and so we need to understand their motivations. As Jenkins (2008) asks, in the absence of a coercive authority structure, why do people 'put up with' power and domination?

Adding a symbolic interactionist lens to this analysis, I suggest that the third dimension of power operates horizontally, through dramaturgically enacted peer surveillance. In the interaction context of an RI, negotiated order is accomplished as members monitor each other's conduct, shaping their progress towards a common goal. Bauman (2000) argued that the most powerful figures were not authoritative leaders but rather peers, for we find inspiration in the stories of people seemingly like ourselves who recount overcoming the same troubles. The discourses that circulate in an RI are powerful largely because of their legitimation by the social body: the inmate is surrounded by a community of others who are undergoing the same transformation and share the same motivation to interpret it positively. As Barker (1989: 27) said of New Religious Movements, regardless of the content of their teachings, 'often it is loyalty to those relationships that have subsequently developed which will keep people in the group.'

Two key features of performative regulation are the *performance of conformity* by individual inmates, as a form of identity work, and the *mutual surveillance* of these performances by fellow inmates in a community of peers. Members play to each other as rule-followers as well as intransigents, performing their commitment to the 'good inmate' role; this may involve the self-presentational strategies of dramatic realization and idealization (Goffman 1959; see Chapter 4 above). These identity claims are scrutinized by the peer group as a critically judgemental audience, who may or may not accept them as sincerely authentic (Weinberg 1996, 2005; Paik 2006). Meanwhile, of course, these audience members are themselves actors, who are engaged in the same projects of reinvention and attempting to convey the same impression of dedication. The overall effect is an emergent, collective team performance (see Chapter 5 above) of obedience, which strengthens each member's motivation for being there and inclination to remain.

The inmate culture is responsible for managing members' moral careers and status passages through the institution (see Chapter 6 above). Actors respond to each other's perceived progress along trajectories of reinvention, challenging and sanctioning those who seem not to be adhering to the rules. Individuals understand their own progress and reinvention not only in terms of the teachings of authoritative leaders and official programme rhetoric, but also in terms of how significant others (fellow inmates) are regarding them and evaluating their conduct; 'progress' is understood in relative terms. Indeed, this may be a motivating factor that explains why people join institutions to transform themselves rather than going it alone: sociability is a potent communicative medium for institutional discourses to flow through and a powerful vehicle of change. Through its dramaturgical deployment and negotiation, therefore, power in the RI is not only discursively constitutive but also *interactively productive* of identities.

## Religious and spiritual communities

The first type of RI includes those that people join as a matter of faith, seeking spiritual enlightenment. There is a quest for knowledge and understanding, a promise of salvation and a willingness to submit to the authority of leaders who provide instruction in the interpretation of doctrines. Wallis and Bruce (1992: 10–11) define religion as the actions, beliefs and institutions people create to orient themselves to impersonal powers that are perceived to have the capacity to intervene in human affairs. However, in spiritual RIs, the object of worship is different: the sacred, mysterious force that inmates ultimately seek to understand is not a transcendent god or spirit but their own self-identities, as idealized potential.

The emergence of these RIs in contemporary Western cultures can be contextualized as a backlash against secularization: '... the process whereby religious thinking, practice and institutions lose social significance' (Wilson 1966: 14). Parallel trends of rationalization – a disenchanted loss of belief in magical, spiritual and supernatural forces (Weber 1922) – and desacralization – the rolling back of the 'sacred canopy' that had provided comforting order and meaning to the phenomenological lifeworld (Berger 1969) – are resisted through a counter-trend of resacralization (Greeley 1973): the resurgence of faith but channelled into secular institutions. Davie (1994) suggests that religion has survived but simply changed form: there has been a decline in belonging but not in believing. In the absence of the supernatural, we develop an amorphous, eclectic interest in all matters spiritual, which Davie calls 'common religion'.

## Seminars of the self

One group of secular 'self-religions' (Heelas 1984) promise to absolve the individual through regimes of holistic improvement, of mind, body and spirit. The 'New Age' dawned in the 1970s as an ideological counter-discourse to the materialism and mass consumption of capitalism, advocating a 'return to nature', traditional or simpler lifestyles and collectivist values. Yet the movement itself suggests values of neoliberalism and individualist self-interest. Identity reinvention is rewarded by the transcendent bliss of self-actualization, but must be fervently worked at. Furthermore, New Age adherents practise their faith through consumption, whether individually, by visiting health food shops, buying crystals or listening to self-hypnosis CDs, or collectively, by attending seminars, groups and workshops. They are often eclectic in their approach, dabbling in the practices like leisure activities (cf. Bellah 1967), to cultivate an overall sense of being 'spiritual'. In what Bruce (1995: 113) calls the 'paradox of naturalism', New Age rhetoric invites individuals to celebrate their uniqueness by using standard, prefabricated consumables.

> We are supposed to 'just be yourself' but we attain that authentic state by working hard to change into the sort of person the instructor or therapist or 'resource person' thinks we ought to be. . . . these modern techniques are not designed to help us conform to an external ethical code and better to glorify god. They are designed to make us happy: to allow us to fulfil our human potential. (Bruce 1995: 113–14)

A subset of these RIs are World-Affirming cults (Wallis 1984) that celebrate the values of individual achievement, career success and financial gain as means of personal fulfilment within the secular world. Transcendental Meditation (TM) involves learning techniques of meditation and developing a personal mantra, in order to achieve a calm, positive and sharply focused state of mind: by channelling one's mental energies into the self, we can become more efficient and effective. Scientology similarly claims to enhance a follower's mental health, confidence and self-efficacy. By following a course of Dianetic Therapy, members are taught ways of erasing 'engrams', or schematic memories that are thought to be preventing them from realizing their true potential: the aim is 'to make the able more able' and 'to confront past failures in order to get on with being successful' (Rolph 1973: 19–20). These belief systems are taught through seminars, workshops and conferences, which members attend like a weekly church service, becoming progressively more committed to their new identity as a moral career trajectory (see Chapter 6 above).

Vipassana Meditation is an ancient Indian technique that has become popular in the West by promising 'the total eradication of mental impurities and the resultant highest happiness of full liberation' (Vipassana Meditation website). However, the passage to this enlightened state is framed as a serious venture demanding hard work. It involves ten-day residential courses at retreat centres, where members are expected to renounce any ritual practices associated with other religions, such as prayer, bead counting, singing and dancing: this is a greedy institution (Coser 1974) that demands total commitment to its teachings. Vipassana students follow a strict 'Code of Discipline' that has Foucauldian overtones. In order to focus completely on meditation, they must remain silent, abstain from sexual activity, intoxicants and eating after midday, and dress modestly without any 'body decoration' such as jewellery. Students are expected to maintain a 'Noble Silence' by avoiding not only speech but also written and non-verbal communication with each other, and even the instructors can only be consulted at certain times of day. Yet the daily schedule here is peppered with sessions of 'Group Meditation', a confounding contradiction in terms.

This latter point highlights an intriguing paradox of spiritual RIs: that people should join a collectivist institution and immerse themselves in such a totalizing social environment, when their aim is to pursue highly individualistic methods of self-reflection. Perhaps members perceive a value in subjecting themselves to the disciplinary gaze of peer surveillance, without which they feel unable to exert sufficient self-control. Performative regulation occurs as members internalize a sense of collective scrutiny, which they then use to discipline themselves.

## Rebranding religion: the Alpha Course

In response to popular conceptions of the faith as being old-fashioned and irrelevant to younger generations, apologists have attempted to repackage Christianity to appeal to a new market of increasingly dubious and disillusioned people, who nevertheless show a thirsty quest for meaning. The Alpha Course is targeted at sceptics, lapsed believers, agnostics and those with a mild curiosity. It lasts ten weeks, incorporating a weekend away, and aims to provide 'an opportunity to explore life and the Christian faith, in a friendly, open and informal environment' (Alpha Course website). Alpha courses are designed to be accessible and inclusive: they are taught by young, dynamic leaders, free of charge, held in civic venues, make frequent references to popular culture, and are tailored to the vernacular language of their target audiences. Thus alongside the standard programme, there are specialist variants such as Youth Alpha, Student Alpha, Senior Alpha, Alpha in the Workplace, Alpha for the Forces and Alpha for Prisons, each of which is advertised using a different discursive style (see Scott 2011).

Started by a charismatic clergyman, Nicky Gumbel, the course has become routinized into a standardized lecture series that can be attended at a variety of institutional outlets: a 'McFaith' of sorts (cf. Ritzer 2004). The lecture topics cover such questions as 'Is there more to life than this?', 'How can we have faith?' and 'Why and how should I tell others?' These are followed by informal discussions in small groups with a facilitator, in which 'guests' (as members are called) are encouraged to question and challenge the lecture content. Critical reflection is the hallmark of the Alpha Course and is used to distinguish it from more traditional Christian instruction: members are positioned not as passive recipients of a message, let alone victims of brainwashing, but rather as equals in an interactive, democratic discussion.

However, the exercise of power here is evident, albeit repackaged in a subtler and more insidious form. Authority stems not from a single charismatic leader, but rather from the actions of peer facilitators (cf. Bauman 2000), who oversee the recruitment of new members and manage their moral careers of reinvention. In a Channel 4 television documentary, gonzo journalist Jon Ronson (2009; see also 2013) pointed to Alpha's marketing strategies of employing friendly, jocular, down-to-earth preachers; the vision of 'young pretty Christian women serving food'; and the publicity generated by celebrity converts, such as Geri Haliwell and Bear Grylls. Ronson argues that the most seductive element of Alpha is the ostensibly benign, non-directive, non-confrontational atmosphere of the small group meetings, through which members believe that they are making a free choice to learn. This manufactured 'niceness' obscures what is in fact a carefully organized scheme for processing inmates through a moral career of religious conversion: 'Alpha is all about rigorously structured, almost mathematical niceness, and this structure is a huge success. It's hard not to feel warm towards these nice people who share their lives in small groups and only put the pressure on once, but even then it's just engagingly flaky' (Ronson 2009).

## Summer camps and festivals

Other Christian retreats hold more of a festival flavour, as worshippers are invited to celebrate and revel in their faith, while welcoming new

members into it. These events evoke Durkheim's (1912) description
of the 'effervescent assemblies' that characterized traditional religious
worship. For example, Soul Survivor is a movement aimed at younger
people, which organizes festivals, fundraising events, community projects and voluntary work schemes around the world, bringing young
people together to worship. It incorporates Soul Action, an awareness-
raising programme, as well as guidance on Bible study, discussion
groups for those new to the faith, a magazine and an online shop.
Equally important as the substantive content of the materials studied
is the socially mediated process through which this is communicated.
Soul Action involves an event called The Noise, in which groups of
teenagers work together on local community projects as an expression
of their faith. The concept of noise is invoked both literally, to refer to
the boisterousness of adolescents, and metaphorically, to refer to the
power of their religious fervour.

Spring Harvest is a more temporally bound, annual event held over
Easter: billed as an interdenominational Christian conference, it is held
in a UK holiday camp and seeks to cultivate a jubilant atmosphere.
The schedule involves communal prayer, Bible readings, seminars
and workshops, but these are integrated with 'fun' sport and leisure
activities, including a carousel, dodgems and an adventure playground.
Spring Harvest, like Soul Survivor, invokes the services of charismatic
preachers and activists, such as Steve Chalke and Tim Hughes, who
are venerated as celebrities within the community for their ability to
communicate with young people. The atmosphere is punctuated by
regular effervescent assemblies of collective worship. For example, the
Big Top is a nightly celebration that brings all campers together for
prayer, public lectures, discussion, song and dance, complementing the
more informal meetings that they have throughout the day in seminars,
lounges and 'café-churches'. The overall effect is to create a warm, supportive atmosphere that encloses the individual and confirms their faith.
Indeed, the power of collective ritual practices is explicitly recognized
by the organizers as being central to the transformative experience:
'Whatever your church background, there's something special about
worshipping our God, our creator, in the company of thousands of
other people, with one heart and one mind – to praise God' (Spring
Harvest website).

## Disciplinary regimes

A very different kind of RI is that based upon the principles of the
military and/or penal institutions. Disciplinary power (Foucault 1975)
is used as a tool of reinvention, in the name of punishment, reform or

character building, and is valued as an end in itself. Members willingly submit to the authority of an expert gaze through displays of uniformity, rehearsals of a discursive rhetoric and mechanisms of peer surveillance. Central to this process are the interaction rituals of observance through which members perform their commitment: drills, orders and regimes are followed with a 'military' precision.

An interesting paradox is that whereas traditional penal TIs, such as prisons, have become increasingly concerned with therapeutic aims and inmates' welfare, some non-penal RIs pride themselves on being harsh and dictatorial, re-mobilizing the very disciplinary techniques that have fallen by the wayside. Rose (2000) points to the rise of new 'technologies of freedom', whereby the net of surveillance is cast wider, so that risk and dangerousness are increasingly identified in law-abiding, healthy populations. A new set of 'control professionals' (Rose 2000) has emerged to map out the terrain of normal problems of living (Szasz 1961), such as relationship breakdown, unemployment and general unhappiness. A common underlying goal is the 'ethical reconstruction of the excluded' (Rose 2000: 335) through processes of responsibilization, remoralization and resocialization.

## Military careers

During peacetime, the decision to join the armed forces is a voluntary career choice pursued in the name of self-improvement, with expressed moral aims of 'character building' (Brookes 2003), 'knuckling down' and 'making a real (wo)man' of oneself (Hale 2008). With its connotations of strength, endurance and toughness, military training provides important symbolic resources (Zittoun et al. 2003) with which to perform masculine identities (Agostino 1998; Connell & Pearse 2015) and is perceived as a rite of passage to male adulthood (Klein 1999; Hale 2008). Through its alignment with the state, the military is regarded as a 'respectable' establishment that can keep wayward youth on the straight and narrow, and repair the damage caused by deviance and criminality. A large proportion of army recruits come from working-class backgrounds and use the career path to perform composite class, gender and national identities (Sasson-Levy 2003). The idea of being willing to fight and die for one's country is of course imbued with symbolic values of heroism and bravery that distinguish military personnel and veterans as objects of veneration (Thomson 1995).

The corporeal effects of physical training undertaken in military service reshape the soldier's body as an emblem of fitness, self-discipline and perseverance – akin to the symbolic meanings embodied by gym fanatics (Crossley 2006a) and anorexics (Bordo 1993). The physically strong, fit body is paraded as a trophy, representing months or years of hard work, discipline and commitment. For many, it is this process that gives military careers their appeal, as much as the end product itself: the idea of gaining control over one's body, mastering instinct, spontaneity and laziness, and being able to follow instructions to the letter, day after day and without complaint. The servicemen in Hale's study felt proudly that the physical and mental arduousness of the work had transformed their masculinities in ways that distinguished them from their civilian counterparts. They performed 'representational labour' (Hale 2008: 309) by constructing self-narratives about making the transition to a new identity. Ronnie, a Royal Marine, said that he had developed 'a pair of bollocks . . . I've matured a lot earlier than my friends' (2008: 326), while army sergeant Graham felt that enduring difficulty had given him a moral advantage: 'It's probably given me a tiny bit of hardship and actually having to overcome the hardship . . . because some people, they don't experience hardship you know. People are born with silver spoons . . . some people probably think that hardship is not being able to use their mobile phone' (2008: 326–7).

The social context of army life also holds a unique appeal, through the forging of meaningful peer relationships. Another respondent in Hale's study, a commissioned officer from the Royal Marine Commandos, reflected on how being confined alongside others to endure a gruelling shared experience created deep bonds of intimacy that were equally important for 'character building':

> If you go through training with a batch of mates, um, it's not the most enjoyable part of life and through that shared hardships. But I liked it because again, playing in a team. Because you have a mutual suffering if you like and without sounding over-hard here, it brings you closer cos it does. I mean guys get worn away to the minimum and everyone struggles at some point and you get together and help each other. So by the end of training, you know someone as well as anyone, probably as well as their girlfriends or whatever. (Hale 2008: 321)

Mechanisms of informal social control operate within the interaction context of military inmate culture. In his ethnographic account of an American army barracks, Westley (1968: 201) observed that 'the ebb and flow of army life was in response to many forces besides army regulation'. Most notably, this meant the ways in which soldiers related to each other as a primary group (Cooley 1902), perceiving their common status and circumstances to engender shared values. Removed from their civilian lives and forced into this strange new situation, the soldiers 'clung to each other and to army discipline' (Westley 1968: 206), finding comfort in routines and predictability (cf. Giddens

1984). New recruits were socialized into the inmate culture, as more experienced members helped them practise the required rituals: they would rehearse drills, test each other in preparation for skills and knowledge tests, check their uniforms and kit boxes, and generally support each other's identity performances. This in turn ensured that the battalion presented an orderly, coherent team impression (Goffman 1959; see Chapter 5 above) to their senior officers: they disciplined both body and mind under the governmental gaze of inspections and examinations.

Interestingly, however, this status hierarchy was more flexible outside the immediate performative context of the working day, indicating processes of negotiated order. When relaxing out of hours, there was an unspoken camaraderie between the sergeants, officers and privates as they colluded in 'working the system' (Goffman 1961a: 189). Alongside the formal system of bureaucratic rules, there was an informal negotiated order of rule-bending and fudging (Day & Day 1977) into which new recruits were socialized, and through which they learned what it really meant to be a member of this society. 'Sergeants never seemed actually to break the rules but rather to bend them to their needs, often to facilitate action which would be obstructed by formal requirements' (Westley 1968: 201). In the sergeants' mess area, men would discuss over breakfast the arrangements and resources they could request to make their duties easier that day, and concoct a suitable cover story: for example, trucks could be secured by persuading the motor pool sergeant to declare a vehicle out of commission and put it aside for the men to collect. This 'staging talk' (Goffman 1959) formed a significant part of the routine work of army existence, and helped to make daily life run smoothly.

Negotiation was further facilitated by an indulgency pattern (Gouldner 1955) of power, whereby senior officers would turn a blind eye to minor rule infractions by their charges, in the interests of practical efficiency and harmonious working relations. For example, coms (lower-status soldiers) would take equipment and supplies from the stores without permission rather than going through the formal channels to obtain written authorization from the lieutenant, and so the contents listed in the official inventory rarely matched what was actually in the stores at any point. Any discrepancies that were discovered could be written off as 'lost in battle', so that no awkward questions were asked. Similarly, the coms indulged their sergeant by arriving punctually for roll call, knowing that he would be blamed if they were late; in return, the sergeant would pretend not to notice any silent responses, or decline to call the name of a soldier he knew to be absent. This is an example of the dramaturgical technique of 'communication out of character' (Goffman

1959; see Chapter 5 above), whereby team-mates collusively present to their audience one ostensible definition of the situation, while tacitly acknowledging that something else is really the case.

## Makeover miracles

Another set of disciplinary RIs is those dedicated to transforming the physical appearance of the body in the name of beauty, fashion and healthiness. They may be institutional sites that facilitate the pursuit of these goals, such as fitness gyms, beauty clinics and spa resorts, or more amorphous collections of ideas, values and activities, such as the discourses and practices of dieting, which consume an actor's consciousness throughout the day. While ostensibly relaxing, even self-indulgent, activities, these simultaneously aim to bring the body into line with culturally normative standards. The paradoxical effect is to 'discipline and pamper' (Black 2004), as revealed, for example, when we speak of self-imposed 'beauty regimes'.

### *Making the body fit*
Discourses of health and fitness pervade everyday life, creating a widespread and normalized belief that the body needs to be disciplined, toned, detoxified, neatly contained and checked through regular monitoring practices (Lupton 1995; Cederström & Spicer 2015). A moral panic surrounds obesity (Monaghan 2007) as the symbolic anathema of self-control, orderliness and containment (Bordo 1993), which is addressed by fad diets, sliming clubs and other regimental interventions. Similar meanings are embedded in discourses of exercise as 'fitness regimes'. Crossley's (2006a) ethnography of a UK gym revealed how patrons saw the pursuit of a toned body as an ongoing project (Shilling 1993), detaching their disciplinary mind from the object to be governed. They would engage in 'motivations talk' with fellow gymgoers, establishing the standards against which they evaluated their own progress in 'post-workout reflections'.

Weight loss retreats, or 'fat camps', are residentially segregated organizations that employ the principles of a military boot camp, albeit in a somewhat tongue-in-cheek way. Members are usually young people, sent by their parents but voluntarily agreeing as they imagine a healthier and happier future self. While these camps have a therapeutic rationale, aiming to address the emotional reasons behind eating behaviour (Walker et al. 2003), this is pursued through a strict regime. The daily timetable of weigh-ins, scheduled outdoor activities, nutritionally balanced meals and counselling, interspersed with designated periods of self-reflection, aims to effect long-term changes in behaviour after residents return home. A typical itinerary is prescribed by the Wellspring Academy in the USA:

> Stretch and morning walk
> Breakfast followed by self-monitoring
> Rock-climbing trip
> Lunch followed by self-monitoring
> Culinary training
> Mid-afternoon snack
> Game of football
> Dinner followed by self-monitoring
> Talent show
>
> (Wellspring Academy (a) website)

Wellspring's references to 'self-monitoring' after each meal suggest that inmates are taught to internalize a surveillant gaze over their attitude to food, in order to reform their thoughts, feelings and behaviour. However, peer interaction is built into the design of the camps' institutional arrangements (through the collective activities of the rock climbing trip, football game and talent show), and this informal support is intended to provide as much motivation as the formal diet and exercise regimes. Parents bear witness to transformations that reinvent not only the child's body, but also their whole identity:

> It was a life time experience for John, he has grown and matured, he is less angry and he doesn't get that easily upset, maybe because he has more self confidence and self esteem. You made an excellent job, you gave him a new image, a new self, and our family life has changed for the better too, since it was one of our major worries and a constant reason to fight with John. (Wellspring Academy (b) website)

*Reality TV*
Reality television shows, which document the lives of supposedly ordinary people undergoing life-changing experiences, hold a voyeuristic appeal: we like to peer in and watch other people, whose behaviour provides a yardstick of moral standards (Kilborn 2003). A famous example is *Big Brother* (Channel 4; Channel 5), a game show based on the dystopic vision of surveillance documented in Orwell's novel *Nineteen Eighty-Four* (1949). The *Big Brother* house is a residentially segregated, impermeable institution to which contestants voluntarily and competitively commit themselves for a number of weeks in the name of psychological experimentation and self-development. Identity reinvention follows the pattern of a temporally compressed rite of passage (Turner 1967; see Chapter 6 above). There is first a stage of separation,

as contestants enter the house, leaving their previous identities behind
and imagining future selves, followed by a transitional or liminal period,
when they are 'betwixt and between' those two statuses, and finally an
emergence of the new self who has learned from the experience.

Housemates willingly submit to the authoritarian gaze of Big Brother
as a disembodied figurehead, who is only accessed in abstraction,
through a voice piped into the Diary Room. Far from resenting being
under surveillance, contestants positively welcome this as a benign and
calming, constant presence. They seek solace in the Diary Room as a
Foucauldian confession booth, and call upon Big Brother to intervene
and adjudicate in arguments, such as the vote-rigging duplicity of
'Nasty Nick' in 2000 (Ritchie 2000) and the media-fuelled 'racism row'
between Jade Goody and Shilpa Shetty in 2007 (Holmwood & Brook
2007).

Another set of reality TV shows address the aesthetic reinvention of
the fashioned body (Entwistle 2015), through morally transformative
correctional training. Overweight bodies and frumpy attire are framed
as symptoms of low self-esteem, and the transformation of appearance
is regarded not as superficial or frivolous, but rather as an opportunity
to liberate one's authentic inner self. Trinny and Susannah, the sarto-
rial gurus of *What Not to Wear* (BBC One), began this trend in the
early 2000s, presenting a united front against unfashionable clothing
as an assault upon dignity and self-respect. Contestants underwent a
Goffmanesque mortification ritual (see Chapter 6 above) by standing,
stripped down to their underwear, inside a three-way mirrored booth
while receiving a brutally honest, critical evaluation of their fashion
sensibility. Body parts were scrutinized for flaws, which were identified
as shameful objects through derogatory terms ('wobbly tummy', 'bingo
wings', 'saddle bags') to be disguised with technologies of discipline
('control pants' being an infamous example). This echoes feminist
critiques of the beauty and fashion industries as vehicles of corporeal
regulation (Bartky 1990; Black 2004).

Correlates of this model focus on eating behaviour as a signifier of
presumed moral character. Gillian McKeith's *You Are What You Eat*
(Channel 4) was perhaps the most infamously harsh and militaristic of
these programmes: an offender who had transgressed cultural norms
of weight and fitness was identified, paid a surprise visit by McKeith
in a mock arrest and carried off to her home for a period of reflection
and reform. The contestant was confronted with a table filled with a
week's worth of their current diet, as well as graphic representations of
its nutritional sinfulness (rows of sugar sacks, blocks of lard), as another
mortifying degradation ceremony (Garfinkel 1956). Breaking down
into tears, they resolved to change their ways by adhering to McKeith's

strict diet and exercise regime. Similar formats can be found in other, more recent British TV programmes, such as Channel 4's *Supersize vs Superskinny* (in which extremely overweight and underweight people swap diets in a totally enclosed 'feeding clinic') and *Secret Eaters* (which uses hidden cameras and secret detectives to spy on families, exposing shameful discrepancies between what they say they eat and what they really eat). By the end of all of these programmes, contestants are shown with flattering photography and a new outfit to emphasize their weight loss (or weight gain for the superskinnies), and make a statement to camera about how radically their quality of life has improved.

Skeggs and Wood (2009) argue critically against these types of shows from a material feminist perspective, pointing to the relevance of social class. Locating reality TV within a wider cultural trend of individualistic lifestyle politics, they argue that the transformations of selfhood taking place are structurally embedded within a 'moral economy' of social values. Drawing on Bourdieusian theory, they argue that this system normatively regulates the reproduction of *classed* identities within a hierarchy of 'taste' and distinction (cf. Bourdieu 1979). Despite often being dismissed as 'trash TV', the reality TV genre allows for the circulation of 'dangerous discourses' that pejoratively represent the values and lifestyles of working-class people. Makeover shows hold up specimens of working-class 'tastelessness' or 'shamelessness' to inspection, criticism and ridicule from middle-class audiences, who enjoy exercising a surveillant gaze over them.

A recent example is the media furore surrounding the programme *Benefits Street* (Channel 4), which depicted the residents of a socially deprived neighbourhood as 'welfare scroungers': claiming state benefits to fund a life of petty crime and unemployment. While left-wing critics argued that this was perpetuating a misrepresentative stereotype of 'poverty porn' (Burrell 2014), the programme-makers also presented a moralistic counter-discourse that emphasized the possibility of escaping such a 'lifestyle'. The series sympathetically depicted certain characters (such as the matriarchal figure White Dee) as working-class heroes, who were striving to transcend their situation by seeking employment or holding onto 'traditional British values' (Brooker 2014).

Skeggs and Wood (2009) observed that these kinds of programmes often have a twofold narrative, involving first this invitation to sneer at, disapprove of and be morally judgemental of the participants, and then a dramatic transformation of them in accordance with middle-class values. Essentially, working-class people are taught how to be more like the middle class, by emulating their values, attitudes and lifestyle behaviours. For example, shows like *Ladette to Lady* (ITV) teach young women the techniques of etiquette and refinement, while others like

*You Are What You Eat* advocate a middle-class understanding of what constitutes a 'nutritious' diet and 'healthy' lifestyle. Skeggs and Wood suggest that the participants, who symbolically represent working-class and middle-class values, are pitted against each other in a battle of wills, authority and moral values. This echoes Skeggs' (2004) analysis of the notion of 'respectability' as a cultural discursive construction associated with the middle class, which is used as a standard by which deviant 'others' are morally evaluated.

## Rehabilitative clinics

A third type of RI is that with a focus on mental health: therapeutic communities, self-help groups and other semi-voluntary organizations function to provide social and emotional support for those who self-define as troubled souls (Gubrium & Holstein 2001) and seek to find meaning in their confusion. In these institutions, recovery is framed as a journey of self-discovery, to be experienced as a personal triumph of identity work.

### Therapeutic communities

Therapeutic communities (TCs) represent a deliberate attempt at detachment from the institutional context of mainstream psychiatry, posing a challenge to its conventional structure, function, leadership patterns, staff–patient relations and distribution of power (Morrice 1979). The movement began in the 1930s with London's Tavistock Clinic, finding its heyday in the 1960s and 1970s anti-psychiatry movement, with notable projects including Kingsley Hall, The Arbours and the Paddington Day Hospital (Spandler 2006). People who had been labelled mentally ill were taught that they were in fact hyper-sane, and that only by indulging in their symptoms could they liberate their true selves. The role of the therapist was to nurture the individual's journey through 'madness' as an existential voyage of self-discovery (Laing 1967), surrounded by a blanket of supportive others.

Contemporary TCs are residential, site-specific homes for those with mental health issues, addictions and personality disorders, and are run in a participatory, democratic manner with clients working alongside staff to negotiate aspects of their treatment. In particular, there is an emphasis on group-based, milieu therapy and co-operation on practical tasks, rather than reliance on medication; clients and staff may share a living space, and both contribute to the organization of the institution's daily running (Whitely 1970). The organizations pride themselves on housing 'democratic citizens' rather than block patients, and responding to the social and moral implications of their behaviour (Talbot & Miller 1971). One of the four key principles of the TC identified by Morrice (1979) is reality confrontation, which takes place in group psychotherapy and milieu therapy sessions, whereby members hold their peers accountable for their actions within the community and issue sanctions against any conduct that breaches their democratically agreed rules.

Mahony (1979) provides a reflective account of his time at the Henderson Hospital in London during 1972–3, when he was 22 years old. He conjectures that the mundane aspects of everyday interaction were as important as the formal therapy sessions in effecting a sense of personal development and therapeutic progress. Here again we see the significance of informal socialization in the RI: peer monitoring occurred backstage (Goffman 1959), during community downtime, when members expressed mutual concern over, but also engaged in ruthless scrutiny of, each other's welfare:

> The groups themselves weren't the places that things 'happened'. They gave cerebral insight and stirred feelings up, but it was during the unstructured times of the day, weekends, night-time, down the pub etc. when the intellectual insights of the day or the week or the month percolated down to the 'gut'. . . . Because of the expectations raised and the fixed notion that we were going to 'do the business', i.e. sort out our own and everyone else's problems, within the meetings you were on your therapeutic guard, expecting, even welcoming, criticism or unfavourable analysis of your behaviour from your fellow members. . . . the fact that we were living together made our relationships much more 'real' and valuable than if we had only met each other for a few hours a day in our therapeutic roles. (Mahony 1979: 86)

Consequently, Mahony began to identify himself as 'one of them' and to accept, even enjoy, his newfound group identity by fraternizing with his fellow inmates as the 'Family'. He found himself rising through the ranks to positions of greater leadership and status, chairing community meetings and organizing games. Despite the stigma he had anticipated, he found it liberating to surrender to the effervescent current of the group (cf. Durkheim 1912): '. . . the worst had happened, yet I felt freer, more relaxed, less on my guard' (Mahony 1979: 85). Eventually, his allegiance shifted so completely that he came to venerate the community as superior to the outside world, and defended this boundary from the inside. This echoes the earlier discussion in this chapter of processes of institutionalization within 'greedy' TIs (Wing 1962; Coser 1974):

> We were a miniature army complete with uniform, codes, rules and degrees of status. The outside – work, work-mates, legal restrictions,

conventions, morality, family, career, the future – all meant nothing. Outsiders' rules didn't apply to us, only to the sheep, the mugs, the grey people who couldn't see the con, the lie. The 'I' became a 'We', yet the 'We' reinforced and perpetuated the 'Them'. Part of our kicks was to shock, horrify and bewilder everyone on first contact. . . . We drew an absolute distinction between Family and outsiders. We had all the resources we needed within the gang. (Mahony 1979: 77)

More recently, Larsen (2007) conducted an ethnography of OPUS, a biopsychosocial early intervention service in Copenhagen for people who had experienced first-episode psychosis. Alongside the experiential crisis evoked by severe mental illness, the process of recovery effected a further transition in the individual's sense of self, insofar as treatment provision was mediated by a social network of peers who provided 'symbolic healing'. The OPUS programme lasted for two years and combined lowest effective dosage medication with individual coun-selling, family therapy, group therapy and social skills workshops, in addition to practical and financial assistance in the areas of housing and employment. Peer mentoring was important: instead of being depend-ent on professional experts, members were taught the requisite skills to analyse themselves and each other:

> In the [family] groups clients and relatives were educated about mental illness, and through concrete problem-solving exercises relatives, mainly parents, but occasionally also siblings, grandparents or partners, were advised how they could support the client. In the social skills training (SST) groups staff were identified as 'trainers' (*trænere*) and the aim was, aside from educating clients about medical notions of mental illness, to train them in using cognitive and behavioural coping techniques. The intention was that clients would use this knowledge and skill in their everyday lives to better identify and control their symptoms to prevent psychotic relapse and improve their quality of life. (Larsen 2007: 339)

As 'totally' encompassing environments, TCs shape not only clients' individual relationships with staff but also their more general percep-tions of social reality (Bloor et al. 1988). In phenomenological terms, they create a new symbolic lifeworld (Berger & Luckmann 1966) of shared meanings and motivations that have an internal logic within the context of the institutional programme and are upheld by its members. Bloor et al. call this process the 'supplantation of the lifeworld', as one vision of reality is replaced by another:

> [Therapeutic work] can transform any mundane event in the community by redefining that event in the light of some therapeutic paradigm. . . . to

so redefine an everyday event as an occasion or a topic of therapy sets it apart and transforms it, much as the profane is transformed into the sacred by religious belief and ceremony. . . . Any and every event and activity in the therapeutic community is potentially open to such redefinition: there is no nook or cranny of resident life that is not open to scrutiny and potentially redefinable in therapeutic terms. (Bloor et al. 1988: 5)

Drawing on Durkheim's (1912) theory of religion, Bloor et al. suggest that the TC develops a reified, sacred status in the eyes of its members, taking on a mystical charisma that charms and seduces potential converts. This was illustrated by Wiley's (1991) ethnography of Quaesta, a private residential TC for people with schizophrenia who had become disillusioned with conventional psychotherapy. Located in an affluent area of California, the community combined luxurious living quarters with countercultural ideals and practices, such as mysticism, hypnosis, meditation, rebirthing and psychedelia. It followed a strictly controlled regime of timetabled activities, including group therapy, special issue groups (on such themes as addiction, sexuality and separation) and community meetings, interspersed with nurturing recreational activities such as cooking, gardening and artwork.

The Quaesta community attempted to create a 'moral milieu' to transform the client's self through a sequence of four stages, echoing Goffman's (1961a) moral career (see Chapter 6 above): Phase One entailed bonding to the community; Phase Two involved assuming responsibility for one's past behaviour; Phase Three was a transitional stage of preparing to live autonomously; and Phase Four was the final stage of enlightenment and self-actualization. The therapeutic milieu provided a new way of seeing that was claimed to be superior to the civilian world: '. . . feelings are the central legitimate focus of talk. If this were done in the everyday world, it would be regarded as inappropriate, in bad taste, or intrusive. In this community, emotion and feeling talk were of the essence' (Wiley 1991: 146).

Wiley suggests that the charismatic authority of the founder was transferred to the community itself, which was venerated as a symbolic expression of his values. Members came to worship the TC as a *sui generis* reified structure (Durkheim 1898), or microcosmic society, which they called 'The Culture'. They began to personify The Culture as an *analyst* (Hinshelwood & Manning 1979), and believe in its magical powers to transform their troubled selves:

. . . the individual journey to the soul becomes the concern of the community. The space of the community provides a home for the lost or disturbed soul of the resident. . . . Quaesta offers a culture or shared value system that provides meaning, and a context for a strong, caring and responsive community. . . . There is a sense of mutuality at Quaesta, a feeling that 'we are in this together'. . . . Your belief system disappears. (Wiley 1991: 147)

However, the group cohesiveness of TCs can have a darker side, as the benign act of 'looking out for each other' slips into the mutual monitoring of conduct. The intense insularity of the totally encompassing peer group means that solidarity can breed conflict, co-dependency and institutionalization. Cliques and divisions may form within the community, so that a once cohesive inmate culture splinters into abrasive subgroups (Whitely 1970). Residents may form a self-imposed hierarchy on the basis of their disorder labels, orientations to the staff and stages of recovery (Hoffmann 2006). Milieu therapy groups can be experienced as uncomfortably confrontational, even degrading, in their demands for total self-disclosure and exposure to peer scrutiny (Burnett 2001). Recovered selves, like the 'cleaned up' drug addicts in Burnett's (2001) study, may feel so immersed in the safe familiarity of their TC's routines that they experience institutionalization and release anxiety (Goffman 1961a) about the prospect of re-entering the civilian world. Many other ex-TC members describe this process of readjustment as a culture shock (Poulopoulos & Tsibouki 1998).

## Self-help groups and Twelve Step programmes

A second type of rehabilitative RI is the self-help or support group, run by and for people who experience a condition. As Crossley (2006b) notes, the twenty-first century has seen a rise in the number of mental health service user-led groups and movements, whose members unashamedly identify with their disorder labels. While such groups may have a leader-facilitator, this tends to be a recovered or recovering member from their midst: as Bauman (2000) suggests, peer guides carry far greater authority than traditional 'experts' in such groups, because of the authenticity implied by their personal experience.

However, critics argue that the insularity of these groups creates a dependency that encourages people to cling to the notion of recovery as a long-term self-narrative, extending beyond the level of local experience to the life course as a whole. Hayes (2000) suggests that some people move from one self-help group to another for a succession of different lifestyle problems, effectively addicted to the idea of addiction – or, rather, to the process of recovery from it. They become serial career addicts, who never finally make it back into the 'healthy', civilian world because of their anxieties about having to be able to cope without the supportive peer group. Furedi describes 'victim addicts' who engage in 'trauma-tourism': regarding themselves as being at the mercy of a series of misfortunes, they appeal to notions of victimhood and vulnerability to substantiate their claims to therapeutic services. He writes critically of this 'fetish of addiction' as involving 'the medicalization of bad habits' (2004: 122), whereby lifestyle behaviours that would previously have been regarded as merely deviant are recast as mental or emotional disorders of impulse control.

'Twelve Step' recovery programmes involve graduated withdrawal from substances, behaviours and relationships that are thought to be damaging. While the model originated from Alcoholics Anonymous (AA) in the 1930s, it has since been applied to a plethora of newly defined addictions, from smoking to shopping, gambling, debt and Internet use. As we saw in Chapter 6, progress along the Twelve Step trajectory is an interactionally managed moral career, whereby the interaction rituals and negotiations of meaning between participants create the emergent 'recovering self' (Denzin 1987). The meetings follow a common formula that is repeated week after week (Hoffmann 2006), constructing and consolidating definitions of addiction and addictive personalities.

Recovery, in these groups, is framed as a state of constant becoming: one can never claim to be fully recovered but rather must remain aware of the potential for relapse. Addiction is personified as the 'trickster within' (Weinberg 1996), who is lurking and seeking opportunities to lure the vulnerable subject back. The inmate's former self must be wilfully discarded and kept at bay by constant self-reflexive identity work; abstinence from the destructive behaviour is framed as a moral responsibility. However, members are encouraged to draw on the support of the group to generate and sustain this motivation: recovery is performatively regulated through peer surveillance and interaction.

For example, Rossol (2001) shows how the 'compulsive gambler' identity was co-constructed in meetings of Gamblers Anonymous (GA). Patient-clients collectively accomplished both the medicalization of their condition as an addiction, by citing clinical terminology in their discussions of 'symptomatic' behaviour, and the reduction of their selves to the master status (Hughes 1945) of an addict, by downplaying their diversity and homogenizing their experiences. A common narrative structure could be found in the way that members recounted their biographies, drawing on this shared and mutually ratified vocabulary of motives (Mills 1940). Accounts of becoming a compulsive gambler followed the same sequential pattern: members spoke firstly of compulsion, then of 'chasing' the desired outcome, then of an escalation in their behaviour that evoked a crisis in their family life, and finally of capitulating when a loved one intervened to confront them.

Rossol argues that this narrative structure was performatively reproduced during GA meetings through the course of members' interactions,
as they engaged in three main stages of mutual biographical reconstruction. Firstly, the meanings of present and former selves were reframed
in medical terms: compulsive gambling was an illness, members were
sick, and their addictive behaviour was symptomatic. Secondly, there
was a discounting of members' backgrounds by shifting the focus to
their present, common state as institutional inmates. If they dwelled too
much upon personal experiences, participants were told, 'you've got
to let go of that. You're here now' (Rossol 2001: 329), and frequently
reminded of how the programme would affect 'us all'. Thirdly, the past
was actively reconstructed by the reinterpretation of members' past
experiences: any memorable life event was incorporated into the narrative of recovery and attributed a symbolic meaning in relation to the
final outcome of that story.

Hoffmann's (2006) study of AA similarly showed the power of peer
group interactions in co-creating members' accounts of progress and
recovery. They did not speak spontaneously, 'from the heart', but rather
gave carefully delivered versions of events according to anticipated
social reactions from the other members. This reminds us of Mead's
(1934) theory of the self as a reflexive inner dialogue between the 'I'
and the 'Me' (see Chapter 1 above), as well as Goffman's dramaturgical
perspective. Self-presentation was evident in the way that they carefully
attended to the challenge of 'telling a good story' (Hoffmann 2006) with
a familiar, convincing narrative that would be validated by their peers:

> While some members are better storytellers than others, this attribute
> is not enough to be recognized as having a good recovery program.
> Members' speech events must also capture the normative and 'stereo-
> typical' structure of speech events in order to be well received by others.
> . . . Members with a good story who embody 'good AA' can acquire
> a celebrity-like status as these 'circuit speakers' are asked to tell their
> recovery stories at local, regional, or national AA meetings . . . . Thus,
> in a somewhat strange twist of fate, the sordid trials and tribulations that
> members experienced during their active alcoholism enhance their status
> in sobriety. (Hoffmann 2006: 677)

Insofar as membership of Twelve Step groups is voluntary, and the
shared definition of the situation is that this is a harmonious, nurturing
environment, there is rarely any overt hostility between individuals.
Instead, social control operates more informally and subtly, through
mechanisms such as gossip (Gellman 1964), resigned tolerance (Mäkelä
et al. 1996) and socialization into preferred modes of identity performance. Hoffmann's (2006) AA study showed that members sought to

eradicate perceived deviations from the programme, such as 'inappropriate' emotions (anger, self-pity, jealousy), cognition (thoughts about
drinking and egocentric attitudes) and behaviour (resorting to drinking,
being dishonest or otherwise deviating from the Twelve Steps). Direct
criticism occurred only rarely, when a person transgressed one of the
group's core principles: for example, Glenda was chastised by two
fellow inmates for presenting herself as a victim and 'making excuses'
rather than taking responsibility for her drinking (Hoffmann 2006:
680). More commonly, however, criticism occurred through subtle,
non-confrontational gestures that gently showed the individual they
were stepping out of line. For example, when Jill spoke for too long,
other members would signal their frustration and annoyance by leaving
the circle to refill their coffee cups or go to the bathroom (Hoffmann
2006: 684).

In another study of AA, Pollner and Stein (2001) pointed to the
importance of *humour* in guiding the transition from an alcoholic self to
a recovering self. The intensely serious atmosphere of meetings would
be interspersed with moments of hilarity, as members laughed about
their previous misdemeanours. They expressed attitudes of shock and
disbelief, standing back from and critically reflecting upon their addictive tendencies with the benefit of hindsight. Humour enabled members
to experience their identities as dualistic, by creating a division between
their current and former selves and positioning the first as a mature and
rational partner. Moreover, by telling jokes, making self-deprecating
remarks and teasing one another, they dramaturgically enacted this division, demonstrating to each other that they had 'moved on'.

### Accomplishing authenticity

However, the publicly shared definition of reality in these groups may
be undermined by members' private interpretations of what is really
going on, implicit status claims and jostles for power. Tensions arise
particularly if members perceive internal power divisions that belie the
pretence of equality. Hoffmann (2006) argues that while groups like
AA may flatten the more obvious hierarchies of wealth, education and
social class, other factors can emerge as significant markers of status.
In particular, a member's length of time in sobriety is regarded as an
indication of their sustained and genuine commitment to recovery;
more established members assume a veteran status, based upon claims
to superior knowledge of the programme and expertise in its delivery.

Such contradictions between privately believed and publicly presented realities (Scheff 1968) remind us of the importance of collectively
upheld 'polite fictions' as a cornerstone of interaction order (Goffman
1983a; see Chapter 2 above). However, because of the importance

of conformity and uniformity within the RI, this discrepancy may be tolerated less here than in other spheres of everyday life. There is an expectation that individuals will be sincerely (Goffman 1959) committed to the programme and the institutional rhetoric, rather than merely complying instrumentally. Interactive work is therefore performed to reduce any incongruence between the two realities, aligning individual members' private beliefs with the publicly asserted team impression or 'party line' (see Chapter 5 above).

This is evidenced by the social reactions that inmates encounter as they strive to perform and be seen as *authentic*, obedient adherents to the regime – however they may feel inside. Weinberg's (1996, 2005) ethnographic study of a skid row drug rehabilitation programme in Los Angeles points to the dramaturgical stress that arises when there is a contradiction between members' avowed commitment to recovery and fellow inmates' perceptions of their true attitudes. Having committed time and energy to the programme, members felt angry and frustrated with those who seemed not to be pulling their weight. Weinberg's participants saw themselves as tough and unforgiving: 'coming from the curb' or being used to street life, their natural inclination was to mistrust others and be suspicious of their motivations. Ironically, however, this street morality contradicted the logic of the programme's emphasis on emotional intimacy: '. . . failing to trust – that is, to disclose one's authentic thoughts and feelings to one's "brothers" in the program – was [seen as] a failure to embrace one's own recovery' (Weinberg 1996: 141).

Demonstrating authenticity is a matter of strategic identity work. Members performed emotion work (Hochschild 1983) not only privately, by managing their own self-presentation, but also publicly, by managing and sanctioning the emotions shown by others, distinguishing between those who were more and less committed to the programme: '[Members] actively intervened to foster or suppress each other's emotional displays so as to bring them more completely into line with what they believed was characteristic of the local appearance of personal authenticity and successful recovery' (Weinberg 1996: 157). Weinberg identified four techniques of 'institutional emotion management' that the members used to enact and appraise authenticity. *Ideology avowal* involved citing the programme rhetoric as if it were a personal set of values, in the hope that others would believe they were speaking 'from the heart'. *Ideology exemplification* involved talking about life events and experiences in relation to this discourse, in order performatively to provide evidence that the programme worked and that they were right to believe in it. A third strategy was to *bracket out scepticism* towards others' performances, taking them at face value: staff counsellors would accept a client's apology for inappropriate behaviour while secretly regarding it with scepticism. By contrast, the fourth strategy of *emotion management* involved calling each other on perceived insincerity, as illustrated by this excerpt from a personal growth workshop:

> Matt [a second phase programme man] said, 'Okay Terry. I don't want you to take this in the wrong way, but, back in New York, we had a word for people who went through their programs and never had no problems at all, didn't relapse or nothin'. We called that skatin', and I don't want to scare you or accuse you of nothin', but the people that skated, in my experience, they fell harder than anybody else. They graduated. But it didn't last, man.'
>
> Terry replied, 'Are you sayin' I'm skating?'
>
> Matt, 'I ain't sayin' you're doin' anything . . .'
>
> Doug [a second phase programme man] interrupted Matt with, 'That's what I'm saying. You are skating, man!'
>
> Terry answered, 'Well I don't mind you sayin' that. We're all entitled to our own opinions . . .' (Though smiling, Terry looked quite uncomfortable and a long pause ensued.)
>
> Paul added, 'You look really uncomfortable right now, Terry. You don't like hearin' these things, do you?' (Weinberg 1996: 152)

### Deepening performed sincerity

Dramaturgical techniques are used in these displays as a collective team performance (Goffman 1959; see also Chapter 5 above). It is crucial to the smooth running of support groups that members act *as if* they are personally committed to recovery, and everybody else is equally committed, regardless of whether or not they actually are. However, the power of such collaborative effort can transform the meaning of the scene during the process of its unfolding. Recalling Thomas and Thomas's (1928: 575) claim that situations defined as real become real in their consequences for interaction (see Chapter 2 above), the show collectively presented can become the subjective reality which actors believe (cf. Scheff 1968). As we saw in Chapter 4, cynical performances can turn into sincere ones, and surface acting can become deep (Hochschild 1983).

This is illustrated by Paik's (2006) ethnography of Project Arise, a drug rehabilitation programme in Los Angeles. Paik describes how staff and clients co-operated in therapeutic encounter groups by using interpretive practices (Gubrium & Holstein 2001) to appraise whether or not clients were authentically reconstructing themselves as 'recovering dope fiends' and taking on the desired institutional self. The practice of 'slips' entailed members writing down observations of each other's deviations from the programme and posting them anonymously to the staff: an act of mutual surveillance. Some clients engaged in this willingly, seizing the idea of 'snitching' on a fellow inmate as a way of making themselves appear relatively obedient.

More often, however, clients felt uncomfortable about breaking ranks in this way, and sought to avoid tension. Although individuals might be challenged for displaying 'wrong' or 'inappropriate' emotions (those that did not fit with the programme or indicated a lack of engagement with it), they were always given the opportunity to redeem themselves through narrative work, which was supported by their fellow inmates. For example, one participant, Andrea, was confronted by the group about her angry outburst at Ken, a counsellor, the previous day. Initially she encountered hostility from her peers, who rose to his defence. However, when she accounted for this by 'confessing' that the anger was really displaced sadness about losing custody of her son, and broke down in tears, the atmosphere within the group changed to one of moral support, as she was seen to have confronted her 'real issues'. She was then applauded for 'getting with the programme' and taking the first step on a therapeutic journey:

> *Isaac*: 'Sometimes I don't know if you are a woman or not. You have this anger that comes out so viciously.'
> *Floyd*: 'Be a woman. Represent what you got to represent. You're on state parole, don't go back to prison. Don't do that to your son – you'll be farther away from him than before.' [As soon as Floyd says 'your son', Andrea starts to get agitated again.]
> *Jorge*: 'You are this close to getting your son back – I know you love him.' Jorge is the first person to say something in a somewhat positive manner – the others' hostile tone did not seem to sit well with Andrea who is looking nervously around the room.
> *Ken (staff) interjects*: 'I refuse to let you play the victim role. Everything is someone else's fault. I refuse to let you do that. I will be consistent – you are on contract [program punishment]. Staff will back me up.'
> (Paik 2006: 226–7)

In order to receive this approbation, however, Andrea was expected to perform contrition and humility by apologizing and substituting the group's interpretation of her behaviour for her own. Just like Goffman's (1961a: 143) asylum inmates, she must '"insightfully" come to take, or affect to take', the institution's view of herself:

> Andrea says that everyone's indictments – except Ken's – were valid and she apologized to Stella for behaving that way. She said to Stella, 'I was mad at you – well you know why but still I shouldn't slam doors like that.' She then addresses the entire group: 'I know I have an attitude problem

but what can I say? I'm working on it. I really am.' Andrea sounds as if she is about to cry; her voice is not angry or spiteful at all. She sounds like she is trying to stay calm and in control of her emotions. (Paik 2006: 227)

From this we can see how powerful a mechanism performative regulation is in governing the reinvention process. Once socialized into an RI's programme rhetoric and its incumbent inmate culture, individuals devise identity performances of obedience and conformity. In some cases, however, doubt is cast on the authenticity of their professed commitment to the regime. Identity claims and 'announcements' of status are not met with ratification and congruent 'placement' (Stone 1962). Collectively, meanwhile, dramaturgical work goes on to construct, enact and reassert the morality of the inmate culture. Inmates comply with RI programmes because they genuinely want to – or at least have convinced themselves to believe that they genuinely want to – and are surrounded by a community of peers who support these motivations. How could this be anything other than benignly beneficial?

## Conclusion

This chapter has examined the processes of identity change that take place when people become members of institutions that 'totally' encompass them. Taking the symbolic interactionist approach to social organizations as formed and routinely recreated by micro-level negotiated order, we looked firstly at Goffman's classic model of the total institution (TI), as depicted in his ethnographic study of a psychiatric asylum. Goffman's model was critical and pessimistic, focusing on processes of coercive, authoritarian social control exercised by staff over inmates. Although we can detect hints of resistance in their reactions to these mortifying circumstances, and thus the resilience of an authentic 'true self', the attempts were ultimately futile. Updating this concept somewhat, I then presented my model of the contemporary reinventive institution (RI), to which members voluntarily commit themselves in pursuit of self-transformation, improvement and identity reinvention. I considered three example types of RI: religious and spiritual communities, military camps and therapeutic communities. Ostensibly, these new 'institutions without walls' suggest much greater agency and a liberating potential, but we can detect an undercurrent of subtler social control, operating horizontally through members' interactions. What I call 'performative regulation' brings together Foucauldian notions of surveillance with the symbolic interactionist model of negotiated order and Goffman's interaction order. It is based on two key mechanisms:

identity performances of conformity to the institution's values, and the peer surveillance and mutual monitoring of members' conduct. Such is the intensity and insularity of RIs, this performance of authentic commitment can become subjectively real for inmates, who shift from cynical self-presentation to deeply acted sincerity. This raises further questions about the ontology and authorship of the reinvented self: is there still an actor behind the character, an agent driving the change, or does this subject get subsumed beneath deceptive discourses and rehearsed rhetoric? In the next chapter, we consider how micro-social processes of deception and fakery pervade everyday life beyond the institutional context, and may, paradoxically, be helpful to the interaction order.

# 8

## Faking identity

### Secrecy, deception and betrayal

This final chapter turns on its head one of the tacit assumptions embedded in the previous seven. So far we have looked at how social actors manage their identities through self-presentation, negotiation, symbolic gestures and interaction rituals, and how this can involve struggles for power and agency in the authorship of the self. However, throughout these discussions we have been working with the assumption that these communications are relatively genuine: people's motives for action reflect their concern with expressing what they see as their true self-identity, creating the best possible impression, or protecting their authentic self from external threats. Symbolic interactionism is often criticized (albeit perhaps unfairly) for its rosy-coloured view of actors harmoniously co-operating to keep everybody in face (Goffman 1955), but there is another side to this precarious interaction order. In this chapter, we critically reconsider that assumption of benevolence, examining the more devious ways in which actors present identities that are false, misleading or socially exploitative. Revisiting some of the concepts discussed in previous chapters but also encountering new ones, we reinterpret the meaning of identity performances, which shift from being merely communicative to calculatedly manipulative. From the polite fictions that facilitate relations in public to the darkly torturous processes of intimate betrayal, we shall see how matters of identity are rarely as straightforward as they seem.

Deception can be defined as the intentional misleading of others (Meltzer 2003). However, this umbrella term encompasses many different acts, which vary in how they are experienced, performed and regarded. The main forms I will consider here are secrecy (the withholding and restriction of information), lying (the verbal telling of an untruth), 'benign fabrications' that protect others' faces or feelings, and self-deception. We can also distinguish between deceptive *action*, which requires only the actor's intention to mislead, and deceptive *interaction*, which depends on the audience's reception and interpretation of the act. In the latter case, deception only occurs if the action is successful: a secret that gets discovered or a lie that is not believed (Barnes 1994) is merely a failed attempt at persuasion. Recalling Blumer's (1969) concept of joint action and Mead's (1934) social act, we can focus on the dynamics of interaction that unfold between the deceiver and the deceived in their symbolic conversation of gestures (Mead 1934).

## Is deception pragmatically useful?

When men [*sic*] confront each other, each cannot always be certain – even when given seemingly trustworthy guarantees – that he knows either the other's identity or his own identity in the eyes of the other.
(Glaser & Strauss 1964: 669)

SI encourages us to consider the paradox that deception might be a socially good thing. In our routine encounters, a dash of tactful pretence or studied non-observance (Goffman 1963b) can oil the wheels of inter-action by facilitating the smooth flow of situations. Dishonesty can even be seen as necessary to the maintenance of micro-social order (McCall & Simmons 1966), for to indulge in total frankness in our dealings with others would be treacherous for interactional harmony (Barnes 1994). Indeed, Barnes suggests, rather than asking what makes people lie, a more pertinent question might be: why do we ever tell the truth? We talk about people being pathological liars but not pathologically honest, even though the truth can hurt and white lies heal. Rather than being unusual, then, deception is endemic to everyday life: '. . . relationships necessarily turn on somewhat misguided and misleading premises about the other parties, social order rests partly on error, lies, deception, and secrets, as well as upon accurate knowledge' (McCall & Simmons 1966: 195–6).

This subverts the conventional wisdom conveyed in primary sociali-zation that honesty is a virtue and lying a sin: one should always tell the truth. Yet as Barnes (1994) points out, in some contexts, lying is expected, culturally normalized, even positively valued. We find sys-tematic deception embedded in some occupational roles – barristers, politicians, estate agents – where it is accepted as necessary to the game-like procedures of the organizations they represent (albeit some-times a cause of their occupational stigmatization [Lofland 2004]). Deception is institutionalized in some cultural traditions, as temporal, spatial and physical markers designate boundaried contexts in which lies are condoned. Barnes (1994) gives the example of parents telling their children about the existence of Santa Claus, and we can think of comparable lies and myths told in the spirit of protecting the innocent: the dead pet dog who has 'gone to live on the farm', or the baby who was 'delivered by a stork'. Meanwhile in the arts, we celebrate as talent the ability to deceive: clever authors draw us into a story, skilled actors build a 'fourth wall' around the stage to convince us their characters are real (Schechner 2002), and comedy relies on audiences perceiving two alternative realities in juxtaposition (Scheff 2011).

The symbolic interactionist approach subverts traditional ways of thinking about deception in moral philosophy, which debates whether and how dishonesty can be justified. Kantian absolutism teaches that a deceptive act is intrinsically unjustifiable, regardless of its outcomes, because of the intention to mislead (Bok 1978). This focus on individual motives may be countered by the utilitarian perspective that focuses on the social consequences of action: deception is morally good if it results in more beneficial than harmful consequences. However, in both of these theories, there is still an emphasis on whether or not one *should* tell untruths. By contrast, SI (and dramaturgical theory) brackets out these questions of the morality of deceptive action, considering only what it *does* for the interaction order. Like utilitarian philosophy, it focuses on the social consequences of deception, but from a more neutral position that analyses only its *procedural effects*. From this perspective, deception can be *socially good*, regardless of whether or not it is morally right or wrong, insofar as it sustains actors' beliefs in shared definitions of reality. Their motivations should be understood in pragmatic rather than ethical terms, as strategic choices made in situated contexts of interaction (Scheibe 1979). As we saw in Chapter 1, pragmatist philosophy influenced the symbolic interactionist focus on what actors do to construct the social world around them, and the objects (including people) they relate to in practical or instrumental ways. From this morally neutral perspective, it does not matter whether deception actually occurs or reality has been distorted, only what the various players involved perceive to have happened, how they orient themselves in response, and what the consequences are for the interaction that unfolds.

## The fascination–fear dialectic

Simmel's (1971) dialectical theory pointed to the dualisms, conflicts and ambivalence that characterize different 'forms' of interaction, as knowledgeable actors perceive multiple views of a situation. In his reading of sociation, one of the interactional forms, we can identify a dialectic of fascination and fear: contradictory responses to the prospect of knowing and being known about by another. Simmel saw the tension between concealing and revealing private information to be a feature of everyday life, insofar as social actors are constantly engaged in making judgements about what and how much to disclose. This fascination–fear dialectic characterizes all kinds of deceptive interaction. On the one hand, Simmel (1908b) suggested that we are intrigued by the private, mysterious, unknowable aspects of people's characters, and take a mischievous delight in discovering what they 'really' think and feel. On the other hand, there is a risk in allowing oneself to be known in the same way. Simmel thought it prudent not to reveal all, but to retain an enclosure of secrecy around the self: 'Whatever we say, as long as it goes beyond mere interjection and minimal communication, is never an immediate or faithful presentation of what really occurs in us during that particular time of communication, but is a transformation of this inner reality, teleologically directed, reduced, and recomposed' (1908b: 329).

Simmel's (1908b) social geometry distinguished between groups of varying size and proximity according to the degree of reciprocal knowledge held by their members. However, I would add that we do not simply *think* about those we meet and form relationships with, but also *feel* (dis)inclined towards them in different ways – and the more we care about them, the harder it is to deceive them. Actors are pulled in different directions by opposing forces of approach and avoidance, trust and vulnerability, which compromise their ability and willingness to engage in strategic game playing. Thus I have superimposed on this a *social geometry of deception*, examining how deceptive processes and consequences vary at different levels of intimacy (Scott 2012). When interaction partners are relatively detached and self-contained, wariness and risk aversion predominate, making it easier and more pragmatic to engage in deception as a course of shrewd, strategic action. In terms of the fascination–fear dialectic, fear (or at least cautious restraint) is the stronger force. As people become closer and more emotionally invested in each other, however, the balance shifts so that feelings of fascination, intrigue and mystique become paramount, over-riding the motivation for instrumental-rational action (cf. Weber 1922). Interactants become increasingly willing to remove the safety net of deceptive communication and engage in honest, direct or self-disclosing modes of communication, whilst being simultaneously aware of the escalating dangers of betrayal.

At one end of Simmel's continuum is the interest group, formed on the basis of a shared, external focus of attention. These members know nothing about each other's personal qualities, and so can engage in deception as a purely rational, strategic act. Next is confidence, or trust in a public figure; conversely, we distrust such people, whom we acknowledge that we do not really know (politicians are an obvious example). Acquaintanceship involves a generalized but superficial knowledge of another's lifestyle and interests; here again the actor may retain enough cool detachment to engage in deception, although there may be the potential for embarrassment if discovered. Further along the continuum, however, friendship is based upon the disclosure and sharing of deeper, more personally meaningful beliefs and values. Deception ceases to be a purely rational enterprise and becomes more emotionally charged, most obviously by feelings of guilt. Love is the next stage of intimacy, wherein partners seek to gain complete knowledge of each other through honest self-disclosure. Now trust becomes of paramount importance, and deception a morally culpable act of betrayal. Finally, Simmel pointed to marriage, or lifelong partnership, as a unique phenomenon through which members relinquish individuality and form a new, joint identity – a brave and hazardous venture of trust.

In the remainder of this chapter, I develop my social geometry of deception from a symbolic interactionist perspective, examining how identity deception occurs at five different levels of interactional intimacy. These are: encounters between strangers; collusion and misrepresentation between teams; strategic game-play between team-mates; betrayal by an intimate accomplice; and self-deception.

## A social geometry of deception

### Encounters between strangers: illusions of intersubjectivity

The first form of deceptive interaction we can recognize is the 'polite fictions' of the interaction order discussed in Chapter 2. These occur in the fleeting, superficial encounters that take place between strangers or the less acquainted, often in public places (cf. Goffman 1963b). Here, deception unfolds as a relatively straightforward technique of praxis, contemplated as strategic rational action that poses little emotional challenge or few malign moral connotations. This is because it reflects a common preoccupation with upholding the interaction order (Goffman 1983a). SI argues that what matters is not whether people perceive reality accurately, but rather that they believe they do, and act on the basis of this belief. Actors co-operatively strive to create a definition of the situation (Thomas & Thomas 1928), accomplishing intersubjective agreement (Schütz 1972) about what is going on and tacitly agreeing to follow the script of normative expectations. Social solidarity, bonding, even intimacy, are anticipated as the fruits of interactional labour, while trust forms the foundation of social relations (Bok 1978).

When situations flow smoothly, we bracket out our awareness of these constructions' precariousness, and the threat of their potential dissolution (Berger & Luckmann 1966). What appears to be micro-social order is a just an illusion, albeit one that is collectively upheld. Definitions of situations are fragile, contingent and reliant on interactional harmony. As Scheff (1968) argued, the 'presented reality' with which we pragmatically operate is only one version of events, and may be contradicted by the 'believed reality' to which participants privately adhere. Meanwhile, over-arching all of this is a collective delusion about agency and responsibility: actors must also bracket out the fact that they have been complicit in this fabrication of reality, and have the power either to uphold or to dismantle it (Berger and Luckmann 1966). Thus we find a meta-illusory belief that the process of deception is not occurring: that 'nothing unusual is going on', even though a great deal really is (Emerson 1970b; Manning 2000).

Polite fictions abound in the behaviour of strangers forced into situations of co-presence in public places (Goffman 1963b), as we saw in Chapter 2. Waiting rooms, elevators and queues evoke displays of studied non-observance (Goffman 1963b) as actors pretend not to see each other in order to avoid interaction (Gueldner 1965; Felipe & Sommer 1966; Fox 2004). My ethnographic study of a swimming pool (Scott 2009a) revealed how swimmers politely disattended to their state of near-nudity so as to avoid embarrassment, while Weinberg's (1965) and Douglas et al.'s (1977) studies of naturist groups showed how members strove to uphold notions of 'decency' by bracketing out sexualized definitions of the situation.

Collective adherence to a false reality is also apparent with *tact* (Goffman 1959; see Chapter 5 above), the symbolic gestures that actors use to demonstrate regard for each other's faces. Party guests introduced as strangers make small talk about innocuous matters about which they do not care, to avoid awkward silences. We exchange pleasantries in the form of ritualized greetings, farewells and 'grooming talk' that we do not mean literally but rather symbolically, as gestures of caring (see Chapter 5 above). The recipient of a gift they do not like feigns delight and thanks the giver insincerely, to protect their feelings. Embarrassing mistakes, such as tripping over in the street, are remedied by actors glossing over the incompetence and carrying on, while sympathetic passers-by collude in pretending the event has not happened (Gross & Stone 1964; Miller 1996).

## Collusion and misrepresentation between teams

At the second level of intimacy, dramaturgy imagines teams of aligned actors, who are disposed to be loyal to one another but not necessarily to outsiders. Team-mates co-operate to uphold a collective 'face', as we saw with Rossing and Scott's (2014) study of exercising colleagues seeking to define themselves as familiar strangers (see Chapter 5 above). More than just co-operation, however, these kinds of performance team dynamics imply processes of *collusion*, dependent on intensely loyal bonds of trust between members. They rely upon deep, intuitive knowledge of each other as actors who have learned the same script, tricks and strategies, often to outwit another team or an external audience. Goffman (1959: 108) likened the performance team to a secret society, flavoured by 'the sweet guilt of conspirators', who supported each other's lines of self-presentation in order to create a collective team impression, and were fiercely protective of each other's dignity.

## Secrecy

Secrecy can be defined as the intentional concealment of information, to prevent others from possessing, using or revealing it (Bok 1989: 6). Simmel (1908b) characterized secrecy by one party's (or team's) concealment of specialized, restricted or privileged knowledge, and another's interest in revealing it. From a symbolic interactionist perspective, this coincides with actors' interests in presenting and sustaining a carefully composed version of themselves. Individual actors use secrecy as a tool of impression management (Goffman 1959) before an audience or generalized other (Mead 1934), to either enhance their own status or repair a damaged face. As we saw in the discussion of Goffman's *Stigma* (1963a; see Chapter 6 above), secret information is that which, if revealed, has the potential to undermine or discredit the actor's identity claims. 'Mystification' is routinely used to keep the audience at a distance and prevent them catching a glimpse behind the scenes (Goffman 1959). Nevertheless, the audience may regard the performer sceptically, doubting the image presented to them, alert to the impressions unintentionally 'given off', and disinclined to gloss over the duplicity. This reminds us how deception is a form of *interaction*, contingent on the mutual perceptions made by both actor and audience of each other's presented identities.

In *The Philosophy of Money* (1900), Simmel posited that the more socially distanced an object or idea is from the beholder, the more valuable it appears; hence wealth is coveted, celebrity sought and money fetishized. The same principle applies to the 'fascination of secrecy' (Simmel 1908b), whereby information that people keep hidden becomes more intriguing. Consequently, gaining access to restricted resources served as a form of 'adornment', bestowing upon the recipient a degree of privilege or vicarious status. Actors ultimately seek to acquire this, rather than the substantive content of the knowledge *per se*: they find value in the meaning of belonging, being an insider or someone in the know. Correspondingly, from the secret-holder's perspective, the 'fascination of betrayal' lurks as a threat, carrying the risk of exposure but also the thrill of trying to outwit the audience: 'The secret puts a barrier between men [*sic*], but, at the same time, it creates the tempting challenge to break through it, by gossip or confession – and this challenge accompanies its psychology like a constant overtone' (Simmel 1908b: 334).

Bok (1989) argues that secrecy forces us to make moral choices in everyday life, which are grounded in social relations. We must decide how far to go in protecting our privacy and concealing what others tell us: making or breaking intimate promises of confidentiality, or 'whistleblowing' about corrupt affairs. Alice Goffman (2014) documents the risks taken by African American mothers in a Philadelphia neighbourhood, who helped their sons to hide whilst 'on the run' from a technological web of police surveillance and arrest warrants. How far should we pry into others' secrets, or gossip about them behind their backs? How do we seek to justify these actions, in private and public accounts? Companies keep trade secrets from each other, and governments rationalize military defence on the basis of the need to protect national security; meanwhile the mass media endorse 'freedom of inquiry' and the 'public's right to know' (Bok 1989: xvii). Making others swear to secrecy creates bonds of obligation, while revelatory confessions empower the listener who receives them (Foucault 1976). Thus secrecy can be used to exercise power, whether coercively or legitimately, just as betrayal of these ties is a symbolic act of resistance.

In his typology of secrets, Goffman (1959) emphasizes their pragmatic functions for impression management. In each of these scenarios, actors are motivated pragmatically rather than malevolently, to sustain lines of self-presentation and keep themselves in face.

Whereas 'dark' secrets are managed by individuals, such as in concealing a discreditable stigma (Goffman 1963a; see Chapter 6 above), 'strategic secrets' are maintained by teams in relation to their tactics for staging a collective performance. In Chapter 5, we encountered the tactic of 'communication out of character' (Goffman 1959), whereby performance team-mates make veiled references to the fact that they are co-constructing a false definition of reality, acknowledging between themselves that 'this is only a performance'. This involves presenting one version of events to the audience while simultaneously contradicting it with information conveyed to one another. As Simmel (1908b) posited, there is a delightful thrill to be found in colluding with fellow group members against an external other, and managing successfully to pull the wool over their eyes.

For example, Geller's (1934) study of a shoe store showed how sales assistants used a 'secret lingo' of code terms for both the products and the customers, which allowed them to talk about the audience in front of them. Old shoes could be presented to the customers as 'premium' or 'vintage' to make them sound more appealing than the unsold stock they really were. When greeting customers, the staff would 'size up the mark' or victim (cf. Goffman 1952) by categorizing them as a certain type, and signal to each other their potential gullibility. 'Wrap ups' were those customers who came into the store prepared to buy, and might be persuaded to take a more expensive shoe, whereas 'turn overs' were those who would browse but refuse to buy anything. Sometimes a customer would bring a 'lawyer' with them into the store: a friend or relative to shop with, who might be more shrewd and attentive to the sales tactics and who should therefore be treated gingerly. All of these code terms were whispered or gestured by the staff and decoded by their team-mates to ensure a smooth, collaborative performance.

'Insider secrets' (Goffman 1959) are those whose possession symbolizes an individual's membership of a special group, echoing Simmel's remarks about identity adornment. For example, gossip is a sneaky practice whereby team-mates demonstrate mutual regard and build solidarity by colluding in the restriction of information from other teams or audiences. Goffman (1959) described it as a common feature of interaction that people were spoken about relatively well to their faces but less kindly behind their backs: there was a duplicitous inconsistency between 'speaking fair' and 'speaking ill'. The audience's detection of this, meanwhile, exemplifies Glaser and Strauss's (1964) suspicion awareness context (see Chapter 2 above).

Finally, 'secrets about secrets' are those that conceal the very fact that deception is taking place, to prevent embarrassing revelations. One example of this is the 'pretence awareness context' (Glaser & Strauss 1964), discussed in Chapter 2: a situation in which both parties understand that an official state of affairs is not really the case, but tacitly agree not to mention it. We saw this in their study of terminally ill patients and their doctors' awareness that the patient was dying. Feigning ignorance of their mutual understanding that things are not as they appear, actors tactfully overlook the 'elephant in the room'.

## Secret societies

When secrecy defines a group as a criterion of membership, it becomes a *secret society*. Simmel (1908b) suggested that these formations were predicated on ideas of separateness, seclusion and exclusivity, distinguishing themselves from other groups who do not share the privilege of being 'in the know'. Members of secret societies develop intensely close bonds, as they are forced into relations of mutual dependency. Suspicious of outsiders, they must be able to trust one another to keep the group's secrets; betrayal hangs over their collective head as a perpetual threat. This resonates with Coser's (1974) model of the 'greedy' institution that demands the total commitment of its members (see Chapter 7 above). Simmel (1908b: 367) wrote of the 'group egoism' through which the secret society pursues its own goals above individual interests, and Hazelrigg (1969: 324) agreed that 'the interests and activities of all its members are totally encompassed' by the protective function of secrecy.

Perhaps the archetypal secret society is the Freemasons, a ritual brotherhood that emerged in seventeenth-century England and took hold across Europe and the USA throughout the eighteenth and nineteenth centuries (Jones 1967). Its members were middle-class white men whose constitution cited moral values of honour, honesty and brotherly loyalty (Webster 1924). Freemasonry was based metaphorically upon the principles of stonemasonry, a medieval craft guild: new recruits learned the appropriate skills and knowledge through apprenticeship to established members, and resided in lodge buildings, where they ate, slept and fraternized (Dumenil 1984). Great emphasis was placed upon the restriction of access to privileged knowledge, through secret symbols, signs, passwords, handshakes, myths, rituals, oath-swearing and initiation ceremonies.

Other secret societies followed in this tradition, emphasizing values of fraternity and loyalty. The late nineteenth century has been described as a golden age (Carnes 1989) in which secret societies flourished because of their emphasis on the Victorian moral values of virtue, honesty, courtesy, dignity and respectability. During this period, between 15 and 40 per cent of American men belonged to a fraternal order, though there were few equivalents for women (Putney 1993). For example, the Knights of Columbus rose to popularity in New England at the turn of the twentieth century: founded by Irish Catholic veterans from the US Civil War, this evolved into a secular order based upon notions of patriotic American manhood (Koehlinger 2004). The duty of a Knight was to be staid, orderly and chivalrous: '. . . gentle to children, to age and to women, courteous to all whatever their station, clothing his words and deeds with politeness' (Koehlinger 2004: 458). Concurrent with the Knights was the Theosophy movement, based on Christian morality and socialist politics, which was organized as concentric circles, the innermost representing the most tantalizingly restricted membership

(Webster 1924). The Rosicrucians were a similarly exclusive group, founded on the principles of the Jewish Kabbalah, which spread from Germany to other parts of Western Europe and the USA. Nicknamed 'The Invisibles', the group held great mystical appeal through its focus on symbols (the rose and the cross), rituals and claims to supernatural powers (Jones 1967).

A contemporary equivalent to the secret society is the American college fraternity or sorority. Students enrol to join chapter houses: residential lodges combining the functions of sleeping, eating and leisure activities, which provide a sense of collective identity. Newcomb's (1961) study of Bennington, a liberal arts college in Michigan, pointed to the process of acquaintance-building between students living in shared halls of residence. This supported Simmel's (1971) view that trust develops over time, mediated by group interaction dynamics: Newcomb found a shift in the students' system of orientation, from individualism to collectivism. Smaller communities may also form within these overall organizations. Gumprecht (2006) gives the example of Cornell University in New York, which had three distinct residential districts. Fraternity Row was a street lined with chapter houses where the majority of freshman students lived, the Student Ghetto was an affectionately named rental district in which senior and independent (non-fraternity member) students lived, and the Faculty Enclave was where the teaching staff lived.

Some fraternities have been created in a spirit of resistance to subvert the conservative bias of the traditional college clique, particularly its perceived ethnocentrism, homophobia and heteronormativity. Hughey (2008) describes how members of online Black Greek Letter Organizations (BGLOs) drew a symbolic boundary between themselves as 'brothers' as distinct from non-black 'others', reversing the direction of the pejorative exclusion they had experienced. Anderson (2008) documented the inclusive ethos of the Troubadors, a male fraternity chapter in an American university, which posed a challenge to hegemonic masculinity (Connell & Pearse 2015). This was cultivated through a cohesive social network, as one student, Alex, explained: 'It's about being a gentleman, polite and respectful. . . . We expect our brothers not to partake in that macho jock mentality. We want to stand out as being intellectual and athletic, but also as being kind and respectful' (Anderson 2008: 609).

Recruitment of members to college fraternities is a selective business. Hazing rituals take place during rush parties and pledge functions, to which freshmen students are invited by prospective housemates. Echoing Garfinkel's (1956) model of the degradation ceremony (see Chapter 6 above), the individual must perform a humiliating feat before

this audience of peers, who scrutinize and judge their strength of character. Typical hazing tests include drinking games, risk-taking stunts,
early morning runs across campus, having one's face or body branded
and having to repeat humiliating phrases. Paradoxically, however, these
rituals function to increase solidarity between members. The rookie
police officers in De Albuquerque and Paes-Machado's study said that
enduring hardship together and showing their vulnerability created a
sense of community: 'From now on, their new family is right here; they
are meant to feel heartily welcomed and sheltered by their classmates
and instructors at the police academy' (De Albuquerque & Paes-
Machado 2004: 188).

However, this cohesiveness can have a darker side. Sanday (1990)
documents the disturbing trend of gang rapes that plague male fraternity houses, arguing that this has been normalized by a culture of male
sexual aggression, misogyny and the objectification of women's bodies.
Phipps and Young (2014) make similar observations of the 'lad culture'
developing in British universities. Media reports about dangerous or
foolhardy 'pranks gone wrong' (Hodges 1995; Korry 2005) focus on
the pressure inmates feel to demonstrate their devotion, resulting in a
momentary loss of self. We might then ask: are fraternities presenting
their collective identity deceptively to new recruits, offering them false
promises of community, belonging and benevolence?

## Strategic game-play between team-mates

However, are we naïve to assume that we can trust our interaction
partners to co-operate with us in building shared definitions of reality?
The 'insider's folly' (Goffman 1974; Burns 1992) refers to this rose-
tinted belief that everybody is on our side in interaction, or indeed that
there are no sides. Competition may be no less fierce between those
who share a superficial loyalty and are obliged to conceal their personal
opinions beneath the façade of team solidarity.

Goffman's view of the actor was of a self-contained, boundaried
agent (Scheff 2006), who rationally appraised social encounters and
strategically designed their responses as calculated moves. Dramaturgy
warns us that the characters we encounter are at best exaggerations
or selective representations of the underlying actor-self, and at worst
completely contrived fabrications. As we saw in Chapter 4, actors may
not fully believe in the parts that they are playing, and can be more or
less immersed in these roles. Goffman (1959) contrasted the 'sincerely'
committed with the 'cynically' detached or role distant (Goffman
1961b: 73–134), while Hochschild (1983) referred to processes of deep
or surface acting. In documenting these devious strategies, Goffman's

*The Presentation of Self in Everyday Life* (1959) has been described by Manning (2000: 287) as 'a textbook of deception', which catalogues the 'manipulative presentations of self that actors build out of impressions and fronts that they design to mislead'.

## Gambling on identity

Game theory was a major influence on Goffman's (1959, 1961b: 15–72, 1963b, 1967: 149–270, 1969, 1983b) work, enabling him to explore actors' devious strategies for competing with, outsmarting and manipulating each other. On the one hand, Goffman (1961b: 15–72) maintained that interaction was 'fun', or at least exciting enough to keep us motivated. Competitive behaviour was playful, driven by positive motivations of sociability and the thrill of successfully outwitting others. Citing gambling as the prototype of interaction (Goffman 1967), he emphasized the pleasure to be found in risk-taking: self-presentation, status displays and selective disclosure are strategies with unpredictable outcomes, namely losses or gains in social status (Smith 2006). The risk of losing face makes interaction more exciting as it is highly 'fateful', or consequential for future relations. Actors are further intrigued by the mysteriousness of others and their potential dishonesty, enjoying the challenge of cracking through their exteriors to discover the 'real' self behind the mask. On the other hand, interaction is risky insofar as there is a real danger of strategies backfiring. We might disclose too much, misjudge the withholding of information or impute the wrong motives to another, all of which leave us vulnerable to criticism, rejection, exclusion and shame. Juggling fun and risk gives actors an edginess in their approach to interaction, and makes honesty and deception matters of paramount importance.

This resonates with debates about risk in contemporary Western societies (Giddens 1991; Beck 1992; Lupton 1999), which are played out at the micro-social level. In contrast to psychological theories that presume risk-taking is a character trait that motivates some individuals, Lyng (1990) argues that the tendency to engage voluntarily in high-risk behaviour is a pervasive social experience with an existential dimension. He adapted the gonzo journalist Hunter S. Thompson's (1971) concept of 'edgework': a human drive to 'live on the edge' by exploring and transgressing the boundaries between states of consciousness and unconsciousness, life and death, sanity and madness. This explains people's motivations for drug-taking, criminal activity, dangerous sports, and so on. It represents 'a type of experimental anarchy in which the individual moves beyond the realm of established patterns to the very fringes of ordered reality' (Lyng 1990: 882). Following this, Lyng identifies two kinds of edgework: testing the endurance limits of technology (e.g. vehicles) or of the body and mind (e.g. sports). Edgework activities demand intense concentration, dedication and courage to withstand fear, as participants face a direct threat to their physical or mental welfare; the challenge is to endure and survive this, transcending the normal boundaries of human existence (Hardie-Bick 2005). They may take additional risks to add to this sensation of thrill, such as rock-climbing without safety equipment, or skydiving while under the influence of hallucinogenic drugs (Lyng & Snow 1986). This can produce an exhilarating sense of self-actualization and self-determination (Lyng 1990: 860).

Voluntary risk-taking may be easiest to see in these 'extreme' activities, but it is a feature of social interaction more generally. In more mundane situations, the same delight in game playing appears in dramaturgical risk-taking. Goffman (1967: 149–270) employs a specific concept of 'action', defined as any social encounter that is either 'problematic' (having an unpredictable outcome and thus requiring a gamble) or 'consequential' (fateful for the person's identity or relations with others). Both features may even be present in some situations (Lyng 2014) that are ostensibly mundane but dramaturgically risky: for example, identity performances of what Goffman calls 'character' (qualities of moral rectitude, such as poise, composure and gallantry) to an audience. These apparently noble qualities may be deceptive, however: Goffman suggests that action is undertaken for what is felt to be its own sake but is actually motivated by self-presentational concerns.

These ideas were developed in Goffman's *Strategic Interaction* (1969), which used metaphors of spying to show how deception was a routine part of everyday life. He emphasized defensive motivations of suspicion, fear and doubt, rather than simple maliciousness, to explain the propensity to 'acquire, reveal and conceal information' (1969: 4), contextualizing deception within a wider range of 'expression games' that were morally neutral. Recognizing and mistrusting the limited amount of information conveyed through self-presentation, actors work like secret agents, trying to discover each other's real intentions or ulterior motives. Moreover, insofar as we can all assume the role of either observer (detective) or subject (under scrutiny) in different situations, we become aware of how other people will be trying to read *us* in the same way, and so become concerned with safeguarding our own private information. We act as double agents, seeking simultaneously to control the impressions we convey, second-guess the intentions behind others' actions, conceal the fact that we are doing this and feign a breezy nonchalance. For example, Grazian (2007) describes the 'hustling' tactics, myths and confidence tricks used in the nightclub industry to lure customers in, by staging exciting scenes and promising risky encounters.

Audiences, however, may be alert to the risk of being deceived. As we saw in Chapter 4, they are attuned not only to the expressions consciously 'given' by their fellow actors, but also to those unwittingly 'given off' through inconsistencies, slips and non-verbal leakage (Goffman 1959). The recipient's advantage (Goffman 1959) refers to the fact that observers can attend to expressions both given and given off, whereas actors can only control the former. Interaction rituals have a game-like quality, wherein each party is fascinated by the idea of finding out what the other really thinks/feels/is: their elusive backstage self. Teams and their audiences engage in tactical manoeuvres to catch each other out, in 'a potentially infinite cycle of concealment, discovery, false revelation and rediscovery' (Goffman 1959: 8), rendering everyday life a 'constant game of concealment and search' (1959: 83).

## Credibility as performance

It is important not to confuse Goffman's cool detachment with a lack of concern for interpersonal ethics. This misconception may have come about through the detached, impassionate style in which he wrote and his morally neutral language (Becker 2003). Lofland (1984) recalls that in person, Goffman had a 'penchant for mentioning troubling truths' about social encounters, which expressed his 'intense concern about being deceived or cheated'. He was also reputedly a terrible poker player because he was incapable of bluffing.

Analytically, Goffman bracketed out questions of morality, focusing more on the processes of deception and their consequences for the interaction order. He was not positively advocating exploitative action, but rather assuming that, as deception would inevitably occur, we should leave its evaluation to philosophers and focus on its practical consequences. Like all micro-sociologists, he was interested not in states of objective truth or falsity, but rather in claims to truthfulness and perceptions or accusations of deceptiveness (Bok 1978): social attributions that are negotiated within contexts of interaction. He considered actors' motives for deceptive action only insofar as they explained the processes of identity performance and self-presentation that could be observed in social conduct. Manning (2000) argues that it is therefore possible to read Goffman as an *amoral* theorist (MacIntyre 1982) rather than an immoral one.

While somewhat Machiavellian, the Goffmanesque actor was not malevolent or cruel: deception was merely a course of action that was rationally decided upon as the most pragmatic means of raising one's standing. Dramaturgy is concerned less with matters of perceptual truth and accuracy than with the motivation to achieve the appearance of such. As Smith (2006: 46) suggests, Goffman saw deception and secrecy as matters of 'situated intelligence', employed strategically to manage social relations effectively and advantageously. There was no gratuitous intention to harm others just for the sake of it; exploitation was pursued only if it was pragmatically useful to oneself. Goffman considered why actors might find it strategically useful to deceive others, as well as to conceal this very deviousness, seeking merely to *appear* honest and trustworthy in the eyes of those around them. His was a 'functional, pragmatic endeavour to locate the meaning of actions in how others respond to them' (Smith 2006: 45).

Consequently, Manning (2000) argues that dramaturgy's real focus of attention is *credibility*, or the quality of appearing believable. This refers both to the (meta-)definition of the situation and the actor's presented character: we strive both to make performances seem real and to convince others of our own trustworthiness. Credibility is a validity claim (Habermas 1981), which contributes to an identity performance: actors are asserting that not only is the content of their behaviour true but also the position from which they execute it is sincere and dependable. Manning suggests that credibility is a mechanism integral to both trust and deception, as two sides of the same coin.

## Cooling-out strategies

In his essay "On cooling the mark out" (1952), Goffman used the confidence trick metaphorically to describe the reparative strategies used by actors (individually or in teams) to appease those whom they have exploited. A convincing cover story helps the mark, or victim, to adapt to a humiliating and involuntary loss of status. However, this is delivered not as an altruistic gesture of sympathy (as with protective facework) but as a self-serving damage-limitation strategy to discourage retaliation. It is deceptive because it involves giving the mark a palatable explanation of events that differs or distracts them from the true state of affairs, thus deliberately 'misframing' the definition of the situation (see Chapter 3 above). Goffman (1952: 452) suggests this is a 'basic social story' that applies to many other situations in which people's hopes and expectations are disappointed, such as customer relations in the service industries. The role of the 'cooler', whose job it is to provide this consolation, can even be formalized in such institutions, by positions such as shop floorwalkers, helpline staff and complaints departments. Meanwhile, in more intimate encounters, cooling out is used to soothe and pacify those who might otherwise feel rejected, such as when turning down a date, initiating a break-up or simply taking leave from a conversation.

Goffman identifies various strategies that can be used to cool out a mark. We can delegate the task of breaking bad news to someone else whose status will mitigate its effects: an authority figure such as a doctor or priest, or a trusted close friend. The mark can be offered an alternative status to the one they have lost or failed to achieve, like a consolation prize: a Ph.D. candidate is offered a Masters degree, an injured dancer becomes a teacher, or a parting lover offers to be 'just friends'. The mark can be offered another chance to qualify for the same role, so that the loss is not definitive: a student failing an exam is told they can try again next year. Alternatively, the mark can be given an opportunity to 'explode' or vent their frustration, but in a way that is limited and hidden from public view: store managers encourage disgruntled customers to write letters of complaint that can be answered privately, without affecting the company image. Pre-emptive measures can even be taken to avoid the awkward loss of status occurring in the first place: companies screen out potential employees before shortlisting for a post, or partners end a relationship 'before it gets too serious'. Finally, the cooler and the mark may reach a tacit agreement that the latter will leave quietly without making a fuss or causing a scene (see Chapter 2 above), with both parties colluding in the polite fiction that the status loss was amicably mutual: employees are offered redundancy packages instead of being sacked, or crime victims are offered out-of-court settlements.

Goffman suggests that cooling out, while devious, is a normal and pervasive social practice. Societies are organized around the need to 'dispose' of cooled-out marks, with designated sites to which those who have lost status can be sent. Prisons, psychiatric hospitals and other total institutions (see Chapter 7 above) serve this function, as do residential homes for the elderly in cultures where old age is regarded as a 'social death' (Howarth 2006). Segregated areas of the city, such as ghettos, skid rows and 'hobo jungles' (Goffman 1952: 460), keep the socially stigmatized away from public view. Some institutions, such as less prestigious universities, blend into the same rank those who have lost status and those who have always been in that stratum, or may even have risen to it, so that outsiders cannot know from which direction they have come. All of this reminds us of the symbolic interactionist argument that deception can be socially functional, regardless of its moral rightness or wrongness.

## 'White lies' and benign fabrications

Another form of deception found between members of the same team is lying: the verbal communication of an untruth to create distorted, false beliefs. The resultant discrepancy of perspectives between the liar and the lied-to (Bok 1978) can be seen as a mutual accomplishment, despite one party's innocent involvement, insofar as it requires an interactive process of 'taking the role of the other' in a reflexive dialogue of social selfhood (Cooley 1902; Mead 1934).

Lying is easily recognizable as a form of deception because it involves a positive action (making a decision to communicate a fabrication) rather than a negative one that may be less discernible (withholding information, being vague and evasive or 'selective with the truth'). Scheibe (1979) defines lying more broadly as the misrepresentation of a factual state of affairs, which occurs in many realms of everyday life. Mirrors, masks and magic tricks, sunglasses and uniforms, all involve some form of claiming one fictional version of reality while concealing another that is 'true'. Lying is an art form, Scheibe argues, which has to be learned and can be executed more or less convincingly, to good or bad effects.

Insofar as lying indicates the deliberate manipulation of another's perception of reality, it invites moral disapproval: children are socialized into the principle that it is morally bad to lie, in contrast to other deceptive forms (polite fictions and tact) that are positively valued. Yet it is possible to see lying, too, as having some pragmatic benefits for identity performance, management and the social interaction order. Simmel (1908b: 314) drily observed the 'expediency of the lie' as a pragmatic solution to some forms of dispute, although he argued that it became increasingly difficult, both practically and ethically, as group size diminished and social bonds became more intimate. Much of the sociological literature on lying, therefore, seeks to distinguish between different types of lie that may be more or less socially beneficial. This pragmatic question is considered separately from the moral implications of lies or the moral intentions of liars.

Typologies of lies attempt to bracket out questions of morality, but in practice, these are hard to disentangle from the ethics of social interaction. Goffman (1974: 87–111) distinguished between 'benign' and 'exploitative' fabrications – the former used positively to build social relations and the latter aimed at advantaging oneself over others – thereby acknowledging that deception does not always benefit team-mates equally. While ostensibly distinct in moral terms, both kinds of fabrication can be seen analytically as rational, pragmatic courses of action that serve to frame situations in socially useful ways. Benign fabrications include those told to spare another's feelings, such as paternalistic constructions by people in authority (e.g. parents or doctors). The category also includes playful forms of deceit, such as hoaxes and practical jokes, which are intended to be found humorous by everyone, including the victim, and thus to draw team-mates together. Exploitative fabrications include confidence tricks, cheating, false advertising (e.g. lying in one's CV) and lies to cover up wrongdoings – all of which involve taking advantage of the trust others put in us, to enhance our own social image.

Scheibe (1979), similarly, makes a distinction between lies that are 'defensive', aiming to protect one's own self-image, and those that are 'offensive', designed to manipulate or exploit another person. The former might involve boasting about one's credentials, hiding embarrassing or discrediting information, or 'malingering' in a role beyond a legitimate period, as well as more seemingly harmless acts like fantasizing or bluffing in a poker game. Meltzer (2003) identifies 'self-enhancement fabrications', such as boasting, being 'creative with the truth' (e.g. in job applications or dating website profiles) and non-verbal acts of beautification to make oneself appear younger or more attractive (e.g. make-up and cosmetic surgery). Offensive lies are more clearly interactive, involving tricks and strategies, such as gaining trust and gathering intelligence before a betrayal, disguising a harmful act beneath a veneer of generosity (the Trojan horse effect) and using flattery to seduce and trap someone into an unwanted obligation (as in the foot-in-the-door sales technique).

'White' lies are those told to protect another's feelings or to save their public face, which facilitates the smooth flow of interpersonal encounters and suggests a sympathetic attitude towards one's fellow actors. However, Bok (1978) warns that white lies can be *morally bad regardless of their social goodness*, a paradox that turns the symbolic interactionist argument on its head. She identifies four common social defences of lying that may be morally questionable: avoiding harm, producing benefits, fairness (balancing power with resistance, or exacting revenge) and veracity (lying to protect the truth or preserve confidence in the liar's honesty: 'surely the most paradoxical of excuses' [1978: 84]). Once we tell a lie, this often leads to a chain of further lies needed to sustain it. With regard to avoiding harm, Bok disputes the notion of 'harmless lying' as a contradiction in terms, because even well-intentioned deception can have harmful social consequences. For example, the use of placebo drugs in medical treatment risks damaging public trust in science or the medical profession. Letters of reference and recommendation gloss over a candidate's laziness with false reassurances of their diligence, which come back to haunt the employer who innocently hires them. 'The veneer of social trust is often thin,' Bok (1978: 26–7) cautions. 'As lies spread . . . trust is damaged . . . the community as a whole suffers; and when it is destroyed, societies falter and collapse.'

Some additional examples challenge the simplistic dichotomy

between 'good' and 'bad' lies, in turn blurring the boundary between social and moral principles. Even self-interested actions performed with the intention to exploit, manipulate and mislead may not harm their victims (particularly if they remain oblivious), and may work to the satisfaction of both parties. For example, Meltzer (2003) suggests that 'ingratiation with the powerful' can take the sting out of hierarchical power relations, making encounters between unequal parties flow more smoothly. Smiling through gritted teeth, paying insincere compliments and sucking up to one's superiors can work wonders to facilitate proceedings with a veneer of charm, even though everyone knows the ugly truth. This often occurs in the enactment of emotional labour in the workplace (Hochschild 2003): for example, when employees cynically perform diligence in front of their boss or feign cheerfulness with clients. 'Fraudulent creative achievements' (Meltzer 2003) include academic plagiarism, or athletes' consumption of performance-enhancing drugs. While there are obvious moral objections to such actions (to cheat or usurp another's work abuses the fairness principle), we might nevertheless say that they are socially benevolent. If audiences do not realize they have been duped and continue to enjoy a work of art, interesting idea or athletic performance, then the result is a harmonious and positive definition of the situation for everyone concerned.

'Noble lies' (Meltzer 2003) are those that invoke impressive moral principles, but, in my view, this does not preclude their being told with pragmatic motivations, such as to escape difficult circumstances or make them easier to bear. A victim appeasing her kidnapper to avoid violence, and a concentration camp inmate talking optimistically to his child, are undoubtedly brave and heroic, but may perceive their own actions as 'just doing what I need to survive' (Bettelheim 1991; Hardie-Bick 2011). Bok (1978) also discusses lying to enemies and lying to unmask another liar as ostensibly noble actions, but these can alternatively be seen as strategic 'uncovering moves' (Goffman 1969), designed to outwit rival game players. Finally, Meltzer (2003) points to 'socially permissible fabrications', whereby acts of distortion and concealment are embedded in the remit of an occupational role or social status (cf. Barnes 1994, see above) and accepted as legitimate. Here, audiences may know that they are being given a distorted version of the truth, but raise no objections because they recognize its social value. This supports Lukes' (2005) three-dimensional theory of power with its emphasis on the willingness of subjects to be governed. It also raises the question of whether the supposed victims of duping might actually be – pragmatically speaking – complicit with their perpetrators, making deception a negotiated, interactional process.

## *Betrayal by an intimate accomplice*

Perhaps the most dramaturgically dangerous and emotionally charged interaction context in which deception can occur is the (romantic, monogamous) intimate relationship. Partners occupy a unique and privileged status within an inner circle of the lifeworld (Schütz 1972), as a person's most trusted team-mate. As an internalized representation of emotional support, they move around with the actor between situations, and are often regarded as a stable, reliable 'other half' of the self. Because of the high degree of emotional investment partners have in each other, they can be relied upon more than any other team-mate to keep the actor in face and support their identity claims; there is an expectation of dramaturgical loyalty (see Chapter 5 above), quite apart from notions of sexual fidelity or moral faithfulness. At times, the pair may even act as a single performative unit, presenting a united front to outsiders (Goffman 1959): in the game of social life each member is an interactional accomplice, a partner in crime.

The flipside of this, however, is that such relationships are highly fateful (Goffman 1967: 149–270) for identity. With more invested in a partner, there is more at stake to lose, and the prospect of betrayal looms large as a threat to personal integrity. The fear of losing a significant other makes it dangerous to become so close, and casts a shadow over the prospect of emotional intimacy. To varying extents, this cautiousness will be reflected in partners' behaviour towards each other and in their strategies for managing their coupledom. The daily rituals of navigating intimate relationships, like any other kind, involve carefully designed moves, bluffing, guessing and risk-taking. Loving, as a social process, is also a game of mutual regard, selective disclosure and taking the role of the other (Mead 1934), as partners calculate the gains and losses they stand to accrue in the trade-off between trust and vulnerability to betrayal.

One example of this is the extraordinary case of Gemma Barker, a British teenage girl who in 2009–10 posed as a boy to seduce, romance and ultimately betray her two close female friends. In the guise of a character called 'Aaron', Gemma first began an online relationship with her friend Alice, declining to meet her in person on the grounds that he was shy. Simultaneously, as 'Luke', she began online dating her friend Jessica, flattering her with how much he seemed to understand her. When Jessica pressed for a meeting, an 'uncovering move' (Goffman 1969) that threatened to reveal the truth, 'Luke' ended the relationship and Gemma created a new character to take his place. 'Connor' arrived on the scene and seemed very sympathetic to Jessica's plight. They eventually met, although again he claimed to be very shy and would only communicate by text message; he also wore a baseball cap pulled down over his face because, he claimed, he had alopecia. 'Aaron' and Alice, 'Connor' and Jessica continued to date, with Gemma playing both of the male roles. The situation came to a head when Jessica was having sex with 'Connor' and finally saw his face: she recognized him as 'Aaron', her friend's boyfriend. Believing she had been raped, Jessica called the police, who went to arrest 'Aaron', only of course to discover that he was in fact Gemma.

This case raises some fascinating questions about the ontology of social identity, outlined in Chapter 1. Gemma was undoubtedly engaging in identity deception, and Jessica and Alice felt betrayed by their friend's disingenuousness. But this assumes that the 'true' self behind the mask was Gemma, and that 'Aaron' and 'Connor' were mere personae. Perhaps to Gemma, though, these male characters felt more 'real' than her female self: was she exploring what she saw as a means to authenticity? What were her motives: was she simply manipulating her friends in a cold-hearted, calculating manner, or was she on a personal journey of biographical sense-making? As we know from symbolic interactionist theory (Mead 1934; Blumer 1969), the meanings we give to our own behaviour and those that others interpret or attribute to us can be discrepant. Meanwhile, who were Alice and Jessica dating, and of which gender were they? Jessica said afterwards that the experience led her to question her own sexuality, as she now wondered if this meant she was 'really' a lesbian.

The prosecuting judge ruled that crimes of sexual violence had occurred because, '[h]ad either of them realised that the "boys" with whom they were having relationships was in fact a girl, they would never have consented to what happened' (*Daily Telegraph* 2012). In symbolic interactionist terms, the 'symbolic objects' towards which they oriented their actions were their imagined fantasies of males, even if an external observer would say that the significant other was Gemma. Should we define intimate relationships in terms of participants' subjective perceptions and constructed realities, rather than any presumed objective reality? As we recall from Thomas and Thomas's adage (1928: 575), SI takes the view that '[i]f men [*sic*] define situations as real, they are real in their consequences.' So if whole definitions of situations can be deceptive, who colludes in sustaining this illusion? Can the victims be culpable (interactionally speaking) in the process of negotiating their own deception?

Simmel (1900, 1908b) considered the tantalizing allure of intimate partnership. Its appeal lay in the prospect of secrecy and collusion: the excitement and fun of creating a magic, fantastical second world alongside the mundane, manifest one. As Cohen and Taylor (1995) argue, the most effective escape routes from the drudgery of everyday life are those built into its very fabric, such as recreational activities and holidays. With this escape from one's own lifeworld comes the thrilling prospect of breaking into another's, and gaining private or backstage knowledge about them. In Goffman's typology, this demonstrates the insider secret, which bestows upon the actor a positive courtesy stigma by association, or Simmelian adornment. The notion of there being something valuable that lies within sight but just out of reach gives love a mysterious, exciting quality, which seduces people into pursuing it. For example, Tavory (2009) suggests that the practice of flirting involves interactants shifting between present and future time frames, to maintain ambiguity about their intentions and create suspense about the possible outcomes. Additionally, Simmel described a vision of partnership as merger, a sacrificing of individuality in exchange for the cultivation of a new, transcendent, joint identity, which is as yet unknowable. This gives intimate relationships an intoxicating appeal and mysticism, familiar to the discourse of romantic love (Evans 2003; Jackson & Scott 2010).

Partnership offers the pleasure and/or comfort of colluding in deceptive self-presentation. This may be directed at external audiences, but it may also take place between the partners themselves to make intimate life run more smoothly. In the daily routines of 'doing' relationships, couples may find themselves colluding in subtle forms of deception in order to make sense of their circumstances – particularly to persuade themselves that these are not of their own making (cf. Berger & Luckmann 1966).

For example, Jamieson (1999) observes how heterosexual couples who share an unequal division of domestic labour often construct narratives to the contrary. Although men have been shown to exercise more power in relationships by controlling the household budget (Pahl 1989) or opting out of housework and childcare responsibilities (Brannen & Moss 1991), this may not be resented, or even perceived, because of the interpretive frame the couple put around it. Accounts and justifications (Scott & Lyman 1968; see Chapter 3 above) serve to rationalize what might otherwise be seen as unfair decisions: a man claims that his wife prepares most of the meals just because she 'happens to be better at cooking' (Jamieson 1999: 484), while she excuses his failure to tidy up because 'he doesn't care about mess.' Likewise, while women may assume more responsibility for performing emotional labour in heterosexual relationships (Duncombe & Marsden 1993), they will often reason to an interviewer that their husbands show affection in other, more practical ways, such as home repairs, and thus that these are different but equal 'practices of intimacy' (Jamieson 1999).

Bittman and Pixley (1997) concur that couples engage in displays of 'pseudomutuality' when telling their stories to external audiences, including social researchers. This term, borrowed from family systems psychotherapy (Wynne et al. 1958; Laing & Esterson 1964), describes the collusive enactment of a story of domestic harmony, which conceals behind-the-scenes experiences of conflict (see Chapter 5 above). Such rationalizations allow the couple to tell themselves a story about democratically negotiated arrangements, in which they fervently desire to believe, to avoid dealing with the harsh reality of inequality. As Jamieson (1999: 487) explains: '. . . collaborative effort can produce a sense of being equal and intimate, in spite of inequalities. What is important is not an intense process of mutual self-disclosure and exploration but a shared repertoire of cover stories, taboos and self-dishonesty.'

However, to engage in such games is decidedly risky, for they depend upon both partners' continued co-operation. Should either falter, the deceptive mechanisms will break down, rendering both partners vulnerable to exposure. Betrayal of this kind can occur in the context of relationship dissolution, but also, paradoxically, as an anticipated event that explains why people form and/or stay in relationships in the first place. This is because of the unique social bonds that are entailed by romantic intimacy. The dyad, or two-person bond, is precariously dependent on the continued commitment of these specific individuals, and threatens to dissolve if either party becomes disengaged (Simmel 1908b). Triads and larger groups, by contrast, have an existence *sui generis* (Durkheim 1898) that can survive changing membership.

Here Simmel anticipated Giddens' (1992) notion of the late modern 'pure relationship', wherein partners focus upon each other's unique characteristics rather than any external support structures; the relationship is self-sufficiently based upon 'confluent love', which endures only to the extent that both partners feel satisfied, or 'until further notice'. In Giddens' view, the pure relationship is vulnerable to dissolution, ontological insecurity being both a driving force for its formation and the threatened consequence of its ending. Partners are thrown together through a shared fear of being alone, their private, fantastical 'second world' with its co-constructed narratives providing an illusory sense of control over existential anxieties (Giddens 1991). This has been read as a reflection of the wider cultural trends of detraditionalization and individualization (Beck & Beck-Gernsheim 2002), whereby the decline of traditional structures and normative institutions forces actors to turn inwards to seek certainty, stability and identity through the intimate spaces of the lifeworld.

For Simmel, the perils of intimacy lay more in coming together than in being alone. Insularity and segregation render the couple vulnerable to the claustrophobic pressures of mutual dependency: danger arises not from external threats but from the internally sourced risk of implosion, the relationship falling in on itself. Total honesty and self-disclosure leave partners vulnerable to complete 'knownaboutness' through surrendering self-guardianship of the internal realm. In this view, coupledom serves as a greedy institution (Coser 1974), demanding total commitment and intense dedication: passionate lovers offering themselves up for consumption allow their ontological boundaries to become dangerously permeable. The state we now describe as 'co-dependency' is a recently constructed problem of late modern therapy culture (Furedi 2004), but echoes Simmel's earlier concerns.

Similar ideas are explored in Bauman's (2003) account of 'liquid love', as an ambivalent drive both to feel intimately connected and to retain a sense of autonomy. He observed the formation of 'top pocket relationships', whereby 'semi-detached couples' remained defensively attached to their individual secret worlds, venturing out only for carefully circumscribed episodes of intimacy. For example, in Baxter's (1986) content analysis of 157 students' written accounts of relationship break-ups, the reasons most often cited were contradictory: divided between, on the one hand, a desire for greater autonomy and time spent apart and, on the other, a wish for more similarity, openness, emotional sharing and time spent together. These responses were also gendered, with men citing the former set of reasons more and women the latter, which suggests that there may be additional dimensions to the cultural dilemma that Bauman identified.

As well as emotional tangles, we can detect a dramaturgical danger in Simmel's vision of partnership merger. To act not merely alongside another but *with* them, as a joint performative unit, is decidedly risky to one's status as a social actor. Once we have let someone else into our private lifeworld, revealed all our secrets and shown all our cards, there can be no going back to the prior state of ignorance, no more bluffing, game playing or careful impression management. Somebody else knows our tricks, the 'true' self behind the character, and has the power to exploit this information, either by revealing it to third parties or by simply holding onto it themselves. This is why relationship break-ups can be so difficult to initiate and painful to endure, as in addition to grieving the loss of the collective identity and the magical second world, there may be a feeling of ontological betrayal, as if parts of the self have been eroded. The transgression of basic relationship 'ground rules' and expectations about openness, equity and loyalty represents a disturbing violation of trust (Baxter 1986). In readjusting to singledom, the boundaries around the self must be redrawn, defences gathered and new methods of deception put in place.

## Transceivership and duplicitous consciousness

A final complication takes us to the deepest level of deceptive intimacy: that which occurs within the self. This is that people are not
simply actors *or* audience members as distinct and absolute types,
but rather move between the two positions according to situational
contingencies. We can all identify with both the active and the passive
or recipient experience of self-presentation, and view the social drama
from different perspectives. Goffman (1963b) described social actors
as 'transceivers': capable of being both transmitters and receivers of
expressive information, at different times and in different interaction
contexts. He wrote of the 'special mutuality' that emerges in situations
of co-presence, as actors can imagine themselves to be both subject and
object, 'I' and 'Me', simultaneously. We can examine the discomfiting
inconsistencies that occur within a person's self as they shift perspective
from performer to audience member, or are aware of playing discrepant
roles on different occasions.

Transceivership implies that any given individual might be a deceiver
in one situation but a deceived party in another. Not only does this
caution us against making essentialist statements about 'deceptive
people' and 'honest people', who are respectively morally bad and good,
but it also challenges the idea that we interpret situations from one of
these perspectives alone, or are oblivious to alternative interpretations.
Goffman's transceiver inhabits a dual perspective, able to take the role
of the deceiver or the deceived with equal ease, moving between and
even holding both views simultaneously. On the one hand, this creates
an unsettling realization of one's own perspective being limited, partial
and incomplete, and a heightened awareness of our vulnerability to
deceptive victimhood. On the other hand, it means that we can evaluate
our own fraudulence from the perspective of the audience, imagining
their responses and the potential social consequences of discovery.

### Cautious co-operation

The implications of this are twofold. Firstly, transceivership engenders
a cynical regard for one's fellow actors, and pessimistically pragmatic
motivations for co-operating with them. Being aware of both the
deceiver and deceived perspectives and recognizing that anyone can
inhabit either, the actor sees the potential for the tables to be turned:
just as we might drift from innocence into guilt, so might significant
others become the perpetrators of deception, and we the victims. Rather
than selfless, collectivist peers, seeking to interact harmoniously, we
now perceive our team-mates as individualist actors who are as shrewd,

calculating and instrumental as we are ourselves. A climate of suspicion and mistrust develops as we recognize that intimate acquaintances may be exploiting us for personal gain, and furthermore using the very same techniques of deception that we have used ourselves.

Co-operation with team-mates must then be pursued cautiously: we exercise dramaturgical discipline (Goffman 1959) as we feign breezy nonchalance while remaining vigilant that we may be being hood-winked. What appear to be expressions of genuine sympathy may turn out to be mere obsequiousness: shallow, empty and phoney displays of surface rather than deep acting (Hochschild 1983, 2003). Co-operation is no longer about the collective pursuit of intersubjectivity, or of harmony between actors' authentic intentions, but, rather, a fitting together of their surface performances to create an aesthetically pleasing appearance: a neatly choreographed dance whose formation collapses as soon as the music stops.

Thus there are occasions when intersubjectivity fostered through intimacy does not facilitate the adoption of the 'natural attitude' (Schütz 1972), but rather encourages its suspension. It is difficult to remain in a state of blissful ignorance when one has too much insider knowledge of dramaturgical tactics. As Becker (1998) argued, learn-ing a performance team's 'tricks of the trade' helps to make us wiser and better equipped for success, but also more cynical and somewhat disillusioned. Dramaturgical experience leads us into a state of disap-pointment (Craib 1994) or depressive realism (Alloy & Abramson 1988), as we become gloomily aware of the Machiavellian tendencies that all actors hide beneath their co-operative veneer. Realizing that the world cannot simply be divided into people who are safe and unsafe, trustworthy or non-trustworthy, friends or enemies, we accommodate to a more pessimistic outlook. This is what Zimbardo (2007) calls the Lucifer Effect: if even good people can do bad things, the potential for 'evil' (or in this case deception) is in everyone, and we can trust no one.

## Self-deception

Secondly, transceivership raises the question of whether self-deception – the ultimate form of intimate betrayal – is possible. Can this scepti-cal regard for others extend to separate components of the self: the deceived object 'Me' failing to reflect on the subject 'I' as an untrust-worthy deceiver? As Mead (1934: 174) said, 'I cannot turn around fast enough to catch myself' (see Chapter 1 above). In moral philosophy and psychology, the answer is affirmative insofar as the actor is presumed to operate on different levels of consciousness. We can deceive ourselves

through 'madness': delusional beliefs, misplaced faith, psychotic symptoms of dissociation or splitting, and defence mechanisms such as
denial or repression. Some cynics argue that romantic love and religious
faith involve the same mental processes (Slater 2006).

By contrast, symbolic interactionist theory casts doubt on whether
these are really cases of self-deception. According to Meltzer (2003),
the term is an oxymoron because of the relational and intentional
character of deception: one must take the role of the other and understand their perception of a situation in order to know how to mislead
them. We cannot do this to ourselves, as it would entail simultaneously
believing and disbelieving in a state of affairs – a logical impossibility.
Similarly, deception involves self-indication, a reflexive awareness of
one's own intention to deceive, and of the mismatch between one's
privately held beliefs and communicative actions. This means that we
cannot lie to ourselves: we cannot be naïve victims while simultaneously
aware of our mischievous intentions. In Meltzer's view, self-deception
is qualitatively distinct from states of madness, religion or superstition,
wherein the actor adheres sincerely and single-mindedly to their beliefs
in 'good faith' (Sartre 1943).


## The Impostor Phenomenon

Nevertheless, SI itself provides some examples of actors engaging in
self-deception. The Impostor Phenomenon (Clance 1985), said to
plague women professionals in particular, describes a (mis)perception
of oneself as fraudulent in one's claimed achievements. Despite tangible
markers of success, such as qualifications and promotions, the liar/
victim is plagued by self-doubt, feeling as if she is not really as intelligent
or skilled as others believe her to be. Perhaps she has been recruited by
mistake: one day she will be found out, exposed and humiliated by those
who are genuinely talented. This attitude is commonly found in those
occupying junior positions within occupational hierarchies or communities of practice (Wenger 1998), such as new university lecturers (Scott
2007b) and college students (Becker et al. 1968).

Clance and Imes (1978) found the Impostor Phenomenon to be
prevalent amongst the 150 'highly successful' women academics they
surveyed, who reported feelings of fraudulence and low self-confidence,
dismissing their successes as the result of luck, mistakes or dogged hard
work, rather than genuine ability. Furthermore, these women also felt
ashamed of this very fraudulence, regarding it as a discreditable stigma
of their backstage selves (cf. Goffman 1963a), which they strove to
keep secret. Self-perceived impostors regard each social encounter in
isolation from the next: the relief at avoiding discovery is short-lived

and precarious. Even if we manage to fool one audience, we might be discovered by the next, and cannot risk letting our guard down.

The daily work of preventing others from finding out one's 'true' identity is tiring, demanding constant attention to information control and impression management (Goffman 1959). The women in Clance and Imes' study devised game-like strategies, such as 'psyching out' the audience (working out what kind of intellectual performance their senior colleagues expected and fulfilling this through specific tasks, such as a well-targeted journal article), 'charming' potential critics with their femininity in the hope of softening harsh attitudes, gaining approval from a top authority figure, and sheer hard work, with long hours and scrupulous preparation.

My study of performance anxiety in academics (Scott 2007b) found that new lecturers dealt with their nervousness by over-preparing and rehearsing lecture material according to a tight script. They lived in dread of forgetting their lines or being floored by a student's difficult question, and sought only to survive from one stressful class to another. Three women lecturers recounted this experience. Hazel said that she dreaded being challenged by a student's question, 'especially when I can't answer immediately . . . I wonder if they're going to think I'm stupid', and Ellen agreed that when she first started teaching, 'I was trying to keep a very tight control over the proceedings . . . the most important thing [was] that I didn't look an idiot!' Joanne summarized the 'impostor' feeling clearly when she recalled that 'my worst fear was not having enough to say, or not having anything to say, or someone asking me something that I didn't know the answer to' (Scott 2007b: 194).

The Impostor Phenomenon highlights an intriguing paradox: on the one hand, there is the feeling of conspicuous individual deviance (it is 'only me' who is the fraud, while 'everyone else' knows what they are doing), and yet, on the other hand, it appears to be a common, if not universal, sensation. As I found with my research on shyness (Scott 2007a), it is easy to imagine a generalized image of the 'Competent Other' who is poised with the requisite social skills, but few, if any, of us privately believe that we possess these. Could it be that we are all faking our way through social life, bumbling along and hoping to avoid discovery, and that no one really is as competent as they appear? What would happen if we had a Competence Amnesty, when everyone confessed to their fraudulence?

Following in this spirit, Becker (1986) debunks some of the myths relating to academic writing, constructed and perpetuated by scholars themselves, which can make it so daunting a prospect. He refutes such notions as there being 'one right way' to compose an argument,

that 'using big words will make you sound smarter' and that 'proper'
academics write near-perfect drafts first time – and points instead to the
mundane processes of work involved in crafting a thesis by laborious
redrafting. Under-confident academics deceive themselves by imagining a row of stern critics, judging their work and looking for the mistakes
that will surely expose them. Writing then becomes a matter of fooling
the audience, by making convincing credibility claims (Manning 2000)
and getting away with it. Scholars ridden with feelings of impostordom
try to affect an authoritative persona, through verbose, impenetrable
and pretentious language, to throw their internal critics off the scent.

Richards (1986), who was one of Becker's postgraduate students,
explains how these feelings of impostordom, though projected onto an
imagined, generalized other, ultimately reflect private misgivings about
the self. In a neat illustration of the I–Me dialogue (Mead 1934), her
agentic 'I' imagines how she might appear to an audience who can see
through her presumed ineptitude, and reflects on the objectified 'Me'
as a shameful fraud:

> [Trusted friends'] responses convince me to trust myself, because for me,
> there's another great risk involved in writing. It's the risk of discovering
> that I am incapable of doing sociology and, by extension, that I am not a
> sociologist and therefore not the person I claim to be. The risk of being
> found out and judged by colleagues is bound up in the risk of being found
> out and judged by myself. The two are so closely interwoven that it is often
> hard for me to separate them. How can you know that you are doing OK,
> that you are a sociologist, unless someone tells you so? It's other people's
> responses that allow me to understand who I am. . . . So there I am, faced
> with a blank page, confronting the risk of discovering that I cannot do
> what I set out to do, and therefore am not the person I pretend to be.
> (Richards 1986: 117)

Richards suggests that the only way to cure the paralysis of self-doubt is
to call oneself on this self-deception, exposing the lies we tell ourselves
to avoid taking academic responsibility. Confidence, the prize at stake,
is really just a matter of believing in one's own credibility; there are no
other, 'real' audiences beyond our imagination. However, to confront
one's own deceptiveness is the ultimate risky venture for the transceiver-
actor, a dangerous gamble on one's own ontological security. Perhaps
Baudrillard (1981) was right when he said that academia was nothing
more than playing games with different stories of reality, none of which
is any more convincing or true than any other. But even so, we would
be wise also to bear in mind Goffman's (1961b: 15–72) sage rejoinder
that the fun we find in games is deadly serious.

## Conclusion

Symbolic interactionist theories of deception, with their consequential-ist focus on its functions for the interaction order, present an important alternative view to that espoused by moral philosophy. Deception can be socially good, regardless of whether it is ethically right or wrong, because of its potential to strengthen social bonds, gloss over the cracks of strained relations and contribute to the smooth orchestration of everyday life. Ironically, however, in the pursuit of greater intimacy, these objectives can be compromised, because actors perceive there to be more at stake in trusting one another, forming and potentially dis-solving relationships. The dialectic of fascination and fear that Simmel identified can be found at every level of intimacy, but its relative propor-tions shift, causing a change in the way in which deception is regarded and allowed to operate between interaction partners. As social relations become closer and more fateful for self-identity, the cautious, pragmatic rationalism that characterized looser interactional forms gives way to a greater propensity to trust and dramaturgical risk-taking, driven by escalating fascination, intrigue and the tantalizing allure of intimacy. Deception may still occur, but becomes more emotionally charged, conveying notions of betrayal by insiders in ever-decreasing circles of collusion. To participate in this game is both deliciously thrilling and perilously risky, posing dramaturgical dilemmas that culminate in the ontological quagmire of transceivership, wherein those brave enough confront the paradox of self-deceptive agency.

# References

Adler, P. & Adler, P.A. (1978) 'The role of momentum in sport.' *Journal of Contemporary Ethnography*, 7, 2, 153–75.

Adler, P.A. & Adler, P. (1990) *Backboards and Blackboards: College Athletics and Role Engulfment*. New York: Columbia University Press.

Agostino, K. (1998) 'The making of warriors: men, identity and military culture.' *Journal of International Gender Studies*, 3, 2, 58–75.

Albas, D. & Albas, C. (1988) 'Aces and Bombers: the post-exam impression management strategies of students.' *Symbolic Interaction*, 11, 2, 289–302.

Albrow, M.C. (1970) *Bureaucracy*. London: Pall Mall.

Alloy, L.B. & Abramson, L.Y. (1988) 'Depressive realism: four theoretical perspectives.' In L.B. Alloy (ed.), *Cognitive Processes in Depression*. New York: Guilford, pp. 223–65.

Allport, G.W. (1961) *Pattern and Growth in Personality*. New York: Holt, Rinehart & Winston.

Altheide, D.L. & Pfuhl, E.H. (1980) 'Self-accomplishment through running.' *Symbolic Interaction*, 3, 2, 127–42.

Andersen, H. (1837) 'The Emperor's new clothes.' In *Hans Andersen: His Classic Fairy Tales* (trans. E. Haugaard). London: Gollancz, 1985, pp. 119–24.

Anderson, E. (2008) 'Inclusive masculinity in a fraternal setting.' *Men and Masculinities*, 10, 5, 604–20.

Anderson, L. & Taylor, J.D. (2010) 'Standing out while fitting in: serious leisure identities and aligning actions among skydivers and gun collectors.' *Journal of Contemporary Ethnography*, 39, 1, 34–59.

Anderson, N. (1923) *The Hobo: The Sociology of the Homeless Man*. Chicago: University of Chicago Press.

Antaki, C. & Widdicombe, S. (1998) 'Identity as an achievement and as a tool.' In C. Antaki & S. Widdicombe (eds), *Identities in Talk*. London: Sage, pp. 1–14.

Athens, L. (1995) 'Dramatic self-change.' *Sociological Quarterly*, 36, 3, 571–86.

Atkinson, P.A. & Housley, W. (2003) *Interactionism*. London: Sage.

Augé, M. (1992) *Non-Places: Introduction to an Anthropology of Supermodernity* (trans. J. Howe). London: Verso, 1995.

Austin, J.L. (1957) 'A plea for excuses.' Presidential address. *Proceedings of the Aristotelian Society*, 57, 1–30.

Austin, J.L. (1962) *How to Do Things with Words*. Oxford: Oxford University Press, 1975.

Backman, C.W. & Secord, P.F. (1968) 'The self and role selection.' In C. Gordon & K.J. Gergen (eds), *The Self in Social Interaction*. New York: Wiley, pp. 289–96.

Bailey, J. (2000) 'Some meanings of "the private" in sociological thought.' *Sociology*, 34, 3, 381–401.

Bakhtin, M. (1965) *Rabelais and His World* (trans. H. Iswolsky). Cambridge, MA: MIT Press, 1968.

Ball, D.W. (1972) 'The definition of the situation: some theoretical and methodological consequences of taking W.I. Thomas seriously.' *Journal for the Theory of Social Behaviour*, 2, 61–82.

Barker, E. (1989) *New Religious Movements: A Practical Introduction*. London: HMSO.

Barnes, J.A. (1994) *A Pack of Lies: Towards a Sociology of Lying*. Cambridge: Cambridge University Press.

Barthes, R. (1957) *Mythologies* (trans. A. Lavers). London: Paladin, 1972.

Bartky, S. (1990) *Femininity and Domination: Studies in the Phenomenology of Oppression*. London: Routledge.

Baudrillard, J. (1981) *Simulacra and Simulation* (trans. S.F. Glaser). Ann Arbor: University of Michigan Press, 1995.

Bauman, Z. (2000) *Liquid Modernity*. Cambridge: Polity.

Bauman, Z. (2003) *Liquid Love: On the Frailty of Human Bonds*. Cambridge: Polity.

Baxter, L.A. (1986) 'Gender differences in the heterosexual relationship rules embedded in break-up accounts.' *Journal of Social and Personal Relationships*, 3, 3, 289–306.

BBC Magazine (2007) 'Love it or hate it,' 13 September. *http://news.bbc.co.uk/1/hi/6992874.stm*

Beck, U. (1992) *Risk Society: Towards a New Modernity*. London: Sage.

Beck, U. & Beck-Gernsheim, E. (2002) *Individualization: Institutionalized Individualism and Its Social and Political Consequences*. London: Sage.

Becker, H.S. (1952) 'The career of the Chicago public school teacher.' *American Journal of Sociology*, 57, 5, 470–7.

Becker, H.S. (1953) 'Becoming a marihuana user.' *American Journal of Sociology*, 59, 235–42.

Becker, H.S. (1963) *Outsiders: Studies in the Sociology of Deviance*. New York: Free Press.

Becker, H.S. (1967) 'Whose side are we on?' *Social Problems*, 14, 3, 239–47.

Becker, H.S. (1986) *Writing for Social Scientists*. Chicago: University of Chicago Press.

Becker, H.S. (1998) *Tricks of the Trade: How to Think About Your Research While You're Doing It.* Chicago: University of Chicago Press.

Becker, H.S. (2000) 'The etiquette of improvisation.' *Mind, Culture and Activity,* 7, 171–6. *http://home.earthlink.net/~hsbecker/articles/improv.html*

Becker, H.S. (2003) 'The politics of presentation: Goffman and total institutions.' *Symbolic Interaction,* 26, 4, 659–69.

Becker, H.S., Geer, B. & Hughes, E.C. (1968) *Making the Grade: The Academic Side of College Life.* New York: Wiley.

Bellah, R.N. (1967) 'Civil religion in America.' *Daedalus,* 96, 1–21.

Berger, P.L. (1969) *The Social Reality of Religion.* London: Faber & Faber.

Berger, P.L. & Luckmann, T. (1966) *The Social Construction of Reality.* New York: Anchor.

Bettelheim, B. (1991) *The Informed Heart: A Study of the Psychological Consequences of Living Under Extreme Fear and Terror.* Harmondsworth: Penguin.

Beynon, H. (1973) *Working for Ford.* Harmondsworth: Penguin.

Billig, M. (1996) *Arguing and Thinking: A Rhetorical Approach to Social Psychology.* Cambridge: Cambridge University Press.

Birenbaum, A. (1970) 'On managing a courtesy stigma.' *Journal of Health and Social Behavior,* 11, 3, 196–206.

Bishop, S. (2013) 'A frame analysis of how the social reality of a pub "regular" identity is presented, upheld and contested in the pub environment.' Unpublished undergraduate student essay, University of Sussex.

Bittman, M. & Pixley, J. (1997) *The Double Life of the Family.* London: Allen & Unwin.

Black, P. (2004) *The Beauty Industry.* London: Routledge.

Bloor, M., McKeganey, N. & Fonkert, D. (1988) *One Foot in Eden: A Sociological Study of the Range of Therapeutic Community Practice.* New York: Routledge.

Blumer, H. (1969) *Symbolic Interactionism: Perspective and Method.* Englewood Cliffs, NJ: Prentice-Hall.

Bok, S. (1978) *Lying: Moral Choice in Public and Private Life.* New York: Vintage.

Bok, S. (1989) *Secrets: On the Ethics of Concealment and Revelation.* New York: Pantheon.

Booth, M. (2014) *The Almost Nearly Perfect People: The Truth about the Nordic Miracle.* London: Jonathan Cape.

Borchard, K. (2011) *Homeless in Las Vegas: Stories from the Street.* Las Vegas: University of Nevada Press.

Bordo, S. (1993) *Unbearable Weight: Feminism, Western Culture and the Body.* Berkeley: University of California Press.

Bourdieu, P. (1979) *Distinction: A Social Critique of the Judgement of Taste* (trans. R. Nice). London: Routledge, 1984.

Braginsky, B.M., Braginsky, D.D. & Ring, K. (1973) *Methods of Madness: The Hospital as a Last Resort.* New York: Holt, Rinehart & Winston.

Brannen, J. & Moss, P. (1991). *Managing Mothers: Dual Earner Households after Maternity Leave.* London: Unwin Hyman.

Brissett, D. & Edgley, C. (eds) (2005) *Life as Theater: A Dramaturgical Sourcebook*. New York: Transaction.

Brittan, A. (1973) *Meanings and Situations*. London: Routledge & Kegan Paul.

Brooker, C. (2014) 'Benefits Street – poverty porn, or just the latest target for pent-up British fury?' *Guardian*, 12 January. *http://www.theguardian.com/commentisfree/2014/jan/12/benefits-street-poverty-porn-british-fury*

Brookes, A. (2003) 'A critique of neo-Hahnian outdoor education theory. Part 1: challenges to the concept of "character building".' *Journal of Adventure Education and Outdoor Learning*, 3, 1, 49–62.

Bruce, S. (1995) *Religion in Modern Britain*. Oxford: Oxford University Press.

Bruner, J. (1991) 'The narrative construction of reality.' Critical Inquiry, 18, 1, 1–21.

Bulmer, M. (1984) The Chicago School of Sociology: Institutionalization, Diversity, and the Rise of Sociological Research. Chicago: University of Chicago Press

Burke, K. (1945) A Grammar of Motives. Berkeley: University of California Press, 1969.

Burnett, K. (2001) 'Self-help or sink-or-swim? The experiences of residents in a UK concept-based therapeutic community.' In B. Rawlings & R. Yates (eds), *Therapeutic Communities for the Treatment of Drug Users*. London: Jessica Kingsley, pp. 138–48.

Burns, T. (1992) Erving Goffman. London: Routledge

Burr, V. (2003) Social Constructionism (2nd edition). Hove: Routledge.

Burrell, I. (2014) ' 'Benefits Street': Channel 4 documentary sparks anger and threats of violence.' *The Independent*, 7 January. *http://www.independent.co.uk/news/media/tv-radio/channel-4s-benefits-street-sparks-anger-and-threats-of-violence-9044880.html*

Bury, M. (1982) 'Chronic illness as biographical disruption.' *Sociology of Health and Illness*, 4, 2, 167–82.

Butler, J. (1990) *Gender Trouble: Feminism and the Subversion of Identity*. London: Routledge.

Butler, J. (1993) *Bodies That Matter: On the Discursive Limits of Sex*. London: Routledge.

Calhoun, C. (1994) 'Social theory and the politics of identity.' In C. Calhoun (ed.), *Social Theory and the Politics of Identity*. Oxford: Blackwell, pp. 9–36.

Carnes, M.C. (1989) *Secret Ritual and Manhood in Victorian America*. New Haven, CT: Yale University Press.

Carrigan, M. (2011) 'There's more to life than sex? Difference and commonality within the asexual community.' *Sexualities*, 14, 4, 462–78.

Cederström, C. & A. Spicer (2015) *The Wellness Syndrome*. Cambridge: Polity.

Charon, J. (2007) *Symbolic Interaction: An Introduction, an Interpretation, an Integration* (9th edition). Englewood Cliffs, NJ: Prentice-Hall.

Chomsky, N. (1965) *Aspects of the Theory of Syntax*. Boston: MIT Press.

Chriss, J.J. (1999) 'Role distance and the negational self.' In G. Smith (ed.), *Goffman and Social Organization*. London: Routledge, pp. 64–80.

Clance, P.R. (1985) *The Impostor Phenomenon: When Success Makes You Feel Like a Fake.* Toronto: Bantam.

Clance, P.R. & Imes, S. (1978) 'The Impostor Phenomenon in high-achieving women: dynamics and therapeutic intervention.' *Psychotherapy Theory, Research and Practice,* 15, 3, 241–7.

Clayman, S. (1992) 'Footing in the achievement of neutrality: the case of news interview discourse.' In P. Drew & J. Heritage (eds), *Talk At Work: Interaction in Institutional Settings.* Cambridge: Cambridge University Press, pp. 163–98.

Clegg, S.R. (1989) *Frameworks of Power.* London: Sage.

Clegg, S.R. (1990) *Modern Organizations.* London: Sage.

Clegg, S.R. (2006) *Power and Organizations.* London: Sage.

Cohen, A.P. (1994) *Self Consciousness: An Alternative Anthropology of Identity.* London: Routledge.

Cohen, S. (1972) *Folk Devils and Moral Panics: The Creation of the Mods and Rockers.* London: MacGibbon & Kee.

Cohen, S. & Taylor, L. (1995) *Escape Attempts: The Theory and Practice of Resistance in Everyday Life.* London: Routledge.

Collins, R. (2005) *Interaction Ritual Chains.* Princeton: Princeton University Press.

Connell, R. & Pearse, R. (2015) *Gender: In World Perspective* (3rd edition). Cambridge: Polity.

Cooley, C.H. (1902) *Human Nature and the Social Order.* New Brunswick, N: Transaction, 1992.

Cooper, D. (1978) *The Language of Madness.* London: Penguin.

Coser, L.A. (1974) *Greedy Institutions: Patterns of Undivided Commitment.* New York: Free Press.

Coupland, J., Robinson, J.D. & Coupland, N. (1994) 'Frame negotiation in doctor–elderly patient consultations.' *Discourse & Society,* 5, 1, 89–124.

Craib, I. (1994) *The Importance of Disappointment.* London: Routledge.

Craib, I. (1998) 'What's happening to mourning?' In his *Experiencing Identity.* London: Sage, pp. 157–68.

Crossley, N. (2006a) 'In the gym: motives, meanings and moral careers.' *Body & Society,* 12, 3, 23–50.

Crossley, N. (2006b) *Contesting Psychiatry: Social Movements in Mental Health.* London: Routledge.

Csikszentmihalyi, M. (2002) *Flow: The Classic Work on How to Achieve Happiness.* London: Rider.

*Daily Telegraph* (2012) 'Woman who tricked two teenage girls into relationships by disguising herself as a boy faces jail,' 17 January. *http://www.telegraph. co.uk/news/uknews/crime/9020184/Woman-who-tricked-two-teenage-girls-into-relationships-by-disguising-herself-as-a-boy-faces-jail.html*

Daun, Å. (1989) *Swedish Mentality.* University Park: Pennsylvania State University Press.

Davie, G. (1994) *Religion in Britain since 1945.* Oxford: Blackwell.

Davis, F. (1961) 'Deviance disavowal: the management of strained interaction by the visibly handicapped'. *Social Problems*, 9, 2, 120–32.

Day, R.A. & Day, J.V. (1977) 'A review of the current state of negotiated order theory: an appreciation and a critique.' *Sociological Quarterly*, 18, 126–42.

De Albuquerque, C.L. & Paes-Machado, E. (2004) 'The hazing machine: the shaping of Brazilian military police recruits.' *Policing & Society*, 14, 2, 175–92.

DeGloma, T. (2010) 'Awakenings: autobiography, memory and the social logic of personal discovery.' *Sociological Forum*, 25, 3, 519–40.

Denzin, N.K. (1968) 'Collective behaviour in total institutions: the case of the mental hospital and the prison.' *Social Problems*, 15, 3, 353–65.

Denzin, N.K. (1969) 'Symbolic interactionism and ethnomethodology: a proposed synthesis.' *American Sociological Review*, 34, 922–34.

Denzin, N.K. (1987) *The Alcoholic Self.* Beverly Hills: Sage.

Dewey, J. (1922) *Human Nature and Conduct.* New York: Holt & Co.

Ditton, J. (1980) 'A bibliographical exegesis of Goffman's sociology.' In J. Ditton (ed.), *The View from Goffman.* New York: St Martin's Press, pp. 1–23.

Dodd, N. & Raffel, S. (2013) 'The everyday life of the self: reworking early Goffman.' *Journal of Classical Sociology*, 13, 1, 163–78.

Douglas, J.D. & Rasmussen, P.K. with Flanagan, C.A. (1977) *The Nude Beach.* Beverly Hills: Sage.

Douglas, M. (1966) *Purity and Danger: An Analysis of Concepts of Pollution and Taboo.* London: Routledge & Kegan Paul.

Dumenil, L. (1984) *Freemasonry and American Culture, 1880–1930.* Princeton: Princeton University Press.

Duncombe, J. & Marsden, D. (1993) 'Love and intimacy: the gender division of emotion and "emotion work".' *Sociology*, 27, 221–41.

Dunham, H.W. & Weinberg, S.K. (1960) *The Culture of the State Mental Hospital.* Detroit: Wayne State University Press.

Durkheim, É. (1898) *The Division of Labour in Society* (trans. W.D. Halls). New York: Free Press, 1997.

Durkheim, E. (1912) *The Elementary Forms of Religious Life* (trans. J.W. Swain). London: Allen & Unwin, 1915.

Ebaugh, H.R.F. (1988) *Becoming an Ex: The Process of Role Exit.* Chicago: University of Chicago Press.

Edwards, D. (2005) 'Discursive psychology.' In K. Fitch & R. Sanders (eds), *Handbook of Language and Social Interaction.* Hillsdale, NJ: Lawrence Erlbaum, pp. 257–73.

Elias, N. (1939) *The Civilizing Process: Sociogenetic and Psychogenetic Investigations* (revised edition, trans. E. Jephcott). Oxford: Blackwell, 2000.

Ellison, N., Heino, R. & Gibbs, J. (2006) 'Managing impressions online: self-presentation processes in the online dating environment.' *Journal of Computer-Mediated Communication*, 11, 2, 415–41.

Emerson, J.P. (1970a) 'Behavior in private places: sustaining definitions of reality in gynecological examinations.' *Recent Sociology*, 2, 74–97.

Emerson, J.P. (1970b) 'Nothing unusual is happening.' In T. Sibutani (ed.), *Human Nature and Collective Behavior: Papers in Honor of Herbert Blumer.* Englewood Cliffs, NJ: Prentice-Hall, pp. 208–22.

Entwistle, J. (2015) *The Fashioned Body* (2nd edition). Cambridge: Polity.

Erikson, E.H. (1959) *Identity and the Life Cycle.* New York: International Universities Press.

Erikson, E.H. (1968) *Identity, Youth and Crisis.* New York: Norton.

Erikson, K.T. (1964) 'Notes on the sociology of deviance'. In H.S. Becker (ed.), *The Other Side: Perspectives on Deviance.* London: Free Press, pp. 9–21.

Evans, M. (2003) *Love: An Unromantic Discussion.* Cambridge: Polity.

Felipe, N.J. & Sommer, R. (1966) 'Invasion of personal space.' *Social Problems,* 14, 206–14.

Ferris, K. (2004) 'Transmitting ideals: constructing self and moral discourse on *Loveline.*' *Symbolic Interaction,* 27, 2, 247–66.

Fine, G.A. (1984) 'Negotiated orders and organizational cultures.' *Annual Review of Sociology,* 10, 239–62.

Fine, G.A. (1987) *With the Boys: Little League Basketball and Preadolescent Culture.* Chicago: University of Chicago Press.

Fine, G.A. (1995) *A Second Chicago School: The Development of a Postwar American Sociology.* Chicago: University of Chicago Press.

Fisher, B. & Strauss, A.L. (1978) 'Interactionism.' In T. Bottomore & R. Nisbet (eds), *A History of Sociological Analysis.* New York: Basic Books, pp. 457–98.

Fiske, J. (1992) 'The cultural economy of fandom.' In L. Lewis (ed.), *The Adoring Audience: Fan Culture and Popular Media.* London: Routledge, pp. 30–49.

Foucault, M. (1961) *Madness and Civilization* (trans. R. Howard). New York: Vintage, 1973.

Foucault, M. (1963) *The Birth of the Clinic* (trans. A.M. Sheridan). London: Routledge, 1997.

Foucault, M. (1971) *The Archaeology of Knowledge* (trans. A.M. Sheridan Smith). New York: Pantheon, 1972.

Foucault, M. (1975) *Discipline and Punish* (trans. A. Sheridan). London: Allen Lane, 1977.

Foucault, M. (1976) *The History of Sexuality: Volume 1: An Introduction* (trans. R. Hurley). New York: Vintage, 1980.

Fox, K. (2004) *Watching the English: The Hidden Rules of English Behaviour.* London: Hodder & Stoughton.

Frank, A. (1995) *The Wounded Storyteller: Body, Illness and Ethics.* Chicago: University of Chicago Press.

Fulcher, J. & Scott, J. (2007) *Sociology* (3rd edition). Oxford: Oxford University Press.

Furedi, F. (2001) *Paranoid Parenting.* London: Allen Lane.

Furedi, F. (2002) *Culture of Fear: Risk-Taking and the Morality of Low Expectation.* London: Continuum.

Furedi, F. (2004) *Therapy Culture: Cultivating Vulnerability in an Uncertain Age.* London: Routledge.

Garfinkel, H. (1956) 'Conditions of successful degradation ceremonies.' *American Sociological Review*, 61, 420–4.

Garfinkel, H. (1967) *Studies in Ethnomethodology.* Englewood Cliffs, NJ: Prentice-Hall.

Gecas, V. & Schwalbe, M.L. (1983) 'Beyond the Looking-Glass Self: social structure and efficacy-based self-esteem.' *Social Psychology Quarterly*, 46, 2, 77–88.

Geller, D. (1934) 'Lingo of the shoe salesman.' *American Speech*, 9, 4, 283–6.

Gellman, I.P. (1964) *The Sober Alcoholic: An Organizational Analysis of Alcoholics Anonymous.* New Haven, CT: College and University Press.

Gergen, K.J. (1968) 'Personal consistency and the presentation of self.' In C. Gordon & K.J. Gergen (eds), *The Self in Social Interaction.* New York: Wiley, pp. 299–308.

Gergen, K.J. (1991) *The Saturated Self: Dilemmas of Identity in Contemporary Life.* New York: Basic Books.

Giddens, A. (1984) *The Constitution of Society.* Cambridge: Polity.

Giddens, A. (1991) *Modernity and Self Identity: Self and Society in the Late Modern Age.* Cambridge: Polity.

Giddens, A. (1992) *The Transformation of Intimacy: Sexuality, Love and Eroticism in Modern Societies.* Cambridge: Polity.

Gilbert, G.N. & Mulkay, M.J. (1984) *Opening Pandora's Box: An Analysis of Scientists' Discourse.* Cambridge: Cambridge University Press.

Giles, D. (2000) *Illusions of Immortality: A Psychology of Fame and Celebrity.* New York: St Martin's Press.

Gilroy, P. (2000) *Against Race: Imagining Political Culture beyond the Color Line.* Cambridge, MA: Harvard University Press.

Glaser, B.G. & Strauss, A.L. (1964) 'Awareness contexts and social interaction.' *American Sociological Review*, 29, 5, 669–79.

Glaser, B.G. & Strauss, A.L. (1971) *Status Passage.* London: Routledge & Kegan Paul.

Glasgow University Media Group (1976) *Bad News.* London: Routledge & Kegan Paul.

Goffman, A. (2014) *On the Run: Fugitive Life in an American City.* Chicago: University of Chicago Press.

Goffman, E. (1951) 'Symbols of class status.' *British Journal of Sociology*, 2, 4, 294–304.

Goffman, E. (1952) 'On cooling the mark out: some aspects of adaptation to failure.' *Psychiatry*, 25, 451–63.

Goffman, E. (1959) *The Presentation of Self in Everyday Life.* Harmondsworth: Penguin.

Goffman, E. (1961a) *Asylums: Essays on the Social Situation of Mental Patients and Other Inmates.* New York: Anchor Books.

Goffman, E. (1961b) *Encounters: Two Studies in the Sociology of Interaction.* Indianapolis: Bobbs-Merrill.

Goffman, E. (1963a) *Stigma: Notes on the Management of Spoiled Identity*. Harmondsworth: Penguin.

Goffman, E. (1963b) *Behavior in Public Places*. New York: Free Press.

Goffman, E. (1967) *Interaction Ritual: Essays in Face-to-Face Behavior*. New York: Pantheon.

Goffman, E. (1969) *Strategic Interaction*. Philadelphia: University of Pennsylvania Press.

Goffman, E. (1971) *Relations in Public: Microstudies of the Public Order*. Harmondsworth: Penguin.

Goffman, E. (1974) *Frame Analysis: An Essay on the Organization of Experience*. New York: Northeastern University Press.

Goffman, E. (1981) *Forms of Talk*. Philadelphia: University of Pennsylvania Press.

Goffman, E. (1983a) 'The interaction order.' *American Sociological Review*, 48, 1–17.

Goffman, E. (1983b) 'Felicity's condition.' *American Journal of Sociology*, 89, 1, 1–53.

Goldthorpe, J.H., Lockwood, D., Bechhofer, F. & Platt, J. (1969) *The Affluent Worker in the Class Structure*. Cambridge: Cambridge University Press.

Gouldner, A.W. (1954) *Patterns of Industrial Bureaucracy: A Case Study of Modern Factory Administration*. New York: Free Press.

Gouldner, A.W. (1955) *Wildcat Strike*. London: Routledge & Kegan Paul.

Gouldner, A.W. (1973) *The Coming Crisis of Western Sociology*. London: Heinemann.

Gramsci, A. (1935) *The Prison Notebooks* (trans. J.A. Buttigieg). New York: Columbia University Press, 2011.

Gray, D.E. (2002) '"Everybody just freezes. Everybody is just embarrassed": felt and enacted stigma among parents of children with high-functioning autism.' *Sociology of Health and Illness*, 24, 6, 734–49.

Grazian, D. (2007) *On the Make: The Hustle of Urban Nightlife*. Chicago: University of Chicago Press.

Greeley (1973) *The Persistence of Religion*. London: SCM Press.

Green, B.C. & Jones, I. (2005) 'Serious leisure, social identity and sport tourism.' *Sport in Society*, 8, 2, 164–81.

Gross, E. & Stone, G.P. (1964) 'Embarrassment and the analysis of role requirements.' *American Journal of Sociology*, 70, 1, 1–15.

*Guardian* (2013) 'Supermarket etiquette: a guide to modern manners,' 3 July. *http://www.guardian.co.uk/lifeandstyle/shortcuts/2013/jul/03/supermarket-etiquette-guide-to-modern-manners*

Gubrium, J.F. & Holstein, J.A. (2001) *Institutional Selves: Troubled Identities in a Postmodern World*. Oxford: Oxford University Press.

Gueldner, J. (1965) 'Behavior in elevators.' Unpublished paper.

Gumprecht, B. (2006) 'Fraternity Row, the Student Ghetto, and the Faculty Enclave: characteristic residential districts in the American college town.' *Journal of Urban History*, 32, 2, 231–73.

Gusfield, J. (1987) 'Passage to play: rituals of drinking time in American society.' In M. Douglas (ed.), *Constructive Drinking: Perspectives on Drink from Anthropology*. Cambridge: Cambridge University Press, pp. 3–90.

Habermas, J. (1981) *The Theory of Communicative Action: Volume 1: Reason and the Rationalization of Society* (trans. T. McCarthy). Boston: Beacon Press, 1984.

Hacking, I. (1999) *The Social Construction of What?* Cambridge, MA: Harvard University Press.

Hale, H.C. (2008) 'The development of British military masculinities through symbolic resources.' *Culture & Psychology*, 14, 3, 305–22.

Halmos, P. (1965) *The Faith of the Counsellors*. London: Constable.

Hall, E.T. (1959) *The Silent Language*. New York: Doubleday.

Hall, S. (1996) 'Who needs identity?' In S. Hall & P. du Gay (eds), *Questions of Cultural Identity*. London: Sage, pp. 1–17.

Hamilton, S. (2014) 'Negotiating roles and making claims as a patient in the psychiatric consultation: a frame analysis.' Ph.D. thesis, University of Sussex. *http://sro.sussex.ac.uk/48726/*

Hardie-Bick, J. (2005) 'Dropping out and diving in: an ethnography of skydiving.' Doctoral thesis, University of Durham E-Theses Online. *http://etheses.dur.ac.uk/2734/*

Hardie-Bick, J. (2011) 'Total institutions and the last human freedom.' In J. Hardie-Bick & R. Lippens (eds), *Crime, Governance and Existential Predicaments*. Basingstoke: Palgrave, pp. 85–107.

Harré, R. (1998) *The Singular Self: An Introduction to the Psychology of Personhood*. London: Sage.

Harris, D.S. & Eitzen, D.S. (1978) 'The consequences of failure in sport.' *Journal of Contemporary Ethnography*, 7, 2, 177–88.

Hausmann, C., Jonason, A. & Summers-Effler, E. (2011) 'Interaction ritual theory and structural symbolic interactionism.' *Symbolic Interaction*, 34, 3, 319–29.

Hayes, T.A. (2000) 'Stigmatizing indebtedness: implications for labelling theory.' *Symbolic Interaction*, 23, 1, 29–46.

Hayman, R. (1969) *Techniques of Acting*. London: Methuen.

Hazelrigg, L.E. (1969) 'A re-examination of Simmel's "The secret and the secret society": nine propositions.' *Social Forces*, 47, 3, 323–30.

Heath, C. & vom Lehn, D. (2008) 'Configuring "interactivity": enhancing engagement in science centres and museums.' *Social Studies of Science*, 38, 1, 63–91.

Hebdige, D. (1979) *Subculture: The Meaning of Style*. London: Methuen.

Heelas, P. (1984) 'Self-religions in Britain.' *Journal of Contemporary Religion*, 1, 1, 4–5.

Heritage, J. (1984) *Garfinkel and Ethnomethodology*. Cambridge: Polity.

Heritage, J. & Clayman, S. (2010) *Talk in Action: Interactions, Identities and Institutions*. Oxford: Wiley-Blackwell.

Heritage, J. & Raymond, G. (2005) 'The terms of agreement: indexing epistemic authority and subordination in assessment sequences.' *Social Psychology Quarterly*, 68, 15–38.

Heritage, J. & Watson, R. (1979) 'Formulations as conversational objects.' In G. Psathas (ed.), *Everyday Language*. New York: Irvington Press, pp. 123–62.

Hewitt, J. (2007) *Self and Society: A Symbolic Interactionist Social Psychology*. New York: Allyn & Bacon.

Hewitt, J.P. & Stokes, R. (1975) 'Disclaimers.' *American Sociological Review*, 40, 1–11.

Hills, M. (2002) *Fan Cultures*. Hove: Psychology Press.

Hinshelwood, R.D. & Manning, N. (1979) 'The community as analyst.' In R.D. Hinshelwood & N. Manning (eds), *Therapeutic Communities*. London: Routledge & Kegan Paul, pp. 103–12.

Hochschild, A.R. (1983) *The Managed Heart: Commercialization of Human Feeling*. Berkeley: University of California Press.

Hochschild, A.R. (2003) *The Commercialization of Intimate Life*. Berkeley: University of California Press.

Hodges, L. (1995) 'Fraternity hazing rituals come to court.' *Times Higher Education*, 13 January. *http://www.timeshighereducation.co.uk/news/fraternity-hazing-rituals-come-to-court/97918.article*

Hodkinson, P. (2002) *Goth*. Oxford: Berg.

Hoffmann, H.C. (2006) 'Criticism as deviance and social control in Alcoholics Anonymous.' *Journal of Contemporary Ethnography*, 35, 6, 669–95.

Holmwood, L. & Brook, S. (2007) 'Big Brother racism complaints soar.' *Guardian*, 16 January 2007. *http://www.guardian.co.uk/media/2007/jan/16/bigbrother.broadcasting*

Holstein, J.A. & Gubrium, J.F. (2000) *The Self We Live By: Narrative Identity in a Postmodern World*. New York: Oxford University Press.

Holstein, J.A. & Miller, G. (1993) 'Social constructionism and social problems work.' In J.A. Holstein & G. Miller (eds) *Reconsidering Social Constructionism*. Hawthorne, NY: Aldine de Gruyter, pp. 151–72.

Hornbacher, M. (1998) *Wasted: A Memoir of Anorexia and Bulimia*. London: Flamingo.

Horne, J. & Wiggins, S. (2009) 'Doing being "on the edge": managing the dilemma of being authentically suicidal in an online forum.' *Sociology of Health and Illness*, 31, 2, 170–84.

Howarth, G. (2006) *Death and Dying: A Sociological Introduction*. Cambridge: Polity.

Hughes, E.C. (1945) 'Dilemmas and contradictions of status.' *American Journal of Sociology*, L, 353–9.

Hughes, E.C. (1957) 'Going concerns: the study of American institutions.' In his *The Sociological Eye: Selected Papers*. Chicago: Aldine, 1971, pp. 52–64.

Hughes, E.C. (1962) 'Good people and dirty work.' *Social Problems*, 10, 1, 3–11.

Hughey, M.W. (2008) 'Virtual (br)others and (re)sisters: authentic black fraternity and sorority identity on the Internet.' *Journal of Contemporary Ethnography*, 37, 5, 528–60.

Hume, D. (1739) *A Treatise on Human Nature*. Oxford: Oxford University Press, 2011.

Hunt, G. & Satterlee, S. (1986) 'Cohesion and division: drinking in an English village.' *Man* (N.S.) 21, 3, 521–37.

Hurdley, R. (2006) 'Dismantling mantelpieces: narrating identities and materializing culture in the home.' *Sociology*, 40, 4, 717–33.

Hutchby, I. (1999) 'Frame attunement and footing in the organization of talk radio openings.' *Journal of Sociolinguistics*, 3, 1, 41–63.

Isherwood, C. (1954) *The World in the Evening*. London: Methuen.

Jackson, S. & Scott, S. (2010) *Theorizing Sexuality*. Milton Keynes: Open University Press.

Jahoda, M. (1982) *Unemployment and Depression*. Cambridge: Cambridge University Press.

James, W. (1890) *The Principles of Psychology*. Cambridge, MA: Harvard University Press, 1983.

Jamieson, L. (1999) 'Intimacy transformed? A critical look at the pure relationship.' *Sociology*, 33, 3, 477–94.

Jeffery, R. (1979) 'Normal rubbish: deviant patients in casualty departments.' *Sociology of Health and Illness*, 1, 40–68.

Jenkins, R. (2004) *Social Identity*. London: Routledge.

Jenkins, R. (2008) 'Erving Goffman: a major theorist of power?' *Journal of Power*, 1, 2, 157–68.

Johnson, J.L. & Best, A.L. (2012) 'Radical normals: the moral career of straight parents as public advocates for their gay children.' *Symbolic Interaction*, 35, 3, 321–39.

Jones, M. (1967) 'Freemasonry.' In N. Mackenzie (ed.), *Secret Societies*. London: Aldus, pp. 152–77.

Kane, M. & Zink, R. (2004) 'Package adventure tours: markers in serious leisure careers.' *Leisure Studies*, 23, 4, 329–45.

Karmel, M. (1969) 'Total institutions and self-mortification.' *Journal of Health and Social Behaviour*, 10, 2, 134–41.

Karp, D.A., Holstrom, L.L. & Gray, P.S. (1998) 'Leaving home for college: expectations for selective reconstruction of self.' *Symbolic Interaction*, 21, 3, 253–76.

Katovich, M.A. & Reese, W.A. (1987) 'The regular: full-time identities and memberships in an urban bar.' *Journal of Contemporary Ethnography*, 16, 3, 308–43.

Keitlen, T. & Lobsenz, N. (1962) *Farewell to Fear*. New York: Avon.

Kilborn, R. (2003) *Staging the Real*. Manchester: Manchester University Press.

Kim, E.C. (2012) 'Nonsocial transient behaviour: social disengagement on the Greyhound bus.' *Symbolic Interaction*, 35, 3, 267–83.

Kitsuse, J. (1962) 'Societal reaction to deviant behavior.' *Social Problems*, 9, 3, 247–56.

Klein, U. (1999) 'Our best boys: the gendered nature of civil–military relations in Israel.' *Men and Masculinities*, 2, 47–65.

Koehlinger, A. (2004) '"Let us live for those who love us": faith, family and the contours of manhood among the Knights of Columbus in late nineteenth-century Connecticut.' *Journal of Social History*, 38, 2, 455–69.

Korry, E. (2005) 'A fraternity hazing gone wrong.' *All Things Considered*, National Public Radio, 14 November. *http://www.npr.org/templates/story/story.php?storyId=5012154*

Kübler-Ross, E. (1969) *On Death and Dying*. London: Routledge.

Kuhn, M.H. & McPartland, T.S. (1954) 'An empirical investigation of self-attitudes.' *American Sociological Review*, 19, 1, 68–76.

Kuhn, T. (1962) *The Structure of Scientific Revolutions*. Chicago: University of Chicago Press.

Laing, R.D. (1960) *The Divided Self: An Existential Study in Sanity and Madness*. Harmondsworth: Penguin.

Laing, R.D. (1967) *The Politics of Experience and the Bird of Paradise*. Harmondsworth: Penguin.

Laing R.D. & Esterson A. (1964) *Sanity, Madness and the Family: Families of Schizophrenics*. Harmondsworth: Penguin.

Larsen, J.A. (2007) 'Understanding a complex intervention: person-centred ethnography in early psychosis.' *Journal of Mental Health*, 16, 3, 333–45.

Lasch, C. (1979) *The Culture of Narcissism*. New York: Norton & Co.

Lawler, S. (2008) *Identity: Sociological Perspectives*. Cambridge: Polity.

Lee, J. (2009) 'Escaping embarrassment: facework in the Rap Cipher.' *Social Psychology Quarterly*, 72, 4, 306-24.

Lemert, E.M. (1962) 'Paranoia and the dynamics of exclusion.' *Sociometry*, XXV, 2–20.

Lemert, E.M. (1967) *Human Deviance, Social Problems, and Social Control*. Englewood Cliffs, NJ: Prentice-Hall.

Lentin, A. & Titley, G. (2011) *The Crises of Multiculturalism: Racism in a Neoliberal Age*. London: Zed Books.

Lerner, G.H. (1995) 'Turn design and the organization of participation in instructional activities.' *Discourse Processes*, 19, 111–31.

Levine, J. & Moreland, R.L. (2006) 'Small groups: an overview.' In J. Levine & R.L. Moreland (eds), *Small Groups*. New York: Psychology Press, pp. 1–10.

Levitin, T.E. (1975) 'Deviants as active participants in the labelling process: the visibly handicapped.' *Social Problems*, 22, 548–57.

Lindesmith, A.R., Strauss, A.L. & Denzin, N.K. (1999) *Social Psychology*. Thousand Oaks, CA: Sage.

Linduska, N. (1947) *My Polio Past*. Chicago: Pellegrini & Cudahy.

Linstead, S. & Höpfl, H. (2000) *The Aesthetics of Organization*. London: Sage.

Linton, R. (1936) *The Study of Man*. New York: Appleton-Century.

Locke, J. (1689) *An Essay Concerning Human Understanding*. New York: Prometheus, 1995.

Lofland, J. (1970) 'Interactionist imagery and analytic interruptus.' In T. Shibutani (ed.), *Human Nature and Collective Behavior: Papers in Honor of Herbert Blumer*, pp. 35–45.

Lofland, J. (1980) 'Early Goffman: style, structure, substance, soul.' In

J. Ditton (ed.), *The View from Goffman*. New York: St Martin's Press, pp. 24–51.

Lofland, J. (1984) 'Erving Goffman's sociological legacies.' *Urban Life*, 13, 1, 7–34. *http://cdclv.unlv.edu/archives/interactionism/goffman/lofland84.html*

Lofland, L.H. (1973) *A World of Strangers: Order and Action in Urban Public Space*. Prospect Heights, IL: Waveland Press.

Lofland, L.H. (2004) 'The real estate developer as villain: notes on a stigmatized occupation.' *Studies in Symbolic Interaction*, 27, 85–108.

Lukes, S. (2005) *Power: A Radical View* (2nd edition). Basingstoke: Palgrave.

Lupton, D. (1995) *The Imperative of Health: Public Health and the Regulated Body*. London: Sage.

Lupton, D. (1998) *The Emotional Self*. London: Sage.

Lupton, D. (1999) *Risk*. London: Routledge.

Lury, C. (2011) *Consumer Culture* (2nd edition). Cambridge: Polity.

Lyman, S.M. & Scott, M.B. (1970) *A Sociology of the Absurd* (2nd edition). New York: General Hall, 1989.

Lyng, S.H. (1990) 'Edgework: a social psychological analysis of voluntary risk-taking.' *American Journal of Sociology*, 95, 4, 851–86.

Lyng, S.H. (2014) 'Action and edgework: risk-taking and reflexivity in late modernity.' *European Journal of Social Theory*, 17, 443–60.

Lyng, S.H. and Snow, D.A. (1986) 'Vocabularies of motive and high-risk behaviour: the case of skydiving.' *Advances in Group Processes*, 3, 157–79.

McAdams, D.P. (1993) *The Stories We Live By: Personal Myths and the Making of the Self*. New York: Guilford Press.

McCabe, T. (2013) 'My fiancé has never seen me without make-up until now.' *Fabulous* magazine, 15 July. *http://fabulousmag.co.uk/2013/07/15/my-fiance-has-never-seen-me-without-make-up-until-now/*

McCall, G. J. & Simmons, J.L. (1966) *Identities and Interactions*. New York: Free Press.

MacIntyre, A. (1982) *After Virtue: A Study in Moral Theory*. London: Duckworth.

McKinlay, A. & Dunnett, A. (1998) 'How gun owners accomplish being deadly average.' In C. Antaki & S. Widdicombe (eds), *Identities in Talk*. London: Sage, pp. 34–51.

Maffesoli, M. (1996) *The Time of the Tribes: The Decline of Individualism in Mass Society*. London: Sage.

Mahony, N. (1979) 'My stay and change at the Henderson Therapeutic Community.' In R. Hinshelwood & N. Manning (eds), *Therapeutic Communities*. London: Routledge & Kegan Paul, pp. 76–87.

Maines, D.R. (2001) *The Faultline of Consciousness: A View of Interactionism in Sociology*. Hawthorne, NY: Aldine de Gruyter.

Maister, D. (1985) 'The psychology of waiting lines.' *http://davidmaister.com/articles/5/52/*

Mäkelä, K., Arminen, I., Bloomfield, K., Eisenbach-Stangl, I., Helmersson Bergmark, K., Kurube, N., Mariolini, N., Ólafsdóttir, H., Peterson, J.H., Phillips, M., Rehm, J., Room, R., Rosenqvist, P., Rosovsky, H., Stenius, K., Świątkiewicz, G., Woronowicz, B. & Zieliński, A. (1996) *Alcoholics*

*Anonymous as a Mutual-Help Movement: A Study in Eight Societies.* Madison: University of Wisconsin Press.

Maltz, D.N. & Borker, R.A. (1982) 'A cultural approach to male–female miscommunication.' In J.J. Gumperz (ed.), *Language and Social Identity.* Cambridge: Cambridge University Press, pp. 196–216.

Manis, J.G. & Meltzer, B.N. (eds) (1978) *Symbolic Interaction: A Reader in Social Psychology* (3rd edition). Boston: Allyn & Bacon.

Manning, N. (1989) *The Therapeutic Community Movement: Charisma and Routinization.* London: Routledge.

Manning, P. (1992) *Erving Goffman and Modern Sociology.* Cambridge: Polity.

Manning, P. (2000) 'Credibility, agency and the interaction order.' *Symbolic Interaction,* 23, 3, 283–97.

Markus, H. & Nurius, P. (1986) 'Possible selves.' *American Psychologist,* 41, 954–69.

Matza, D. (1964) *Delinquency and Drift.* New York: Wiley.

Mead, G.H. (1934) *Mind, Self, and Society.* Chicago: University of Chicago Press.

Meltzer, B.N. (2003) 'Lying: deception in human affairs.' *International Journal of Sociology and Social Policy,* 23, 6/7, 60–79.

Meltzer, B.N., Petras, J.W. & Reynolds, L.T. (1975) *Symbolic Interactionism: Genesis, Varieties and Criticism.* London: Routledge & Kegan Paul.

Milgram, S. (1977) 'The familiar stranger: an aspect of urban anonymity.' In S. Milgram (ed.), *The Individual in a Social World.* Reading, MA: Addison-Wesley, pp. 51–3.

Miller, R.S. (1996) *Embarrassment: Poise and Peril in Everyday Life.* London: Guilford Press.

Mills, C.W. (1940) 'Situated actions and vocabularies of motive.' *American Sociological Review,* 5, 904–13.

Mills, C.W. (1959) *The Sociological Imagination.* New York: Oxford University Press.

Mishler, E. (1984) *The Discourse of Medicine: Dialectics of Medical Interviews.* Norwood, NJ: Ablex.

Mitchell, D. (2013) 'Phone etiquette at a shopping till is a grey area, but basic politeness isn't.' *Observer,* 7 July. *http://www.guardian.co.uk/commentis free/2013/jul/07/sainsburys-jo-clarke-david-mitchell*

Monaghan, L.F. (2007) 'McDonaldizing men's bodies? Slimming, associated (ir)rationalities and resistances.' *Body & Society,* 13, 2, 67–93.

Morrice, J.K.W. (1979) 'Basic concepts.' In R. Hinshelwood & N. Manning (eds), *Therapeutic Communities.* London: Routledge & Kegan Paul, pp. 49–58.

Morrill, C. & Snow, D.A. (2005) 'The study of personal relationships in public spaces.' In C. Morrill & D.A. Snow (eds), *Together Alone: Personal Relationships in Public Places.* Berkeley: University of California Press, pp. 1–22.

Moscovici, S. (1984) 'The phenomenon of social representations.' In R.M.

Farr & S. Moscovici (eds), *Social Representations*. Cambridge: Cambridge University Press, pp. 3–69.

Newcomb, T.M. (1961) *The Acquaintance Process*. New York: Holt, Rinehart & Winston.

Orwell, G. (1949) *Nineteen Eighty-Four*. London: Penguin, 2008.

Pahl, J. (1989). *Money and Marriage*. London: Macmillan.

Paik, L. (2006) 'Are you truly a recovering dope fiend? Local interpretive practices at a therapeutic community drug treatment program.' *Symbolic Interaction*, 29, 2, 213–34.

Park, R.E. (1950) *Race and Culture*. Glencoe, IL: Free Press.

Parsons, T. (1951) *The Social System*. New York: Free Press.

Patrick, D.R. and Bignall, J.E. (1987) 'Creating the competent self: the case of the wheelchair runner.' In J.A. Kotarba & A. Fontana (eds), *The Existential Self in Society*. Chicago: University of Chicago Press.

Paulos, E. & Goodman, E. (2002) 'Familiar stranger project: anxiety, comfort, and play in public places.' *http://www.paulos.net/research/intel/familiarstranger/index.htm*

Perinbanayagam, R.S. (1985) *Signifying Acts: Structure and Meaning in Everyday Life*. Carbondale: Southern Illinois University Press.

Phipps, A. & Young, I. (2014) 'Neoliberalisation and "lad cultures" in higher education.' *Sociology* (online first). *http://dx.doi.org/10.1177/0038038514542120*

Plummer, K. (1995) *Telling Sexual Stories: Power, Change and Social Worlds*. London: Routledge.

Plummer, K. (2003) *Intimate Citizenship: Private Decisions and Public Dialogues*. Seattle: University of Washington Press.

Pollner, M. & Stein, J. (2001) 'Doubled over in laughter: humor and the construction of selves in Alcoholics Anonymous.' In J. Gubrium & J. Holstein (eds), *Institutional Selves: Troubled Identities in a Postmodern World*. Oxford: Oxford University Press, pp. 46–63.

Potter, J. (1996) *Representing Reality: Discourse, Rhetoric and Social Construction*. London: Sage.

Potter, J. (2004) 'Discourse analysis.' In M. Hardy & A. Bryman (eds), *Handbook of Data Analysis*. London: Sage, pp. 607–24.

Potter, J. & Wetherell, M. (1987) *Discourse and Social Psychology*. London: Sage.

Poulopoulos, C. & Tsibouki, A. (1998) 'The origins and evolution of Greek therapeutic communities for drug addicts.' *Social Work in Europe*, 5, 2, 29–33.

Psathas, G. (1995) *Conversation Analysis: The Study of Talk-in-Interaction*. Thousand Oaks, CA: Sage.

Psathas, G. (1996) 'Theoretical perspectives on Goffman: critique and commentary.' *Sociological Perspectives*, 39, 3, 383–91.

Putney, C. (1993) 'Service over secrecy: how lodge-style fraternalism yielded popularity to men's service clubs.' *Journal of Popular Culture*, 27, 1, 179–90.

Raudenbush, D.T. (2012) 'Race and interactions on public transportation:

social cohesion and the production of common norms and a collective black identity.' *Symbolic Interaction*, 35, 4, 456–73.

Ribeiro, B.T. & de Souza Pinto, D. (2005) 'Medicine and language: oral medicine discourse. Medical discourse, psychiatric interview.' In K. Brown (ed.), *Encyclopaedia of Language and Linguistics* (2nd edition). Oxford: Elsevier.

Richards, P. (1986) 'Risk.' In H.S. Becker, *Writing for Social Scientists*. Chicago: University of Chicago Press, pp. 108–20.

Riggins, S. H. (1990) 'The power of things: the role of domestic objects in the presentation of the self.' In S.H. Riggins (ed.), *Beyond Goffman*. Hawthorne, NY: Aldine de Gruyter, 2010, pp. 341–68.

Ritchie, J. (2000) *Big Brother: The Official Unseen Story*. London: Macmillan.

Ritzer, G. (2004) *The McDonaldization of Society*. London: Sage.

Rock, P. (1979) *The Making of Symbolic Interactionism*. London: Macmillan.

Rolph, C.H. (1973) *Believe What You Like*. London: Deutsch.

Ronson, J. (2009) *Revelations: How to Find God*. Channel 4 television documentary, 28 June.

Ronson, J. (2013) 'A message from God.' In his *Lost at Sea*. London: Picador, pp. 45–65.

Rose, N. (1989) *Governing the Soul: The Shaping of the Private Self*. London: Routledge.

Rose, N. (1990) *Inventing Our Selves*. London: Routledge.

Rose, N. (2000) 'Government and control.' *British Journal of Criminology*, 40, 321–39.

Rosenberg, M. (1979) *Conceiving the Self*. New York: Basic Books.

Rosenhan, D.L. (1973) 'On being sane in insane places.' *Science*, 179, 250–8.

Rossing, H. & Scott, S. (2014): 'Familiar strangers: facework strategies in pursuit of non-binding relations in a workplace-based exercise group.' *Studies in Symbolic Interaction*, 42, 161–84.

Rossol, J. (2001) 'The medicalization of deviance as an interactional achievement: the construction of compulsive gambling.' *Symbolic Interaction*, 24, 3, 315–41.

Roth, J.A. (1966) 'The public hospital: refuge for damaged humans.' *Transaction*, 3, 5, 25–9.

Rubin, G. (1975) 'The traffic in women: notes on the "political economy" of sex.' In R. Reiter (ed.), *Toward an Anthropology of Women*. New York: Monthly Review Press, pp. 157–210.

Ryle, G. (1949) *The Concept of Mind*. Chicago: University of Chicago Press.

Sacks, H. (1992) *Lectures on Conversation*. Oxford: Blackwell.

Sacks, H., Schegloff, E.A. & Jefferson, G. (1974). 'A simplest systematics for the organization of turn-taking for conversation.' *Language*, 50, 696–735.

Sage, G.H. & Loy, J.W. (1978) 'Geographical mobility patterns of college coaches.' *Journal of Contemporary Ethnography*, 7, 2, 253–80.

Said, E. (1978) *Orientalism*. New York: Pantheon.

Sanday, P. (1990) *Fraternity Gang Rape: Sex, Brotherhood, and Privilege on Campus*. New York: New York University Press.

Sandvoss, C. (2005) *Fans*. Cambridge: Polity.

Sartre, J.P. (1943) *Being and Nothingness: An Essay on Phenomenological Ontology* (trans. H. Barnes). New York: Washington Square Press, 1984.

Sasson-Levy, O. (2003) 'Military, masculinity, and citizenship: tensions and contradictions in the experience of blue-collar soldiers.' *Identities: Global Studies in Culture and Power*, 10, 319–45.

Saussure, F. de (1916) *Course in General Linguistics* (trans. R. Harris). New York: Bloomsbury, 2013.

Scambler, G. (2005) *Epilepsy*. London: Routledge.

Scambler, G. & Hopkins, A. (1986) 'Being epileptic: coming to terms with stigma.' *Sociology of Health and Illness*, 8, 26–43.

Scaramanga, J. (2013) 'Are fundamentalist schools up to standard?' *Guardian*, 27 March. *http://www.theguardian.com/commentisfree/belief/2013/mar/27/ fundamentalist-schools-accelerated-christian-education*

Schechner, R. (2002) *Performance Studies: An Introduction*. London: Routledge.

Scheff, T.J. (1966) *Becoming Mentally Ill: A Sociological Theory*. New York: Aldine, 1984.

Scheff, T.J. (1968) 'Negotiating reality.' *Social Problems*, 16, 3–17.

Scheff, T.J. (2006) *Goffman Unbound!* Boulder, CO: Paradigm.

Scheff, T.J. (2011) 'Social-emotional world: mapping a continent.' *Current Sociology*, 59, 3, 347–61.

Scheff, T.J. & Retzinger, S. (1991) *Emotions and Violence*. Lexington, MA: Lexington Books.

Schegloff, E.A. (1968) 'Sequencing in conversational openings.' *American Anthropologist*, 70, 6, 1075–95.

Schegloff, E.A. (1992) 'On talk and its institutional occasions.' In P. Drew & J. Heritage (eds), *Talk at Work*. Cambridge: Cambridge University Press, pp. 101–36.

Schegloff, E.A. (2007). *Sequence Organization in Interaction: A Primer in Conversation Analysis* (Volume 1). Cambridge: Cambridge University Press.

Scheibe, K.E. (1979) *Mirrors, Masks, Lies, and Secrets: The Limits of Human Predictability*. New York: Praeger.

Schneider, J.W. (2009) *Having Epilepsy: The Experience and Control of Illness*. Philadelphia: Temple University Press.

Schneider, J.W. & Conrad, P. (1981) 'Medical and sociological typologies: the case of epilepsy.' *Social Science and Medicine*, 15A, 211–19.

Schur, E. (1971) *Labeling Deviant Behavior*. New York: Harper & Row.

Schütz, A. (1964) 'The well-informed citizen.' In his *Collected Papers: Volume II: Studies in Social Theory*. The Hague: Martinus Nijhoff, pp. 120–34.

Schütz, A. (1971) 'The stranger: an essay in social psychology'. In F. Anthias & M.P. Kelly (eds), *Sociological Debates: Thinking about 'the Social'*. Dartford: Greenwich University Press, 1995, pp. 339–49.

Schütz, A. (1972) *The Phenomenology of the Social World*. London: Heinemann.

Schwartz, B (1970) 'Notes on the sociology of sleep.' *Sociology Quarterly*, 11, 485–99.

Schwartz, B. (1975) *Queuing and Waiting: Studies in the Social Organization of Access and Delay*. Chicago: University of Chicago Press.

Scott, M.B. & Lyman, S.M. (1968) 'Accounts.' *American Sociological Review*, 33, 46–62.

Scott, S. (2005) 'The red, shaking fool: dramaturgical dilemmas in shyness.' *Symbolic Interaction*, 28, 1, 91–110.

Scott, S. (2007a) *Shyness and Society*. Basingstoke: Palgrave.

Scott, S. (2007b) 'College hats or lecture trousers? Stage fright and performance anxiety in university lecturers.' *Ethnography and Education*, 2, 2, 189–205.

Scott, S. (2007c) 'Erving Goffman.' In J. Scott (ed.), *Fifty Key Sociologists: The Contemporary Theorists*. London: Routledge, pp. 113–18.

Scott, S. (2009a) 'Re-clothing the emperor: the swimming pool as a negotiated order.' *Symbolic Interaction*, 32, 2, 123–45.

Scott, S. (2009b) *Making Sense of Everyday Life*. Cambridge: Polity.

Scott, S. (2011) *Total Institutions and Reinvented Identities*. Basingstoke: Palgrave.

Scott, S. (2012) 'Intimate deception in everyday life.' *Studies in Symbolic Interaction*, 39, 251–79.

Scott, S., Hinton-Smith, Härmä, V. & Broome, K. (2013) 'Goffman in the gallery: interactive art and visitor shyness.' *Symbolic Interaction*, 36, 4, 417–38.

Semin, G.R. & Manstead, A.S.R. (1983) *The Accountability of Conduct: A Social Psychological Analysis*. New York: Academic Press.

Seymour, W. (2002) 'Time and the body: re-embodying time in disability.' *Journal of Occupational Science*, 9, 3, 135–42.

Shamir, B. (1992) 'Some correlates of leisure identity salience: three exploratory studies.' *Leisure Studies*, 24, 4, 301–23.

Shaskolsky, L. (1970) 'The development of sociological theory in America – a sociology of knowledge interpretation.' In L.T. Reynolds & J.M. Reynolds (eds), *The Sociology of Sociology*. New York: McKay, pp. 6–30.

Shaw, C. (1934) *The Jack Roller: A Delinquent Boy's Own Story*. Chicago: University of Chicago Press

Shilling, C. (1993) *The Body and Social Theory*. London: Sage.

Shuy, R.W. (1982) 'Topic as the unit of analysis in a criminal law case.' In D. Tannen (ed.), *Analyzing Discourse: Text and Talk. Georgetown University Round Table on Languages and Linguistics 1981*. Washington, DC: Georgetown University Press, pp. 113–26.

Simmel, G. (1900) *The Philosophy of Money* (trans. T. Bottomore & D. Frisby). London: Routledge & Kegan Paul, 1978.

Simmel, G. (1902–3) 'The metropolis and mental life'. In K.H. Wolff (trans. & ed.), *The Sociology of Georg Simmel*. London: Free Press, 1950, pp. 409–24.

Simmel, G. (1908a) 'The stranger.' In K.H. Wolff (trans. & ed.), *The Sociology of Georg Simmel*. London: Free Press, 1950, pp. 402–8.

Simmel, G. (1908b) 'The secret and the secret society.' In K.H. Wolff (trans. & ed.), *The Sociology of Georg Simmel*. London: Free Press, 1950, pp. 307–74.

Simmel, G. (1971). *On Individuality and Social Forms: Selected Writings* (trans. & ed. D.N. Levine). Chicago: University of Chicago Press.

Skeggs, B. (2004) *Class, Self, Culture*. London: Routledge.

Skeggs, B. & Wood, H. (2009) 'The transformation of intimacy: classed identities in the moral economy of reality television.' In M. Wetherell (ed.), *Identity in the 21st Century: New Trends in Changing Times*. Basingstoke: Palgrave, pp. 231–49.

Slater, L. (2006) 'True love: the chemical reaction.' *National Geographic*, 209, 32–49.

Smart, C. (2004) 'Changing landscapes of family life: rethinking divorce.' *Social Policy and Society*, 3, 4, 401–8.

Smith, B. & Sparkes, A.C. (2008) 'Changing bodies, changing narratives and the consequences of tellability: a case study of becoming disabled through sport.' *Sociology of Health and Illness*, 30, 2, 217–36.

Smith, D.E. (1978) 'K is mentally ill: the anatomy of a factual account.' *Sociology*, 12, 1, 23–53.

Smith, G. (2006) *Erving Goffman*. London: Routledge.

Smith, P., Philips, T.L. & King, R.D. (2010) *Incivility: The Rude Stranger in Everyday Life*. Cambridge: Cambridge University Press.

Smith, S.E. (2014) 'Kevin Grow and disability as inspiration.' *Disability Intersections*, 24 February. *http://disabilityintersections.com/2014/02/kevin-grow-and-disability-as-inspiration/#more-282*

Snow, D.A. & Anderson, L. (1987) 'Identity work among the homeless: the verbal construction and avowal of personal identities.' *American Journal of Sociology*, 92, 1336–71.

Sontag, S. (1964) 'Notes on camp.' In her *Against Interpretation and Other Essays*. London: Penguin, 2009, pp. 275–92.

Spandler, H. (2006) *Asylum to Action: Paddington Day Hospital, Therapeutic Communities and Beyond*. London: Jessica Kingsley.

Sparkes, A.C. (2002) *Telling Tales in Sport and Physical Activity: A Qualitative Journey*. London: Human Kinetics.

Spender, D. (1980) *Man Made Language*. London: Routledge & Kegan Paul.

Spiers, J.A. (1998) 'The use of facework and politeness theory.' *Qualitative Health Research*, 8, 1, 25–47.

Stebbins, R. (1992) *Amateurs, Professionals, and Serious Leisure*. Montreal: McGill-Queen's University Press.

Stein, K. (2011) 'Getting away from it all: the construction and management of temporary identities on vacation.' *Symbolic Interaction*, 34, 2, 290–308.

Stokes, R. & Hewitt, J.P. (1976) 'Aligning actions.' *American Sociological Review*, 41, 838–49.

Stone, G. (1962) 'Appearance and the self.' In A. Rose (ed.), *Human Behavior and Social Processes*. Boston: Houghton-Mifflin, pp. 86–118.

Strauss, A.L. (1969) *Mirrors and Masks*. London: Martin Robertson.

Strauss, A.L. (1978) *Negotiations: Varieties, Contexts, Processes, and Social Order*. San Francisco: Jossey-Bass.

Strauss, A.L., Schatzman, L., Ehrlich, D., Bucher, R. & Sabshin, M. (1963) 'The hospital and its negotiated order.' In E. Freidson (ed.), *The Hospital in Modern Society*. New York: Free Press, pp. 147–69.

Stryker, S. (1968) 'Identity salience and role performance.' *Journal of Marriage and the Family*, 4, 558–64.

Stryker, S. (1980) *Symbolic Interactionism: A Social Structural Version*. Menlo Park, CA: Benjamin Cummings.

Sykes, G.M. & Matza, D. (1957) 'Techniques of neutralization: a theory of delinquency.' *American Sociological Review*, 22, 664–70.

Szasz, T. (1961) *The Myth of Mental Illness*. St Albans: Paladin, 1972.

Tajfel, H. (1982) 'Social psychology of intergroup relations.' *Annual Review of Psychology*, 33, 1–39.

Talbot, E. & Miller, S.C. (1971) 'The mental hospital as a sane society.' In S.E. Wallace (ed.), *Total Institutions*. New Brunswick, NJ: Transaction Press, pp. 131–9.

Tangney, J.P. & Fisher, K.W. (eds) (1995) *Self-Conscious Emotions: The Psychology of Shame, Guilt, Embarrassment, and Pride*. New York: Guilford Press.

Tannen, D. (1993) 'The relativity of linguistic strategies: rethinking power and solidarity in gender and dominance.' In M. Wetherell, S. Taylor & S.J. Yates (eds), *Discourse Theory and Practice: A Reader*. London: Sage, pp. 150–66.

Tavory, I. (2009) 'The structure of flirtation: on the construction of interactional ambiguity.' *Studies in Symbolic Interaction*, 33, 59–74.

Thomas, M. (2005) '"What happens in Tenerife stays in Tenerife": understanding women's sexual behaviour on holiday.' *Culture, Health and Sexuality*, 7, 6, 571–84.

Thomas, W.I. (1923) *The Unadjusted Girl*. Boston: Little, Brown & Co.

Thomas, W.I. & Thomas, D.S. (1928) *The Child in America*. New York: Alfred Knopf.

Thomas, W.I. & Znaniecki, F.W. (1918) *The Polish Peasant in Europe and America*. Chicago: University of Chicago Press.

Thompson, H.S. (1971) *Fear and Loathing in Las Vegas*. London: Flamingo, 1993.

Thomson, A. (1995) *ANZAC Memories: Living with the Legend*. Oxford: Oxford University Press.

Thomson, R., Kehily, M.J., Hadfield, L. & Sharpe, S. (2009) 'The making of modern motherhoods: storying an emergent identity.' In M. Wetherell (ed.), *Identity in the 21st Century: New Trends in Changing Times*. Basingstoke: Palgrave, pp. 197–212.

Thrasher, F. (1927) *The Gang: A Study of 1,313 Gangs in Chicago*. Chicago: University of Chicago Press.

Travisano, R.V. (1967) *Alternation and Conversion in Jewish Identities*. Minnesota: University of Minnesota Press.

Turner, R.H. (1962) 'Role-taking: process versus conformity'. In A. Rose (ed.), *Human Behavior and Social Processes*. Boston: Houghton-Mifflin, pp. 20–40.

Turner, R.H. (1968) 'The self-conception in social interaction.' In C. Gordon & K.J. Gergen (eds), *The Self in Social Interactionism*. New York: Wiley, pp. 93–106.

Turner, V. (1967) 'Betwixt and between: the liminal period in rites de passage.' In his *The Forest of Symbols: Aspects of Ndembu Ritual.* Ithaca, NY: Cornell University Press, pp. 93–111.

Van Dijk, T.A. (1993) 'Principles of critical discourse analysis.' *Discourse & Society,* 4, 249–83.

Van Gennep, A. (1909) *The Rites of Passage.* London: Routledge, 2010.

Van Maanen, J. (1990) 'The smile factory: work at Disneyland.' In P.J. Frost (ed.), *Reframing Organizational Culture.* London: Sage, pp. 58–76.

Voysey, M. (1972) 'Impression management by parents with disabled children.' *Journal of Health and Social Behavior,* 13, 80–9.

Walby, S. (1997) *Gender Transformations.* London: Routledge.

Walker, L.L.M., Gately, P.J., Bewick, B.M. & Hill, A.J. (2003) 'Children's weight loss camps: psychological benefit or jeopardy?' *International Journal of Obesity,* 21, 748–54.

Wallace, S.E. (1971) 'On the totality of institutions.' In S.E. Wallace (ed.), *Total Institutions.* New Brunswick, NJ: Transaction Press, pp. 1–7.

Wallis, R. (1984) *Elementary Forms of the New Religious Life.* London: Routledge & Kegan Paul.

Wallis, R. & Bruce, S. (1992) 'Secularization: the orthodox model.' In S. Bruce (ed.), *Religion and Modernization.* Oxford: Oxford University Press, pp. 8–30.

Waskul, D. & Lust, M. (2004) 'Role-playing and playing roles: the person, player, and persona in fantasy role playing.' *Symbolic Interaction,* 27, 3, 333–56.

Weber, M. (1904) '"Objectivity" in social science and social policy.' In his *The Methodology of the Social Sciences* (trans. & ed. E.A. Shils & H.A. Finch). New York: Free Press, 1949, pp. 50–112.

Weber, M. (1922) *Economy and Society* (trans. & ed. G. Roth & C. Wittich). Berkeley: University of California Press, 1978.

Webster, N.H. (1924) *Secret Societies and Subversive Movements.* London: Boswell.

Weeks, J. (2003) *Sexuality* (2nd edition). London: Routledge.

Weinberg, D. (1996) 'The enactment and appraisal of authenticity in a Skid Row therapeutic community.' *Symbolic Interaction,* 19, 2, 137–62.

Weinberg, D. (2005) *Of Others Inside: Insanity, Addiction, and Belonging in America.* Philadelphia: Temple University Press.

Weinberg, M.S. (1965) 'Sexual modesty, social meanings, and the nudist camp.' *Social Problems,* 12, 3, 311–18.

Wenger, E. (1998) *Communities of Practice: Learning, Meaning and Identity.* Cambridge: Cambridge University Press.

West, C. & Zimmerman, D. (1983) 'Small insults: a study of interruptions in cross-sex conversations between unacquainted persons.' In B. Thorne, C. Kramarae & N. Henley (eds), *Language, Gender, and Society.* Rowley, MA: Newbury House, pp. 103–18.

West, C. & Zimmerman, D. (1987) 'Doing gender.' *Gender and Society,* 1, 2, 125–51.

West, P. (1986) 'The social meaning of epilepsy: stigma as a potential explanation for psychopathology in children.' In S. Whitman & B.P. Hermann (eds), *Psychopathology in Epilepsy*. New York: Oxford University Press, pp. 245–66.

Westley, W.A. (1968) 'The informal organization of the army: a sociological memoir.' In H.S. Becker, B. Geer, D. Riesman & R.S. Weiss (eds), *Institutions and the Person*. Chicago: Aldine, pp. 200–7.

Wetherell, M. (ed.) (2009) *Identity in the 21st Century: New Trends in Changing Times*. Basingstoke: Palgrave.

Whalen, J. & Zimmerman, D.H. (1987) 'Sequential and institutional contexts in calls for help.' *Social Psychology Quarterly*, 50, 172–85.

Whiteley, J.S. (1970) 'The response of psychopaths to a therapeutic community.' *British Journal of Psychiatry*, 116, 534, 517–29.

Wiley, J. (1991) 'A refracted reality of everyday life: the constructed culture of a therapeutic community.' *Symbolic Interaction*, 4, 2, 139–63.

Wilkinson, I. (2001) *Anxiety in a Risk Society*. Hove: Psychology Press.

Wilkinson, I. (2004) *Suffering: A Sociological Introduction*. Cambridge: Polity.

Williams, R. (2000) *Making Identity Matter*. Durham: sociologypress.

Williams, S.J. & Bendelow, G.A. (eds) (1998) *The Lived Body*. London: Routledge.

Willis, P. (1977) *Learning to Labour: How Working Class Kids Get Working Class Jobs*. London: Routledge.

Willmott, P. & Young, M. (1960) *Family and Class in a London Suburb*. London: Routledge & Kegan Paul.

Wilson, B. (1966) *Religion in a Secular Society*. Harmondsworth: Pelican.

Wing, J. (1962). 'Institutionalism in mental hospitals.' *British Journal of Social and Clinical Psychology*, 1, 38–51.

Wirth, L. (1938) 'Urbanism as a way of life.' *American Journal of Sociology*, 44, 1–24.

Woodward, K. (2002) *Understanding Identity*. London: Hodder.

Woofitt, R. (1992) *Telling Tales of the Unexpected: The Organization of Factual Discourse*. Hemel Hempstead: Harvester Wheatsheaf.

Wortham, S.E.F. (1996) 'Mapping participant deictics: a technique for discovering speakers' footing.' *Journal of Pragmatics*, 25, 3, 331–48.

Wulbert, R. (1965) 'Inmate pride in total institutions.' *American Journal of Sociology*, 71, 1, 1–9.

Wulff, H. (1998) *Ballet across Borders: Career and Culture in the World of Dancers*. Oxford: Berg.

Wynne, L., Irving, C., Ryckoff, M., Day, J. & Hirsch, S.I. (1958) 'Pseudomutuality in the family relations of schizophrenics.' *Psychiatry*, 21, 205–20.

Young, K.G. (1987) *Taleworlds and Storyrealms*. Boston: Martinus Nijhoff.

Zerubavel, E. (1981) *Hidden Rhythms: Schedules and Calendars in Social Life*. Chicago: University of Chicago Press.

Zerubavel, E. (2007) 'Generally speaking: the logic and mechanics of social pattern analysis.' *Sociological Forum*, 22, 2, 131–45.

Zimbardo, P.G. (2007) *The Lucifer Effect: How Good People Turn Evil*. London: Rider.

Zimmerman, D.H. (1992) 'The interactional organization of calls for emergency assistance.' In P. Drew & J. Heritage (eds), *Talk at Work: Social Interaction in Institutional Settings*. Cambridge: Cambridge University Press, pp. 418–69.

Zimmerman, D.H. (1998) 'Identity, context and interaction.' In C. Antaki & S. Widdicombe (eds), *Identities in Talk*. London: Sage, pp. 87–106.

Zimmerman, D.H. & Wieder, L. (1970) 'Ethnomethodology and the problem of order: comment on Denzin.' In J. Douglas (ed.), *Understanding Everyday Life: Toward the Reconstruction of Sociological Knowledge*. Chicago: Aldine, pp. 285–98.

Zittoun, T., Duveen, G., Gillespie, A., Ivinson, G. & Psaltis, C. (2003). 'The use of symbolic resources in developmental transitions.' *Culture & Psychology*, 9, 4, 415–48.

## Websites

Alpha Course: *http://www.alpha.org/*

Spring Harvest: *http://www.springharvest.org/* (quotation no longer online)

Vipassana Meditation: *http://www.dhamma.org/en/vipassana.shtml*

Wellspring Academy (a): *http://www.wellspringcamp.co.uk/schedule.html*

Wellspring Academy (b): *http://www.wellspringcamp.co.uk/parentcommentsabout-weightloss.html*

# Index